NEUTRALISM

NEUTRALISM

by

PETER LYON
B.Sc. (Econ.), Ph.D.

*Lecturer in Politics
in the University of Leicester*

LEICESTER UNIVERSITY PRESS

1963

PRINTED IN GREAT BRITAIN
BY BLACKFRIARS PRESS LTD
FOR
LEICESTER UNIVERSITY PRESS

TO ALISON

PREFACE

THIS is a book about the major meanings and significance of neutralism in contemporary international politics. As it is a short study of a large and complicated subject, it may be helpful to indicate the main concerns and aims of the book by outlining the contents of the six main chapters.

What is 'neutralism'? Does such a question lead to an enquiry into the uses of a word, or to an investigation of an aspect of international politics? It can be both, but this enquiry is concerned far more with the latter than the former. Even so, terminology is important. Chapter I points to some of the difficulties that arise in studying neutralism, draws attention to common verbal and semantic puzzles and perplexities that often occur concerning 'neutrality', 'neutralism', 'non-alignment', and other kindred terms, and tries to make clear and explain the intended use of the term 'neutralism' in this study, pointing out too that a prime purpose is to make each contextual meaning clear.

Chapter II outlines the main features and phases of the Cold War, in which the main rivals are the two 'superpowers' the Soviet Union and the United States, and thus describes the setting in which neutralism occurs and is shaped. The origins of the Cold War struggle, the growth of the rival military alliances, the emergence of new states, and the growing strength of neutralist currents, are all traced. As neutralism can only be understood by reference to the Cold War struggle, particular attention is paid in this chapter to the official attitudes and policies of the two superpowers to neutralism in general and to certain significant neutralist states and leaders in particular. This may be familiar ground to some readers but it does provide the setting for the whole study.

As the Cold War is, in part at least, an ideological as well as a power struggle, Chapter III is concerned with neutralism as an ideology or doctrine. It endeavours to point out what are the main precepts of the leading neutralists, and why; tries to determine whether these are novel or time-honoured, and to suggest why they are so popular today.

Chapters IV and V are both concerned with neutralism as state policy. Chapter IV gives an overall view of the contemporary inter-state system, distinguishes the neutralist from the aligned states and outlines a six-fold division of the types of neutralist policy. These six types of neutralist policy are: new state neutralism; pioneer neutralism; neutralization; buffer status; traditional neutrality; and erstwhile isolationism. Each of these types of policy represents different ways in which a state can become neutralist. It is suggested how many states fall into

7

each of these classes, what are their distinctive characteristics, and the necessary conditions for pursuing such policies. The treatment in this chapter is necessarily general and comparative. Chapter V examines some particular examples of neutralist states in greater detail than was possible in the preceding chapter, showing the mutual interaction of neutralist diplomacy and pressures of the international environment.

Chapter VI is a study of the Belgrade Neutralist Conference in September 1961, the largest and most important neutralist conference to date.

This is a modified version of a thesis presented for the Ph.D. degree of London University, early in 1962. It then seemed to me that the natural *terminus ad quem* was the Belgrade Conference of September 1961. Since, I have been tempted to regard the Chinese invasion of India in October 1962 as the end point instead. In fact, of course, there is no natural end for any 'contemporary' study, and it is a vain quest to seek to be fully up-to-date. In the main, we are here concerned with events between 1945 and December 1962. References to events outside these limits are mostly incidental. As this short study aims at a general perspective of neutralism in international politics between 1945 and 1962 it has been necessary to be ruthless in deciding what are central issues and in rejecting what is often interesting but is, in my view, peripheral. So far, surprisingly little has been written which centres attention on neutralism in international politics. The most valuable of such writings as I have discovered are virtually all short and highly specialized, symposia or articles widely scattered in learned periodicals, especially American periodicals. I have tried to make clear my debts to these, and to many other studies, in my notes and bibliography. Though there is much here which must be tentative and conjectural, it is hoped that this general and comparative analysis of neutralism in international politics may be of some use in clarifying discussions about the nature of neutralism and in suggesting some lines for future enquiry.

Leicester   PETER LYON
April 1963

CONTENTS

CONTENTS

ACKNOWLEDGEMENTS

I am grateful to the editor of *The Review of Politics* for permission to reproduce some small portions of an article of mine that he published in April 1960. For the help I have received in my work my grateful thanks are due: to Leicester University Press for publishing this book, and to the University Research Board for financial assistance; to my past and present colleagues — Professor Bruce Miller, Professor Christopher Hughes, Maurice Hookham, John Day, Harry Hanak and Richard Chapman; to my former teachers—Professor C. A. W. Manning and Professor Martin Wight; to my brother Michael; to the staffs of many libraries and embassies; to the many colleagues, friends and students who have helped me in various ways. To Professor Jack Simmons I owe a special debt. He read the whole of my untidy manuscript at short notice and did much to expedite publication. And last, but most of all, I am indebted to my wife. I am alone responsible for all the faults that remain.

P.L.

ABBREVIATIONS*

A.A.A.P.S.S.	*The Annals of the American Association of Political and Social Science*
A.J.I.L.	*The American Journal of International Law.*
Akzin	Benjamin Akzin (ed.), *New States and International Organizations.* A Report prepared on behalf of The International Political Science Association (U.N.E.S.C.O., Paris, 1955).
A.P.S.R.	*The American Political Science Review.*
Campbell	John C. Campbell, *Defence of the Middle East. Problems of American Policy* (Frederick Praeger, New York, revised edition, 1960).
† C.S.M.	*The Christian Science Monitor.*
D.S.B.	*The Department of State Bulletin* (Washington, D.C., fortnightly).
Fifield	Russell H. Fifield, *The Diplomacy of South-East Asia: 1945-1958* (Harper Bros., New York, 1958).
Goodwin	Geoffrey L. Goodwin, *Britain and the United Nations* (Oxford University Press for R.I.I.A., 1957).
J.M.H.	*The Journal of Modern History* (Chicago).
Lenczowski	George Lenczowski, *The Middle East in World Affairs* (Cornell University Press, New York, second edition, 1956).
M.S.P. 1961	The Mutual Security Program. Fiscal Year, 1961. *A Summary Presentation.* (Department of State, Washington, D.C., March 1960).
Oppenheim-Lauterpacht	L. Oppenheim (ed. by H. Lauterpacht), *International Law,* 2 vols. (Longmans, 1948).
O.U.P.	Oxford University Press.
R.I.I.A.	The Royal Institute of International Affairs.
The Middle East	*The Middle East. A Political and Economic Survey.* 3rd edition, edited by Sir Reader Bullard (O.U.P. for R.I.I.A., London, 1958).
The World in March 1939	Survey of International Affairs 1939-1946. *The World in March 1939,* edited by A. Toynbee and F. T. Ashton-Gwatkin (O.U.P. for R.I.I.A., London, 1952).
The War and the Neutrals	Survey of International Affairs 1939-1946. *The War and the Neutrals,* edited by A. and V. M. Toynbee (O.U.P. for R.I.I.A., London, 1956).
U.S.W.A.	*The United States in World Affairs* (Annual volumes. Harper Bros. for the Council on Foreign Relations, New York).
Y.B.U.N.	United Nations, *Yearbook of the United Nations.*
Y.B.W.A.	*The Year Book of World Affairs* (London, Stevens for London Institute of World Affairs).

* This list does not include such familiar abbreviations as N.A.T.O., S.E.A.T.O., U.N., *op. cit.,* etc.

† The reference here, as with all other American newspapers cited in this study, is to the European edition.

"The study of general contacts and relations and of general resemblances and differences is the only avenue to a general perspective without which neither profit nor pleasure can be extracted from historical research."

POLYBIUS

"The historian may applaud the importance and variety of his subject; but, while he is conscious of his own imperfections, he must often accuse the deficiency of his materials."

EDWARD GIBBON

CHAPTER I

WHAT IS NEUTRALISM?

"It will be good for all concerned if neutralism ceases to be simply an international cliché." *The Times*, leader, 26 October 1959.

"We must therefore use ordinary words. They separate us least from the past, which we are trying to understand, and from the present, with its Babel of tongues, in which and to which we must tell what we have understood. But let us not imagine that ordinary words are easy to use. To split the ism demands clarity of thought and constant watchfulness." Sir Keith Hancock, *Country and Calling*.

"Neutralism is, of course, one of those rather rotund words which does not readily admit of definition." Mr Menzies to the U.N. General Assembly, 5 October 1960.

SINCE the end of the Second World War the political neologism[1] 'neutralism' has been used so often by so many people, in such different circumstances and with such different intentions, that its meaning seems to change, chameleon like, depending on the context in which it appears. Contemporary usage has not produced any real consistency in definition, though it is clear that the word invariably has reference to the Cold War struggle between the United States and its allies on the one hand, and the Soviet Union and its associates on the other. It is the aim of this study to try to distinguish what are the main kinds of neutralism, by reference to what states do, and what statesmen say, to draw attention to their distinguishing features, and to assess their importance in contemporary international politics.

As 'neutralism' is now such a protean term, it is necessary at the outset to say something about the words with which it is commonly confused or at least associated, and to clarify its intended use here.

An exchange which took place in the Indian parliament[2] just after Mr Nehru returned from the Belgrade Conference for 'The Heads of State or Government of Non-Aligned countries' illustrates some of the verbal confusions which now surround the use of the word 'neutralism':

Shri Hem Barua "All types of neutralism—positive neutralism, un-committed neutralism, unaligned neutralism, etc.—were represented

---

[1] The emergence of this neologism is traced in Peter Lyon, "Neutrality and the Emergence of the Concept of Neutralism": *Review of Politics*, Apr. 1960, pp. 255-68.
[2] *Lok Sabha Debates*, 15th Session, vol. LIX, No. 1, 20 Nov. 1961, cols. 31-4.

at Belgrade. What basic policy did our Prime Minister adopt to steer
through the rough weather at Belgrade?"

Shri Jawaharlal Nehru "Obviously when a large number of countries
get together they represent often in minor matters or even in major
matters differences of opinion. People do not come together merely to
say ditto to each other, because they do not agree on everything.
That is obvious. In the Belgrade Conference a great majority of the
countries were from Africa and from the Arab countries. They were
influenced by local considerations, this, that, and the other. In forming a policy — it was not high policy — geography counts; these
things are discussed and ultimately something emerges. Here a com-
munique emerged, which was ultimately passed unanimously".

Quite apart from the fact that the world's leading neutralist statesman here described the hitherto most important neutralist conference
as 'not high policy', this desultory parliamentary exchange showed
that 'non-alignment' had not emerged as the sole favourite synonym
for 'neutralism'. For present purposes 'neutralism' is taken to mean
dissociation from the Cold War. This working definition is sufficiently
broad in reference to take account of such popular expressions as 'non-
alignment', 'active and peaceful co-existence', 'active policy for peace',
'independent policy', 'positive neutrality', 'positive neutralism'. Some
of the favourite euphemisms, circumlocutions and synonyms for
'neutralism' will be indicated where appropriate. Indeed, the very loose-
ness with which the term is used today has endowed it with an element
of metaphor. Neutralism is often compared and contrasted with such
similarly equivocal terms as 'colonialism', 'nationalism', 'socialism' and
'communism', and though this draws attention to the overlapping
and interaction of important political forces, it cannot be said that
the necessary introduction of these other 'ism' terms reduces the
ambiguities that arise in discussions of neutralism. But it is important
to bear in mind all the time the difference between the central concern
here—which is to try to describe the main ways in which since 1945
there has been dissociation from the Cold War—and the fact that the
label 'neutralist' is used tendentiously and varyingly, both by Cold
War protagonists and by self-avowed neutralists. Inevitably, the
approach adopted here necessarily involves controversial attribution of
the label 'neutralist' to states or persons where others might deny that
this is a permissible usage. It is hoped that the reasons for such attribu-
tions will be clear in each context. Though this is not a lexicographic
study, the reader who wishes to would find it possible to compile a list
of definitions in use, and to note the origin of some kindred and
currently fashionable polemical terms, by reference to the index to this
book. Obviously, there are many forms of dissociation from the Cold

War. It is the task of this enquiry to try to suggest which have so far been the major ones, and why.

Though there is much popular confusion between 'neutrality' and 'neutralism', in this study they are regarded as quite distinct. And so it is worth while at this point to say something about neutrality in order to dispose of the need for further discussion, and, by contrast, to say something further about neutralism in order to draw attention to some perplexities which are central to this study.

Neutrality has a strictly legal[3] as well as a general diplomatic or political[4] connotation. This is what distinguishes neutrality most sharply from neutralism, for no one has suggested that the latter should be construed as a legal[5] as well as a political term. The history of war and of the changing balance-of-power shows that the practical value of the legal right to be neutral has varied in different ages. On the whole, such a right was well respected throughout the nineteenth century, but it was hardly respected at all, and had only a rather shadowy existence, even in theory, in the seventeenth and eighteenth centuries, and it has certainly not been greatly respected so far in the twentieth century. Thus the period was a short one during which neutrality was generally respected, and the rules of international law had little to do with the matter one way or the other. The chances of maintaining a neutral policy successfully have always been governed by the character of warfare, and they have varied with the variations of warfare in different ages. The conditions in which wars were fought in the nineteenth century (strictly, between 1815 and 1914)—the one period during which neutrality seems to have been an effective policy for avoiding involvement in a war—were of a very special kind. Virtually all the wars of that century were fought for limited aims, and were undertaken for the settlement of fairly well defined issues. They were not wars of the kind we now call ideological or totalitarian, struggles in which at least one side aims to vindicate a faith or to achieve the complete and unconditional submission of its antagonist. Then again, whereas before the French Revolutionary-Napoleonic wars central Europe was split into so many small weak states, that if every one of them had been allowed to decide for itself whether it would be neutral or not, belligerents could not have waged their wars effectively, that state of affairs was altered as a result of Napoleon's work. With the transformation of this

[3] Definitions of legal neutrality are legion. Some representative references are cited in T. Komarnicki, "The Place of Neutrality in the Modern System of International Law": *Recueil des Cours, Académie de droit international de la Haye* (1952), I.

[4] Diplomatic or political neutrality connotes a state of fact, two parties in conflict and a third adopting a policy or attitude of being on neither side.

[5] C. G. Fenwick, "The legal aspects of neutralism", *AJIL*, Jan. 1957, pp. 71-4.

B

'Kleinstaaterei' and the subsequent greater consolidation of the European states-system, it became possible in the nineteenth century for European belligerents, with the instruments of war and in the conditions of mobility then available, to carry on war and at the same time to respect the wishes of states desiring to be neutral without seriously impairing their own military efficiency. And what was more important, there was then a multiple balance-of-power system of several great powers. Each belligerent was anxious not to provoke a non-belligerent great power to join with its antagonist, and this was a factor encouraging respect for neutral rights. The net result of these conditions was that a policy of neutrality came to be generally regarded, with some justification, as an effective means of limiting the area of war by drawing a ring round the belligerents and letting them fight out their quarrel inside it, and the special and temporary nature of the conditions which made this possible attracted little attention. The First World War re-taught, and the Second World War re-emphasized the lesson of the French Revolutionary-Napoleonic Wars: that in any widespread and prolonged war the rights of neutrals will be little regarded. Today, as has always been the case, the law on the rights and duties of neutrals is neither undisputed nor unchanging. It is full of uncertainties and it has constantly changed. Even so, there has never yet been a war where there were no neutrals left at all; and, given a hot war, every state that stays out of it is *eo ipso* neutral.

Just as neutrality varies with the character of warfare, so neutralism varies with the changing character of the Cold War. Cold War is a situation in which each side continually envisages war with an acknowledged rival, it is a state of continuous preparation for war, a continuous war alert; and *the* Cold War, in which the Soviet Union and the United States are the principals, has been compatible with all forms of organized violence short of direct encounters between the armed forces of the two superpowers. Although the world balance of preponderant power has been roughly bi-polar since 1947, the significance of this in terms of military technology and the responses of the allies of the two superpowers has changed considerably. Neither the Soviet Union nor the United States are equally involved and interested at every point on the globe, but as the only truly world powers they each have at least a token interest in all of the world all of the time; and increasingly they have come to have substantive interests in a large part of the world most of the time. A Cold War binocular view of any international problem may not always be the most penetrating or pertinent, but at least it is always one possible view. The occurrence of wars, widely so-called, in Korea, Algeria, Indo-China, Malaya, the Congo, South Vietnam, and elsewhere, in prevailing global Cold War conditions, underlines the point that a clear distinction between war and Cold War, any more than that between war and peace, is not easy to apply to the real world. Hence the widespread use of such adjectives as 'general', 'local', 'limited', 'conventional', 'guerrilla', attached to war to describe various forms of organized violence. War, peace and Cold War cannot adequately be regarded as points on a single scale, but should perhaps be seen as items in a cluster or constellation of alternatives, each of which needs describing carefully in the context in which they are used.

With the onset of the Cold War it was from France that the word neutralism came into political vocabulary, after the brief period of French mediation between the superpowers had passed.[6] During 1949 and 1950 Etienne Gilson and Hubert Béuve-Méry in Le Monde, and Claude Bourdet in Combat and later in L'Observateur, became widely regarded as the exponents of neutralism;[7] though Gilson eventually made clear that for him, at least, the difference between neutralism and neutrality was "only unfortunately over words".[8] Indeed, the term neutralism was not embraced readily by the so-called proponents of the doctrine, and in a letter to the editor of Le Figaro Littéraire Gilson strongly denied that he was a "champion of neutralism".[9] His denial provoked the counter comment from the editor, Pierre Brisson, that Gilson "having launched the idea refuses to accept the word".[10] Gilson's refusal was not unique. Support for neutralism in France seemed to be far greater than the liking for the label. Bourdet's ironical formula "I'm not a neutralist, but——" then seemed aptly to describe the mood of a large number of Frenchmen.

In the summer of 1958 Bourdet, in the new journal of his British counterparts, described the genesis of this rather unwelcomed term as it emerged during 1947-8: "It was unpopular at that time to be a 'neutralist'. The name, which we did not choose, was picked for us by our opponents and by the pressmen. Rather than deny the title, which was not a particularly fortunate choice because of the aura of sit-back-and-do-nothing that surrounded it, we preferred to take it up and try to popularize it. 'Neutralism' very quickly had people worried."[11]

Bourdet describes how the stigma attached to neutralism began to diminish among "serious-thinking people" (sic) as India and Yugoslavia became popularly identified as neutralist states. As if to acknowledge the expansiveness of neutralism and with a Humpty-Dumpty-like insouciance towards the meanings of words, Bourdet claims that by 1958

[6] Dorothy Pickles, French Politics (London, 1953), pp. 186-91; and below p. 33.
[7] John Marcus, "Neutralism in France", Review of Politics (July 1955).
[8] Étienne Gilson, "Querelles de Mots", Le Monde, 31 Aug. 1950.
[9] Le Figaro Littéraire, 17 Feb. 1951.
[10] Ibid.
[11] Claude Bourdet, "The Way to European Independence", The New Reasoner (Summer 1958), pp. 12-13.

both sides in the cold war "seemed prepared to agree that active neutrality, or disengagement—the name is unimportant—was not such a bad thing . . . as long as it did not spread within their own ranks. The growth in the acceptance of these ideas has been astonishing when one remembers that it has taken place over a period of only ten years." [12]

For present purposes, neutrality and neutralism are in general regarded as quite distinct. By neutrality is meant non-involvement in war, while by neutralism is meant non-involvement in *the* Cold War. And while the tenuous distinction between war and peace is central to the concept of neutrality, it is the fact of freedom from or commitment to the military arrangements—the alliances—of the Cold War camps which has so far been central to the difference between Cold War alignment and non-alignment. These definitions of mine have no sanction in popular usage but they do, I think, draw attention to some important differences in fact. Very occasionally where I have felt the need to slur this distinction, though only verbally, this is because (as with Sweden and Switzerland) an alternative popular usage is already deeply entrenched, which it would be pedantic to dispute. I have then relied on making my contextual meaning clear. Though use of the phrase 'Cold War' to describe recent Soviet-American relations rightly avoids the superficial view that war and peace are stark antitheses, it is important to remember that it is quite possible for a state to be neutralist in its policy in the Cold War while at the same time being neutral with regard to a given local hot war. Also, a state can be involved in a local hot war while remaining neutralist in the Cold War. While the fact that a state is neutralist in the Cold War is, of course, no guarantee that it would be able to be neutral in a global hot war. And, however plausible is the view that the contemporary global Cold War is a state of affairs earlier characterized by Trotsky as "neither war nor peace", one must not lose sight of the fact that *the* Cold War still means international peace in the sense that it has not yet meant thermonuclear or world war.

Some other perplexities must be briefly mentioned. While it is convenient, and often unavoidable, to write of "the Western" or "the Eastern" "bloc", "the uncommitted world", "*le tiers-monde*", or "the non-aligned area", it must be remembered that these are simplifying generalizations which in each case mask great diversities and embrace widely varying patterns and possibilities. In using those indispensable notions "State" and "Nation" if there is real danger of illicit "reification" —of mistaking words for things, metaphors for realities—there is at least equal danger in rejecting these popularly postulated presences as utterly insignificant. There is no easy way of resolving these difficulties, nor are

[12] *Ibid.*

they *merely* verbal. For students of politics must try to follow Professor J. L. Austin's injunction and use "a sharpened awareness of words to sharpen an awareness of the phenomena". Where terminology is loose, where common usage inadequately expresses notions and distinctions which we feel important, our best precision is found in being aware of the nature of our tools, of the different senses in which the same words are used, in trying to keep as sharp as possible distinctions we believe to be crucial, and in trying to keep each contextual meaning as clear as possible.

Yet all this is easier to recommend than to practise. Consider such questions as: is neutralism a specific condition or state of affairs, or merely something imputed to some states at particular times by other states? Is neutralism a doctrine or a policy or both? How many neutralist states are there? What are the significant similarities and differences between various neutralists? None of these questions admit of easy answers. This is why they are important and interesting.

Clearly, the abstract noun 'neutralism' (or even its adjective 'neutralist') may serve in the title of a book but to attempt answers to any of the questions outlined above requires further analysis and explanation.

CHAPTER II

NEUTRALISM, THE SUPERPOWERS AND THE COLD WAR

"For Warre consisteth not in Battell onely, or the act of fighting;
but in a tract of time, wherein the Will to contend by Battell is
sufficiently known: and therefore the notion of Time is to be considered in the nature of Warre; as it is in the nature of weather.
For as the nature of foule weather, lyeth not in a showre or two of
rain; but in an inclination thereto of many dayes together; so the
nature of War, consisteth not in actual fighting; but in the known
disposition thereto, during all the time there is no assurance to the
contrary."   Thomas Hobbes, *Leviathan* (1651), Chapter 13.

THE roots of the contemporary Cold War go deep. Although the
rivalry between the Soviet Union and the United States did not
become intense, openly acknowledged on both sides, and of world-
wide significance until after the Second World War, the seeds of their
antagonism and rivalry were sown at the birth of the new Soviet State.

In Tsarist days relations between Russia and the United States were
few, and were for both countries secondary.[1] In general, the two countries were, in Walter Lippmann's words, "separated by an ideological
gulf and joined by the bridge of national interest".[2] Before 1917 they
had never clashed in war and, despite the differences between Tsarist
autocracy and Presidential democracy, each regarded the other, in effect,
as "a potential friend in the rear of potential enemies".[3] Then, following
the Bolshevik Revolution in November 1917, the new Soviet regime,
through the unofficial agency of Colonel Robins, sought diplomatic
recognition and aid from America against Germany. The United States,
which had previously made a substantial loan to Kerensky's provisional
government, refused both requests. Instead, for three years following
the separate peace of Brest-Litovsk with Germany in March 1918, the
Soviets, while cherishing vain hopes of world revolution, had to fight
for survival in the face of American and Allied intervention and
blockade. The view, so precious to Soviet historiography, that the intervention had from the very beginning the single deliberate motive to
"strangle Communism at birth" is tenable only if one neglects the actual
records of allied muddle and misunderstanding, of conflicting thoughts

[1] See W. A. Williams, *American-Russian Relations, 1781-1947* (New York, 1952).
[2] This *mot* is quoted in Edward R. Stettinius, Jun., *Roosevelt and the Russians*
(London, 1950), p. 16; but the illustration of this point is in chapter 8 of
W. Lippmann, *U.S. Foreign Policy* (London, 1943), esp. pp. 85-8.
[3] *Ibid.*, p. 88; see also pp. 89-94.

and aims, arising during the stress and heat of war.[4] It is, nevertheless, true that the immediate and lasting effect of intervention was to confirm Lenin in everything he had hitherto preached about the inevitable hostility of 'Capitalism' towards 'Communism'. Wilsonian and Leninist messianism thus became not complementary, as had seemed possible for a short while during 1917, but opposed; and the decision for conflict, taken unwillingly in July 1918, prefigured the antagonisms of the post-1945 period. It was ironic that in 1920 the United States was the only truly world power, and repudiated the rôle; while the Soviets, who so yearned to play a world rôle, lacked the capacity to do so. When each of them became active world powers after 1945, it was as implacable rivals.

Active participation in the later part of the First World War did not persuade the United States to depart finally from its traditional policy of diplomatic aloofness from Europe, and with the end of the war the Senate rejected the Versailles Treaty, refused to countenance United States membership of the League of Nations, and the country relapsed into isolationism. This return to what was somewhat nostalgically described as "normalcy" was not in the 1920s so absolute a policy of isolation as it became in the next decade. Nor was hostility towards the Soviet Union completely unremitting. It seems that by the time of the Washington Conference in 1922 the United States had begun to act on the assumption that the territorial integrity of the Soviet Union was an American national interest.[5] This did not mean that 'Bolshevism' was deemed any the less abhorrent. What it did mean was that the Soviet State should be allowed to exist, but should be treated as a pariah. Such attitudes found ambiguous expression in economic relations which between 1924 and 1930 produced small but increasing trade (so that by 1930 the United States was the biggest single source of Soviet imports), and a diplomatic policy which, until 1933, was determinedly one of non-recognition. Deciding how, in the words of Washington's *Farewell Address*,[6] "our interest, guided by justice, shall counsel", in inter-

[4] For a masterly, detailed, study, see George F. Kennan. *Soviet-American Relations, 1917-1920*: vol. i, Russia Leaves the War (London, 1956); vol. ii, The Decision to Intervene (London, 1958).

[5] See Lippmann, *op. cit.*, p. 87, n. 2.

[6] See James D. Richardson, ed., *Messages and Papers of the Presidents 1789-1905* (Washington, 1907), vol. i, pp. 213-24. The Address is read annually on Washington's birthday in each House of Congress. In the second volume of his memoirs ex-President Truman comments on the significance of this, pointing out that for "the isolationists this address was like a Biblical text". Truman rightly remarks that the isolationists relied on a very selective reading of Washington's advice. See Harry S. Truman, *Years of Trial and Hope, 1946-1953* (London, 1956), p. 107. The famous phrase "entangling alliances with none", was from Jefferson's First Inaugural and not from Washington's *Farewell Address*. See also below, p. 73.

national matters was no easy task, and the strength of isolationism suggested that the United States was unprepared to assume an active world rôle. Yet no matter how persistently American leaders clung to the national ideal of isolationism,[7] there was no denying that by now their country had the undoubted capacity of a great power, it was difficult, if not impossible, to remain remote from the mainstreams of international politics. Domestic decisions, such as revaluing the dollar and increasing the stringencies of immigration quotas, and domestic events such as the Wall Street "crash" of 1929, had their immediate repercussions throughout the world. Yet the moral drawn from these demonstrations of world influence was not that isolationism should be abandoned for a more actively international rôle, but the reverse. The Great Depression undoubtedly strengthened domestic preoccupations and throughout the 'thirties foreign relations were deemed secondary and intrusive. Though the loosely worded Roosevelt-Litvinov agreements of November 1933[8] ended U.S. non-recognition of the U.S.S.R., and seemed to promise future co-operation, especially in the Far East, resurgent American isolationism foredoomed all such expectations.[9] American debate about issues of war and peace centred round successive Neutrality Acts. There was wide agreement as to the desirability of keeping the country out of war. What was contentious was whether or not federal legislation was in itself a sufficient and practical way to avoid involvement—a question which received a decisive answer with the Japanese attack on Pearl Harbour on 7th December 1941. In Senator Vandenberg's words, "that day ended isolationism for any realist".

In 1917 the Soviet Union, like the United States in the late eighteenth century, was born of a revolution proclaiming international ideals; but whereas the American revolution was directed against the overseas metropolitan power and soon embraced a modest and cautious foreign policy of "no entanglements", the Soviet revolution was aimed not only at overthrowing the Tsarist dynasty but at sparking off world revolution. The Tsars had developed no tradition of isolationism comparable with that of the United States, and the leaders of the new Bolshevik state had neither the inclination nor the opportunity to adopt either an

[7] "Isolationism, the ideology or the body of doctrine emanating from the original and deeply rooted belief, not really shaken until 1941, in the geographical remoteness and security of the country, is the underlying expression of American nationalism. Indeed it is nationalism, and like the nationalism of other countries (or perhaps even more) it is a coat of many colours": Richard W. van Alstyne, *The American Empire. Its Historical Pattern and Evolution* (Hist. Assoc. pamphlet G.43, London 1960), p. 27.
[8] See *Foreign Relations of the U.S.* (Washington, 1933), vol. ii, pp. 785, 789, 790, 793-4.
[9] A. Nevins, *The New Deal and World Affairs, 1933-1945* (New Haven, 1950).

ideological or a diplomatic impartiality towards Europe. The deepest motif of Soviet policies between 1917 and 1941 was the preservation of the integrity of Soviet power within Russia.[10] This was less obvious in the early years after 1917 while hopes of world revolution still ran high, but it became clear after Stalin assumed leadership—for the slogan "socialism in a single country" was, as Isaac Deutscher[11] has remarked, nothing but a doctrine of isolationism expressed in Bolshevik idiom. It was a brand of isolationism very different from that of America: whereas the United States was separated from the main conflicts of world politics by two great oceans, Russia's frontiers lay open to any invader. While American isolationism grew out of security and self-sufficiency, that of the Soviets grew out of insecurity and fear (both fed by Soviet doctrine as well as by experiences since 1917) and absorption in internal tasks. Soviet determination to secure the safety of their frontiers resulted in a number of treaties of non-aggression and "neutrality" with neighbouring states.[12] These not only had the direct advantages of relieving pressure on Soviet borders, but these treaties with Germany, Turkey, Persia and Afghanistan against Western "imperialist" powers, were one way of forwarding Soviet "revolutionary" aims outside the Soviet Union too. Official Soviet attitudes towards the United States were ambivalent. The United States was undoubtedly a "capitalist" state and, therefore, a member of the camp rivalling the Soviet Union,[13] but American technical efficiency was openly envied.[14]

[10] See Louis Fischer, *The Soviets in World Affairs* (2 vols., London, 1930); Max Beloff, *The Foreign Policy of Soviet Russia 1929-1941* (2 vols., London, 1947-9); and G. F. Kennan, *Soviet Foreign Policy, 1917-1941* (Anvil books, New York, 1960).

[11] Isaac Deutscher, *The Great Contest* (London, 1960), p. 45. Communists themselves prefer the term Socialism to describe their present condition. Communism is a higher phase which still lies in the future.

[12] "In addition to converting the conception of a neutral obligation from a passive one such as marked nineteenth century neutrality to one of an active and positive character, the Soviet Union insisted on giving and receiving specific guarantees of non-aggression and non-interference." M. W. Graham, "The Soviet Security System", quoted in Beloff, *op. cit.*, vol. i, p. 12. The U.S.S.R. concluded neutrality treaties with Germany, Turkey, Persia, Afghanistan, Latvia, Lithuania, Estonia and Finland—see Beloff, esp. chapter 2. Such treaties may be regarded as forerunners of Cold War "Peaceful Co-existence" treaties. See R. N. Carew-Hunt, *A Guide to Communist Jargon* (London, 1957), pp. 26-33—Coexistence, and below p. 44.

[13] Thus Stalin in his Political Report to the 14th Party Congress of the U.S.S.R., 18 Dec. 1925—"Two dominant and mutually antagonist poles of attraction have come into existence, so that the world over, sympathies are diverging towards one pole or the other: the sympathies of the bourgeois governments tending towards the British-American pole, and the sympathies of the workers of the West and of the revolutionists of the East tending towards the Soviet Union pole": in J. Stalin, *Problems of Leninism* (London, 1938 ed.), pp. 369-70.

[14] *Ibid.*, 1954 ed., pp. 109-11.

As early as May 1918, Lenin had predicted that America would check the movement of Japanese imperialism against Russia, and with the realization of this prediction by 1922 it seemed that the chances of direct Soviet-American clashes were remote. Indeed, before 1933 relations between the two countries were virtually non-existent. Even after the Litvinov-Roosevelt agreements, and throughout the ensuing years down to the involvement of both powers in World War II, relations remained troubled, distant, and devoid of real political content.[15] From 1933, with the growth of Fascist power and the consequent development of a third bloc in world politics, the Soviet Union became the most active verbal champion of "collective security" and a sneering denigrator of the "non-intervention" and "neutrality" policies of "capitalist" states.[16] The 1939 edition of the *Great Soviet Encyclopaedia* recorded that "the position of neutrality within the contemporary imperialist system is, under all conditions, not only a dangerous illusion which in no way prevents a neutral state from being drawn into war, but is in fact a justification of aggression, and a contributing factor to the unleashing of war". The article said further that the Soviet Union regards its "neutrality pacts" as "a weapon in the struggle for the destruction of the front of Imperialist States against the U.S.S.R.".[17] These points were underlined when on 23 August 1939 Molotov signed the German-Soviet Pact of Non-Aggression and Neutrality.[18]

Both the United States and the Soviet Union only entered the Second World War fully and formally as a result of direct attack on their own territories. Even so, while both sides were officially neutral for some time after the German attack on Poland in September 1939, they both in fact tilted their neutrality policies in favour of one of the belligerents, though their favours were given to opposite camps. Before the attack on Pearl Harbour on 7th December 1941, and despite the strength of American isolationism, President Roosevelt's pro-British neutrality[19] was shown in such acts as Lend Lease and the transfer of American destroyers to the Royal Navy. Ostensibly, the Soviet Union was scrupulously neutral till she suffered German invasion in June 1941.[20] In fact,

[15] Beloff, *op. cit.*, vol. i, chapter 10.
[16] See J. Stalin, *op. cit.* (above), 1954 ed., pp. 753-4. John Foster Dulles, who always urged his countrymen to make a close study of *Problems of Leninism*, quotes this passage in his *War or Peace* (London, 1950), pp. 24-35.
[17] I am indebted for this translation to my colleague, Professor Ilya Neustadt.
[18] Text in *Nazi-Soviet Relations, 1939-1941* (Dept. of State, Washington, D.C., 1948), pp. 76-8. See also *ibid.*, pp. 105-7, for text of the further German-Soviet Treaty of 28 Sept. 1939.
[19] See W. L. Langer and G. E. Gleason, *The Undeclared War, 1940-41* (London, 1953).
[20] David J. Dallin, *Soviet Russia's Foreign Policy, 1939-1942* (Yale U.P., 1942), George Ginsburgs, "The Soviet Union as a Neutral, 1939-41" in *Soviet Studies*

she faithfully pursued her collaboration with Germany, as entailed in the secret protocols to the agreements of 1939. Her policies were further marked by successive retreats in the Balkans in face of German advances, by the Neutrality Pact with Japan[21] signed on 13 April 1941, and destined to last until the Yalta Conference four years later, and by territorial expansion: eastern Poland in September 1939, followed by Latvia, Lithuania and Estonia, Bessarabia, also certain parts of Finland, all during 1940. These contrasting activities pursued by the two greatest neutrals, preceding their direct participation in general war, reaffirmed a lesson taught during the French Revolutionary-Napoleonic and First World Wars: that no great power can remain completely outside any prolonged war involving the other great powers.

From 1941 a common determination to fight the Fascist powers forged the Grand Alliance. Nevertheless, throughout World War II contacts of all kinds between the Soviet Union and her allies were strictly regulated by the Soviet government. Allied representatives who had to deal with Soviet Russia during the war resented the restrictions and lack of real cordiality in such relations.[22] This essentially military alliance between states of such diametrically opposed outlooks was dictated by, and limited to, short run considerations of mutual advantage. With the defeat of Germany in sight, individual political considerations began to take precedence over the requirements of a common strategy, and the Alliance began to break up. This was partly masked up to the time of the Yalta Conference, in February 1945, with the continuance of the three great wartime leaders—Roosevelt, Stalin and Churchill—in power. But by the time of the Potsdam Conference, July-August 1945—with Roosevelt now succeeded by Truman, and with Churchill superseded by Attlee during the Conference—the rift between the Soviet Union and its former allies became patent, and reverted to the pre-1941 condition of mutual suspicion and hostility. This situation was appro-

---

(Glasgow) July 1958, pp. 12-35. Ginsburgs points out that "it is a consistent point of dogma with the Soviets that a bourgeois state is incapable of genuine neutrality and that the U.S.S.R. is infinitely superior in preserving *bona fide* neutrality".

[21] For the terms and significance of this treaty, see F. C. Jones, *Japan's New Order in East Asia, 1937-45* (London, 1954), p. 214, *et seq*. It is interesting to note what Mao Tse-tung was writing in his Yenan retreat at this time: "As the conflict between the socialist Soviet Union and imperialist powers becomes further intensified it is inevitable that China must stand either on one side or on the other. Is it possible to incline to neither side? No, this is an illusion. All the countries in the world will be swept into one or other of these two camps, and in the world today 'neutrality' is becoming a deceptive phrase": "On New Democracy" (Jan. 1940) in vol. iii of *Selected Works of Mao Tse-tung* (London, 1954), p. 135; see also p. 125.

[22] For the ambiguities in Soviet relations with her major allies, see W. H. McNeil, *America, Britain and Russia, Their Co-operation and Conflict*, R.I.I.A. *Survey of International Affairs, 1939-46* (London, 1953), esp. chapter 1, section 3.

priately symbolized in the deliberately non-committal way in which
Stalin was told of American possession of the first atomic bomb.[23] Now,
not only were the nineteenth century prophecies[24] of Alexis de Tocqueville, Sir John Seeley and Henry Adams soon to be emphatically realized
with the undeniable emergence of the United States and Russia as the
two Titans of the post-war world, but their growing rivalry, under the
looming shadow of nuclear weapons, ushered in what became widely
known as the Cold War.

Though the phrase[25] only became current after 1945, neither the idea
nor the state of Cold War—intense international tension in a continual atmosphere of rumours and rumbles of war—was new. Indeed,
it has been one of the main purposes of the preceding pages to show
that the Soviet Union (indeed each Communist power) always regards
itself in a state of Cold War with the "capitalist" world, and that
"neutrality" in Communist theory and practice is a device to be used or
vilified in light of current needs. Furthermore, such different men as
Thucydides, Machiavelli, Hobbes, Clausewitz, Bismarck, Hitler and
Lenin all knew and wrote about different versions of Cold War. What
is special about the contemporary Cold War is its extent, for the two
chief adversaries, in terms of territory and tactics, and that it is waged
in the presence of nuclear weapons.

The main vicissitudes of the Cold War can be conveniently outlined
in terms of four fairly distinct phases. Each of these phases is characterized by changes: in the most intense areas of Cold War conflict, in
the formation and fortunes of the Cold War alliance systems, in the
emergence of new states, and in the policies of the superpowers[26]
towards neutralism. It is in no way the aim here to attempt a full
narrative acount, but merely to sketch what appear to be the major

[23] See Herbert Feis, *Between War and Peace. The Potsdam Conference* (London,
1960), esp. pp. 173-8.

[24] Alexis de Tocqueville in *De la Démocratie in Amérique* (in 1835); Sir John
Seeley in *The Expansion of England* (1883), and Henry Adams in a letter to his
brother Brook Adams in 1898.

[25] The phrase was first used publicly by Mr. Bernard Baruch, the American
financier. The phrase was coined for him by one of his speech writers, a veteran
newspaper man Herbert Bayard Swope. See Eric F. Goldman, *The Crucial Decade
and After, America 1945-1960* (Vintage Books, New York, 1961), p. 60. Undoubtedly the phrase was first popularized by Mr Walter Lippmann during 1947
in a series of fourteen articles originally published in the *New York Herald-
Tribune*, critical of Mr Kennan's "containment" thesis. See also a Soviet writer
G. Dadyants, "The Cold War: Past and Present", in *International Affairs*
(Moscow), June 1960, pp. 5-10, who also attributes the phrase "cold war" to
Bernard Baruch.

[26] The term was the invention of an American scholar, W. T. R. Fox; see his
book *The Super-Powers* (New York, 1944). To Fox in 1944 it seemed that there
would be three post-war superpowers—the U.S., the U.S.S.R. and the British
Commonwealth.

developments in the continuing Cold War struggle in relation to neutralism. Following Hobbes' example of meteorological metaphor, these four main Cold War phases may be described as (1) the great freeze-up (1945-9), (2) constant cold (1949-53), (3) partial thaw (1953-7), (4) variable weather (1957-December 1962). Though these four headings mark major Cold War phases, they also, and perhaps more accurately, mark changes in Soviet policies towards neutralist states.

(1) THE GREAT FREEZE-UP, 1945-9

At first sight the growth and consolidation of the two rival Cold War blocs takes on the delusive appearance of inevitability. This view could be sustained by appropriate selections from Soviet 'classic' writings, but a reading of the memoirs of such prominent Americans as Senator Vandenberg[27] and President Truman[28] conveys a much more confused picture, showing the mixture of nostalgia and resolution with which Americans turned their backs on the national tradition of isolationism, the at first faltering but soon unavoidable recognition of Soviet expansionist policies, and the gradual but quite determined assumption of leadership to stem Communist advances. These immediate post-war years saw a revolution in the conduct of American foreign policy, not only in her willingness to assume a permanent rôle of leadership in world politics, but also, domestically, in the deliberate forging of a bi-partisan, or non-partisan, foreign policy. But such early American moves, between 1945 and 1947, as the abrupt termination of Lend Lease, rapid demobilization, and the beginnings of a system of staged withdrawal of her troops from overseas, suggested to many Europeans ominous parallels with American policies after 1919. It was Soviet intransigence[29] and growing American reaction to it, quickly becoming

[27] See *The Private Papers of Senator Vandenberg* (London, 1953). Until Pearl Harbour in 1941 Vandenberg was a symbol and a leader of isolationism, or, as he preferred to say, "insulationism"; after 1941 he became a firm advocate of an international role for the U.S. His papers give, as his son attests, "a narrative account of the decade 1941 to 1951, in which the mass mind of America reluctantly forsook its isolationist traditions and accepted the challenge to world leadership". Herbert Agar draws attention to Vandenberg's importance in his brief book *The Unquiet Years. U.S.A. 1945-1955* (London, 1957).

[28] Harry S. Truman, *Year of Decisions, 1945* (London, 1955), *Years of Trial and Hope, 1946-1953* (London, 1956). Truman and Stalin are the dominant figures of the first two phases of the Cold War.

[29] Of course, the Soviet view is different. G. Dadyants, *op. cit.*, p. 6, who divides up the Cold War into four phases, similar to the divisions used in this chapter, writes: "The causes of the Cold War should be sought not in the alleged desire of the Soviet Union to impose a new order of things upon other countries, but in the real desire of some Western Powers to impose the old order upon peoples who did not want them. The Cold War was caused by the reckless plans of the most aggressive circles of imperialism which, overestimating their own strength, seriously sought to turn back the march of history".

a process of mutual interaction, which soon made these analogies irrelevant.

Soviet influence, operating from a secure base inside Russia, and despite enormous wartime losses in resources and manpower, was from 1945 onwards pressing outward in all directions. She had three main theatres of operation. These were, in ascending order of importance, the Far East, the Middle East, and Europe.

In the Far East the Soviet Union secured, during the latter half of 1945, the Kuriles and South Sakhalin, and her troops occupied Manchuria. In accordance with the Potsdam agreements, she also occupied Korea north of the 38th parallel; with U.S. forces to the south. Towards China she pursued right up to 1949 an equivocal policy of giving slight support to the Chinese Communists, while recognizing and dealing more fully with the Kuomintang.[30] In the Middle East traditional Russian pressure on Turkey and on Persia was renewed and attempts to embarrass Western interests in this area led to the Soviet Union casting the first veto in the U.N. Security Council. However, Europe was the prime area of Soviet concern, and where she made her greatest post-war territorial advances. She regained the territories initially obtained during the period of Nazi-Soviet alliance. In addition, she acquired the province of Petsamo, with its valuable nickel mines, from Finland; part of Ruthenia from Czechoslovakia; and a piece of East Prussia, including the port of Kaliningrad, from Germany. Moreover, most of the countries of Eastern Europe fell under Soviet sway — whether they were the 'liberated' territories of Czechoslovakia, Yugoslavia, Albania, and Poland, or the ex-enemy states of Bulgaria, Hungary, Roumania, and Finland. With the two exceptions of Yugoslavia, which was to successfully assert her freedom from Cominform control in June 1948, and Finland, which enjoyed a severely circumscribed freedom under the terms of the Finno-Soviet treaty of April 1948, all these states became Soviet satellites. An interlocking network of treaties[31] developed to bind them to each other and to the Soviet Union in particular. Russia's direct sphere of control also included the Soviet zones of occupation in Germany and Austria. In areas outside the sway of Soviet armies, especially in Western Europe and South-East Asia, Communist efforts concentrated on building up the strength of local parties and on fomenting internal unrest against "bourgeois-capitalist" governments — policies which found doctrinal expression in Zhadnov's speech[32] at the founding conference of the Cominform in September 1947.

[30] See Hugh Seton-Watson, *The Pattern of Communist Revolution* (London, 2nd ed., 1960), pp. 271-90.

[31] See Z. K. Brzezinski, *The Soviet Bloc: Unity and Conflict* (Praeger, New York, 1961), esp. chapter 6.

[32] For text, see R.I.I.A., *Documents for 1947-8*, pp. 125 *et seq.*

Zhadnov reaffirmed the celebrated Leninist-Stalinist doctrine of "two camps", stressed that a world revolutionary situation now existed, and proclaimed that all Communist parties had to go over to the offensive. At the same time a world-wide peace campaign[33] was launched to provide cover for this aggressive policy. As the U.N. became part of the diplomatic equipment of the Cold War, Stalin's World Peace Movement seemed intended to create alternative international organizations to a U.N. dominated by American power.[34]

As the American reaction to Soviet threats began to crystallize, after the uncertainties of 1945-6, a pattern of bipolarity developed. Official American strategy came to be based on taking up positions all along the perimeter of the Soviet world to resist any further Soviet advance. Translated into operational policy terms, such a "containment" thesis[35] eventually led the United States to assume commitments over a wide arc stretching from North Cape in Norway, through Central and Southern Europe, North Africa, the Middle East, South and South-East Asia, then northwards through the Philippines, the Ryukyu and Ronin islands, Japan and Korea to Alaska. Such long Cold War frontiers became fortified, though gradually, in response to each Soviet challenge and by such actions as seemed dictated by the circumstances.

Before 1949, Soviet breakthroughs seemed to be most likely in Western and South-Eastern Europe, and American Cold War policies began in these areas with emergency programmes of extensive economic and military aid to combat the twin dangers of Communist subversion and Russian military pressure: first, to Greece and Turkey, under the "Truman Doctrine" of March 1947; then, more comprehensively, under the Marshall Plan from June 1947 onwards. The Marshall Plan initially was limited to economic aid, had no overt anti-Communist overtones and was ostensibly aimed at increasing inter-European co-operation, peace, order and stability. But, subjected to the pressure of political controversy, it took on a markedly anti-Communist aspect and in so doing pioneered a way for a good deal of later American foreign economic policies. (In July 1947 the Soviets rejected the application of the Marshall Plan within her sphere of control. In January 1949 Bulgaria, Czechoslovakia, Hungary, Roumania and the Soviet Union formed a Council for Mutual Economic Assistance (Comecon or C.E.M.A.) as a

[33] For a short Soviet history of the Peace Movement, see "Ten Years of the World Peace Movement", *New Times* (Moscow), Apr. 1959, pp. 27-9.

[34] See Martin Wight, *The Power Struggle in the U.N.* (Los Angeles, 1957).

[35] The author of the containment thesis was George F. Kennan. His thesis was first made public in *Foreign Affairs*, July 1947, under the title "The Sources of Soviet Conduct". Up to 1953 Kennan was a steady advocate of the primacy of the problem of limited war, as his analysis of Soviet policy led him to the view that Stalin would be exceedingly cautious about risking major war.

counter-weight to the Marshall Plan; and during 1949 the armies of the
satellites were rebuilt and re-equipped under Soviet direction.) The
Berlin Blockade, from early 1948 until May 1949, was the first open test
the Soviet Union made of American determination and strength.[36] It
was a struggle fought with weapons of blockade and air lift, and not
only did this test harden American resolution to carry containment
through to completion, it also helped to bring about the birth of the
North Atlantic Treaty Organization (N.A.T.O.) in April 1949.[37]
N.A.T.O. thus became the second post-war multilateral security pact in
which the U.S. was to play a leading rôle. The Rio Pact of 1947[38] was
the first, but this was designed for an area still outside the main areas of
Cold War conflict, though it was not without relevance to Cold War
activities, as over a third of the original members of the U.N. were Latin-
American countries and at this time they tended to vote with the U.S.
on all Cold War matters.

Direct confrontation between the two main Cold War protagonists,
apart from encounters at various U.N. meetings, was rare. Even more
rarely, when they found themselves on the same side (as with the birth
of Israel in 1948) their mutual embarrassment was obvious. At the
inaugural meetings of the U.N. there had been a general feeling that the
legal status of neutrality would be redundant with the institution of
the U.N. collective security system;[39] and there was a widespread feeling
that the status of neutrality was, in itself, immoral. Though two wartime neutrals, Argentina[40] and Turkey[41] were among the fifty-one
original members of the U.N., there was general agreement in ostraciz-
ing Franco's Spain, and Switzerland did not apply for membership.
Soviet pressure on Turkey between 1945 and 1949 well illustrates the
coincidence of Soviet post-war distaste for Second World War neutrals
and her shrewd expectation of satisfying territorial ambitions at the

[36] See R.I.I.A., *Survey for 1947-8*, pp. 241 *et seq.*
[37] With twelve founder members—Belgium, Canada, Denmark, France, Iceland,
Italy, Luxemburg, the Netherlands, Norway, Portugal, the U.K. and the U.S.
For details and text, see Lord Ismay, N.A.T.O. *The First Five Years, 1949-54*
(Utrecht, 2nd impression, 1956).
[38] The Inter-American Treaty of Reciprocal Assistance signed at Rio de Janeiro
25 Sept. 1947, by all states of the American hemisphere except Nicaragua, Ecuador
and Canada. For this treaty, see R.I.I.A., *Survey for 1947-8*, pp. 465-76, and
Documents for 1947-8, pp. 773-9.
[39] See *Documents of the United Nations Conference on International Organization* (San Francisco, 1945), vol. vi, p. 459; vol. vii, p. 327. For an analysis of
changing legal attitudes, see H. J. Taubenfeld, "International Actions and
Neutrality", A.J.I.L., vol. xlvii (1953), pp. 377-96.
[40] See *The Memoirs of Cordell Hull* (London, 1948), vol. i, chapters 23-5 and
vol. ii, chapter 99.
[41] See Lenczowski, *op. cit.*, pp. 147-50.

expense of the supposedly compromised neutrals.[42] As the Cold War struggle developed and U.N. collective security measures were clearly inoperative, not only was the earlier assumed redundancy of the law of neutrality seen to be premature but Cold War necessities, as seen by the two main protagonists, made the question of behaviour during the Second World War less important than present intentions, as each side sought to enlist support and gain strength against her chief adversary. Neither the United States nor the Soviet Union appeared ready to accept the idea of genuine non-attachment to either cause; the only essential difference was that the United States could distinguish in practice between active and passive allies, that is, between those with whom she concluded treaties and those others which were, nevertheless, part of the non-Communist world.

It was in France in the years 1947-9 that the word neutralism first emerged and became widely used publicly. The French neutralists straddled a wide segment of opinion and were far from agreed among themselves. At this time the word neutralism became primarily associated with expressions of war-weariness, of pessimism, or nihilism, of distrust and dislike of alliances and indeed of all foreign policy, of passivity or je-m'en-fichisme (I could not care less-ism). In Europe generally professions of neutralism, however articulate,[43] were the concern of impotent cliques not of governments. Neutralist advocacy centred on opposition to the formation of N.A.T.O. and apparently had no significant effect on policies. States either fell under Russian sway, became formal allies of America, or stayed isolated. In this latter class were Ireland, Spain, Sweden, and Switzerland—all neutrals of the Second World War[44]—and they were joined by Yugoslavia after its break with the Cominform in 1948.

[42] Before Dec. 1955 only nine states gained admission to the U.N. following the original fifty-one. These were Afghanistan, Iceland and Sweden (Nov. 1946); Thailand (Dec. 1946); Pakistan and the Yemen (Sept. 1947); Burma (Apr. 1948); Israel (May 1949); and Indonesia (Sept. 1950). The first three were wartime neutrals, two of them became neutralist, while Iceland joined N.A.T.O. Thailand, an ex-enemy state of World War II, became an ally of the Western Powers. Pakistan was neutralist until 1954 and then an American ally. The Yemen, independent but isolationist since 1918, became neutralist. The last three were new states and all became neutralist, though Israel's neutralism took on a marked Western orientation. All other applications were refused. For details, see Y.B.U.N., passim. Concerning neutralist policies see below, chapter 4.

[43] See John Marcus, Neutralism and Nationalism in France (New York, 1958); Marina Salvin, Neutralism in France and Germany (New York, 1951); and I. William Zartman, "Neutralism and Neutrality in Scandinavia" in Western Political Quarterly, vol. vii (2), June 1954, pp. 125-60.

[44] Twenty European states declared their neutrality in 1939, but only five— Ireland, Portugal, Spain, Sweden, and Switzerland—were able successfully to maintain it.

C

In Asia ten new states emerged—Israel, Jordan, Syria, Lebanon,[45] Pakistan, India, Ceylon, Burma, Indonesia, and the Philippines.[46] All of them at this time were mainly absorbed in internal tasks. The governments of Burma, Indonesia and the Philippines each faced internal Communist insurrection. The Philippines became the great exception to the general rule that the new states of the post-war world do not enter Cold War alliances. India, by far the largest and most influential of the new states, in her efforts to speed Indonesian independence, and by her reaction to the situations in Indo-China and Malaya, made clear that Indian concern was more with 'colonial' struggles than with Cold War rivalries. This soon became a standard neutralist claim throughout Asia and Africa. Great Britain was still the dominant power in the Middle East and appeared as the chief 'protector', however unwelcome, in this area. Iraq, though formally independent at least since 1932, was, like Egypt, still closely linked by treaty to Britain. But the rejection of the unratified Anglo-Iraqi Treaty of Portsmouth in 1948, following public riots and demonstrations against it in the streets of Baghdad, underlined the point that opposition to what were believed to be grossly 'unequal' treaties could easily be mobilized in Middle Eastern countries. The Soviets[47] openly regarded the governments, though not the 'toiling masses', of all the new states as 'puppets' of their former colonial masters; while American policy makers erred in assuming too readily that if an Asian state was non-Communist it was naturally ready to take part in American led anti-Communist measures.[48] On the whole, though, these new states were not much involved in Cold War matters, and their desire to be neutralist was not yet a matter of much international significance.

In the main areas of Cold War concern divisions hardened, both Moscow and Washington enlisted partisans and helped to seal off frontiers or to resolve civil strife. In Germany, east and west became completely cut off from each other (with West Berlin a small island in a Communist sea); in China, the Communists won a conclusive victory over the Kuomintang, and Chiang Kai-Shek's forces had to evacuate,

[45] Independence in Jordan, Syria and Lebanon had been declared during the Second World War but only became effective after 1945.

[46] The emergence of the Philippines as an independent state was accompanied by a complex set of agreements binding her to the U.S. See Fifield, *op. cit.*, pp. 60-5.

[47] See George Ginsburgs, "The Soviet Union, Neutrality and Collective Security, 1945-1959" in *Osteuropa Recht*, Oct. 1959, pp. 77-98, and the same author's "Neutrality and Neutralism and the Tactics of Soviet Diplomacy" in *American Slavic and East European Review* (New York, Dec. 1960). These two articles are based on Soviet publications.

[48] See K. S. Latourette, *The American Record in the Far East, 1945-1951* (New York, 1952), esp. pp. 40-2.

mostly to Formosa; in Korea, the Russian dominated north faced the American occupied south. In Greece, Turkey and Iran,[49] Communist pressures were successfully resisted. The only overt loss of an ally suffered by either side during this period was Yugoslavia's defection from the Communist camp; Kuomintang China was not formally an ally of the West, though the victory of the Communists was widely represented as a great American defeat.[50]

This first phase of the Cold War was a time of American atomic monopoly and of the Soviet Union's overwhelming superiority in conventional armaments. It is difficult to see what particular diplomatic advantages atomic monopoly gave to the United States. Probably it was a restraining influence on the Soviets, though Stalin constantly denied that there was any special value in the possession of atomic bombs.[51] America's exclusive atomic monopoly ended in September 1949 with the first explosion of a Soviet bomb, though the world had to learn of it through an American announcement;[52] and this event, coming shortly after the signature of the N.A.T.O. treaty and the conclusive victory of the Communists in China, gave dramatic point to the idea of bipolarity which by now had come to be the dominant pattern of world affairs.

(2) CONSTANT COLD, 1949-53

If the first phase was dominated by events in Europe, then the second was equally dominated by developments in eastern Asia, and particularly by the Korean War.[53] China had been exempted from the developing bi-partisanship of American policy, and though the Korean War began in June 1950 as a U.N. operation designed to repel a north Korean invasion south of the 38th parallel (a little earlier Soviet troops had withdrawn from north Korea, and American troops from south Korea to Japan), by January 1951 it had become converted, essentially, into a Sino-American conflict, fought solely on Korean soil. In these years American involvement in world affairs deepened, while at the same time domestic criticisms, the obvious misgivings of allies and the

[49] See Lenczowski, op. cit., pp. 181-90, esp. pp. 188-9, for an account of U.S.-Iranian economic and military agreements.

[50] See Latourette, ibid., chapter 8—"The Great American Defeat". (In 1949 Mao Tse-tung wrote: "Not only in China but also in the world without exception, one either leans to the side of imperialism or to the side of socialism. Neutrality is mere camouflage and a third road does not exist": "On the People's Democratic Dictatorship", reprinted in A Documentary History of Chinese Communism (Harvard U.P., 1952), pp. 453-4.)

[51] See Henry A. Kissinger, Nuclear Weapons and Foreign Policy (New York, 1957), pp. 362-9.

[52] Ibid., p. 369.

[53] See Guy Wint, What Happened in Korea (London, 1954).

distrust of neutralist nations added to the difficulties of American policy makers. Anglo-American relations were openly strained at times, especially over Far Eastern issues, and President Truman later revealed that in 1950 the British Prime Minister, Mr Attlee, thought there was a good chance of China becoming the Yugoslavia of Asia,[54] thus breaking with the Soviet bloc.

In fact, throughout this phase the Soviet Union pursued a far less obviously active international rôle than did its main Cold War opponent, perhaps because of Stalin's preoccupation with purging 'Titoism' within the Soviet empire[55] — and Sino-Soviet co-operation[56] seemed to increase rather than to suggest strains. Throughout the Korean War, the Soviet Union not only claimed all the privileges and immunities of an officially neutral state, but championed similar claims for Communist China, even though the latter was implicated in the war through the presence of contingents of so-called 'Chinese volunteers' on the side of the north Koreans.[57] Indeed, one consequence of Korea was the growing identification of Communist China and the Soviet Union, so that for a number of years after most Western observers regarded Peking as Moscow's most faithful ally. The sense of Communist menace, which had been a prime factor in European affairs right up to 1950, and lingered thereafter as a constant background threat, did not have the same intensity or effect in non-Communist Asia. Europeans feared the U.S.S.R. more than Asians feared China. Though in 1950 China began to absorb Tibet, this apparently caused less concern to most of the Asian neutralists than did the continuance of the 'colonial' struggle in Indo-China (and growing identification of French and American interests in this question), while it was increasingly felt that American policies were bringing and spreading the Cold War into Asia.

Libya was the only new state to emerge from a dependent status during this stage of the Cold War, for economic and military reasons she was still virtually an Anglo-American dependency, and the intensity of Soviet-American rivalry in the U.N. Security Council, as elsewhere, prevented any increases in U.N. membership.

Though ostensibly a U.N. collective security endeavour, only fifteen

[54] See Truman's *Memoirs*, vol. ii, p. 427.

[55] See Hugh Seton-Watson, *The Pattern of Communist Revolution*, pp. 265-6.

[56] Formally based on the Sino-Soviet agreements of Feb. 1950; see R.I.I.A., *Documents for 1949-50*, p. 96, and *Survey for 1949-50*, pp. 339-43.

[57] See Ginsburgs, "The Soviet Union, Neutrality and Collective Security 1945-1959", *loc. cit.*, pp. 83-7. The legal aspects of the Korean war and the significance of the war in relation to neutrality in international law is dealt with extensively in Julius Stone, *Legal Controls of International Conflict* (2nd ed. with supplement, London, 1959), *passim*.

U.N. members[58] joined with the United States in the Korean fighting, and these formed a roughly accurate list of the states that were by now America's closest allies. A number of neutralist states tried, at first, to reconcile their faith in the U.N. and their Cold War non-alignment by aiding U.N. forces with measures short of becoming active combatants.[59] When, early in October 1950, General McArthur's troops pushed north-wards across the 38th parallel, neutralist misgivings about the war increased. When, in February 1951, the United States sponsored a U.N. resolution[60] condemning Communist China as an aggressor, most neutralist states considered that the war had taken an aggressively anti-Chinese turn and many expressed their loud disapproval. By 1953 American dominance in U.N. General Assembly matters was past its peak, and an Arab-Asian bloc,[61] neutralist in Cold War matters, had begun to cohere.

Neutralist misgivings about U.S. policies heightened as growing American concentration on the Cold War as a quasi-military operation found expression in increasing emphasis on foreign military aid,[62] in the consolidation of her existing alliances and in the extension of her commitments in Latin America, the Middle East and the Far East.

In 1950 the United States sent a survey mission to South East Asia to offer military aid, but Burma refused to receive it and Indonesia per-mitted the mission's entrance with reluctance. Only Thailand signed an agreement with the United States, in October 1950, for military aid. In Latin America during 1952 and 1953 treaties of mutual aid were signed by the U.S.A., with Colombia, Ecuador, Chile, Brazil, the Dominican Republic, Peru, Cuba, and Uruguay. Although there were varying degrees of opposition to these treaties in all the signatory states, only Mexico actually refused an American offer to conclude a mutual aid

[58] These were: Australia, Belgium, Canada, Colombia, Ethiopia, France, Greece, Great Britain, Luxembourg, Netherlands, New Zealand, Philippines, S. Africa, Thailand, and Turkey.

[59] For instance, medical aid was sent by Denmark, India, Italy, Norway and Sweden. Here the differences between the neutralists and some aligned states were not sharp. A full list of aid offered to U.N. forces in Korea is given in Y.B.U.N., 1950, pp. 226-8. Goodwin, *Britain and the United Nations*, pp. 126-54, well conveys the main U.N. voting trends on Korea, see esp. pp. 138-9, showing that in voting matters the differences between the aligned and the non-aligned were more pronounced.

[60] The U.S. resolution was adopted by the General Assembly on 1 Feb. 1951 by forty-four votes to seven (Soviet bloc, India and Burma) with nine abstentions (Afghanistan, Egypt, Indonesia, Pakistan, Saudi Arabia, Sweden, Syria, Yemen, and Yugoslavia).

[61] See Harry N. Howard, "The Arab-Asian States in the United Nations", in *The Middle East Journal*, Summer, 1953.

[62] See table of U.S. Foreign Aid 1946-53 in Reitzel, Kaplan and Coblenz, *United States Foreign Policy, 1945-55* (Washington, 1956), p. 483.

agreement. The Mutual Security Act of 1951[63] made it a prerequisite of American assistance that the recipient country should unequivocally place itself in support of the U.S. in the Cold War. In fact, the beginning of American aid to Yugoslavia in 1949 and the Indian grain bill of 1952 showed that there were not unqualified conditions even if American preferences[64] for formal allies, rather than 'ambivalent' neutralists, were now patently clear. Even so, most neutralist nations, as primary producers, benefited substantially from the upswing of world commodity prices as a consequence of the Korean War.

These years saw the heyday of the neutralism of European public opinion.[65] Ironically, it was probably American enthusiasms for consolidating N.A.T.O. as a means of raising European morale[66] and countering "creeping neutralism"—the growth of neutralist feeling, sentiment, and ideas in a state whose foreign policy is not ostensibly or avowedly neutralist—that gave European neutralism most succour. In retrospect, ideological neutralism still seems to have been an insignificant force in Europe and American fears of "creeping neutralism" exaggerated. In early 1952 Greece and Turkey joined N.A.T.O. thus extending the treaty area of the "North Atlantic" alliance further; and in September 1953 Spain was linked to the United States in three bilateral agreements known collectively as the Madrid Pact.[67]

Indeed, it seemed to be more and more the aim of American policy to spread the N.A.T.O. pattern of alliances and bases around the whole periphery of the Communist bloc. If this were so, only at the extremities of eastern Asia did American policies meet with any real success, and even here she concluded only bilateral pacts. The United States pushed through a treaty of peace and reconciliation with Japan, despite strong opposition from behind the Iron Curtain, and from some Asian

---

[63] See R.I.I.A., *Survey for 1952*.

[64] American attitudes are brilliantly portrayed in Eric F. Goldman, *The Crucial Decade—and After. America, 1945-1960* (Vintage Books, New York, 1961). For Korea, see chapters 8 and 9.

[65] See the studies cited in p. 33, n. 43.

[66] Thus, General Eisenhower in his *First Annual Report to the Standing Group* N.A.T.O. (Paris, 2 Apr. 1952): "There was serious question as to the state of public morale among the European members of the North Atlantic Treaty Organization. . . . It was extremely difficult for the average European to see any future in an attempt to build defensive forces which might offset this real and formidable threat. There seemed to be too much of a lead to be overtaken. The doubts of the European peoples gave birth to the false but glittering doctrine of neutralism, through which they hoped to preserve the things they had always held dear . . . the cumulative effects of repeated failure to make any headway in conferences with the Soviets produced an intellectual defeatism, in some quarters bordering upon despair".

[67] See R.I.I.A., *Documents for 1953*, pp. 126-32.

neutralists.[68] The Japanese Peace Treaty, signed at San Francisco in September 1951—but, more particularly, the simultaneous signing of the U.S.-Japanese Security Treaty—aroused the fears of several states who were most likely to be threatened in the event of renewed Japanese expansion and aggression, and the opposition of Asian, including Japanese, neutralists.[69] It was in order to quieten some of these fears that the United States entered into the Philippine-American Defence Pact in August 1951,[70] and the A.N.Z.U.S. treaty with Australia and New Zealand in September 1951.[71] As the French position in Indo-China worsened, American anxiety increased, and American relations with Indonesia, as well as with India and Burma, became increasingly distant. The idea pursued in 1951-2 of a comprehensive regional pact for the Middle East (M.E.D.O.) was stillborn.[72] Although proposals for this pact were jointly sponsored by the United States and Great Britain, Britain here played the leading rôle. For a number of reasons—historical, economic and strategic[73]—British sensitivity to nationalist and neutralist fears and hopes in south and south-east Asia were not paralleled by a similar appreciation of Middle Eastern nationalism and neutralism. Britain's conflicts with Iran[74] (over British oil interests in Iran) and with Egypt (mostly about the Canal base and the future status of Sudan) were sufficient at this time to prevent the realization of M.E.D.O. However, arrangements were made for U.S. air bases in Morocco[75] in Libya[76] and in Saudi Arabia.[77] The May 1950 Tripartite Declaration—France, Britain and the United States—aimed at guaranteeing existing Arab-Israeli frontiers and maintaining a balance of forces in the area, had not endeared the Western powers to the Arab states. As it was, this policy

[68] See R.I.I.A., *Survey for 1951*, pp. 378-433.
[69] *Ibid.*
[70] See Fifield, *op. cit.*, pp. 77-80.
[71] See R.I.I.A, *Survey for 1951*, pp. 384-5, 478-80.
[72] See Campbell, *op. cit.*, chapters 3 and 4.
[73] *Ibid.*
[74] Lenczowski, *op. cit.*, pp. 192-202.
[75] In July 1951 the French government announced that the U.S.A. was to have use of seven Moroccan airfields. See R.I.I.A., *Survey for 1951*, p. 25. Morocco became an independent state on 2 Mar. 1956 and was admitted to the U.N. in Nov. 1956. See R.I.I.A., *Survey for 1955-6*, pp. 85-7 and 290-5.
[76] Libya, an Italian colony from 1912 to 1942, was in effect a British protectorate from 1945 until her independence in Dec. 1951. She joined the U.N. in Dec. 1955. Both G.B. and the U.S. give extensive economic aid to Libya and in return are permitted to maintain military bases. In July 1953 G.B. signed a treaty of alliance with Libya promising financial aid for twenty years. See R.I.I.A., *Survey for 1953*, p. 119, and *Daily Telegraph*, 14 July 1960.
[77] The U.S. agreement for an airfield at Dhahran in Saudi Arabia dates from the Second World War. It was re-written in 1951, renewed in 1956, and was due to expire in 1962. See *The Times*, 18 Mar. 1961.

depended on the condition that these powers could monopolise the supply of arms to the Middle East—a condition shattered by Egypt's arms deal with the Soviet bloc in 1955.

The first six or eight months of 1953 saw the closing of this Cold War phase and began a series of shifts and changes which eventually affected the whole pattern of international relationships. These changes were symbolized in a change of personalities. First, with General Eisenhower's accession to the American Presidency in January 1953, pledged to end the fighting in Korea, to promote "liberation" in eastern Europe, and to reduce expenditure overseas. Mr Dulles, President Eisenhower's Secretary of State, now became the dominant figure in American foreign policy. Second, and more significant, was the death of Stalin on 5th March 1953, the end of an era in Soviet history. August 1953 saw the explosion of the first Soviet H-bomb; the first U.S. experimental H-bomb had only been exploded in November 1952, and it seemed that the gap in nuclear weaponry between the two superpowers was rapidly narrowing, in qualitative terms, at least.

In the summer of 1953 an armistice was signed to end the war in Korea, more than two years after truce talks had opened. The representatives of Sweden and Switzerland,[78] as two of the five-member commission of "neutral" nations, found themselves in the uncomfortable position of being cast in the rôle of "neutrals" wholly on the side of the West, while Poland and Czechoslovakia were openly "neutral" on the Communist side. Only India, as Chairman of the commission, seemed able to avoid charges of blatant partisanship. As it was, the end of the Korean War brought no settlement, only military stalemate, and did not lead to any political resolution of the essential issues at stake.[79]

(3) PARTIAL THAW, 1953-7

For the greater part of this third phase of the Cold War there was a marked contrast in apparent Soviet and American priorities, and in most neutralist eyes the post-Stalin policies of the Soviet leaders probably were preferable to the Eisenhower-Dulles policies, at first declaredly based on "massive retaliation"[80] and "brinkmanship".[81] America, aided

[78] See Jacques Freymond, "Supervising Agreements. The Korean Experience", in *Foreign Affairs*, Apr. 1959, pp. 496-503; also "Speeding Korea's Guests" in *Economist*, 9 June 1956.

[79] See R.I.I.A., *Survey for 1953*, pp. 188-230.

[80] Mr Dulles first propounded the principle of "massive and instant retaliation" on 12 Jan. 1954. See R.I.I.A., *Survey for 1954*, p. 98. The author of the 1954 R.I.I.A. *Survey* points out (p. 98) that American strategy seemed to presage " a reversion to the pre-Korean reliance on air-atomic power, but with differences—the addition of tactical atomic weapons, and the substitution of the hydrogen for the atomic bomb". See *ibid.*, pp. 96-123.

at times by her chief allies, Britain and France, seemed determined to extend the range and membership of her military alliances and to give foreign aid only to allies, and then mostly for military purposes. At the same time the Soviets, pursuing a 'new look' policy, began to try openly to encourage the spread of neutralism outside the Soviet bloc and to woo several leading neutralist nations with offers of aid, and, in certain respects, with diplomatic support. It seemed that just as the Americans were offering 'swords', and then only on condition that a state was, or became, a formal ally, the Soviets were offering 'ploughshares' to neutralist nations and were asking for no formal undertakings in return. These contrasts, dramatized by Soviet propaganda, had some foundation in fact—though Soviet bloc arms to Egypt in 1955 were hardly 'plough-shares', even if Egypt was not required to join in a military alliance with the Soviet bloc. As it was, the neutralist nations were growing in numbers and self-confidence and were becoming increasingly independent factors in international politics, with consequent effects on the nature of Cold War rivalries.

The fluctuations and contrasts of this phase can be conveniently conveyed in terms of the major developments in Europe, the Middle East, the rest of Asia, in questions of foreign aid, and in U.N. matters. An overall chronological treatment would give a better impression of the conjunction of certain events but would make it more difficult to show their significance in relation to neutralism.

The first significant sign of changing Soviet policies occurred when, at the Berlin Conference of Foreign Ministers in January-February 1954, Mr Molotov suggested, *inter alia*, bringing into being a re-unified Germany by prohibiting its participation in any alliances and coalitions, by strictly limiting its armaments, by barring all foreign military bases from its territory and by withdrawing all foreign troops. These measures would, according to Mr Molotov, provide a satisfactory basis for a re-unified, neutralized Germany. A similar status for Austria was advanced by Mr Molotov at the same time. However, the Soviet proposals were unacceptable to West Germany and her allies, and after more than a year of diplomatic preparations, Western Germany became the fifteenth member of N.A.T.O. in May 1955.[82] The Soviets' reply to this further consolidation of N.A.T.O. was to announce the knitting

---

[81] See *ibid.*, p. 25. Mr Dulles first approved the art of going to "the brink" of war in relation to Indo-China. See Coral Bell, *Negotiation from Strength* (Chatto & Windus, London, 1962), which is a scholarly analysis of the origins, different formulations, presuppositions and weaknesses of the methods Dulles used, showing too that both the idea and practice of negotiation from strength were known and used by Dean Acheson, Dulles's predecessor as American Secretary of State.

[82] See R.I.I.A., *Survey for 1954*, pp. 131-7 and 137-48, and *Survey for 1955-8*, pp. 37-44, 108-9, 138-47.

together of pre-existing bilateral arrangements in Eastern Europe in a newly comprehensive Warsaw Pact.[83] Even so, Soviet abandonment of previous claims that the German and Austrian problems must be considered together was able to facilitate Austria's independence by neutralization during 1955. Soviet endeavours to stimulate support among west European political opinion in favour of military disengagement were shown not only in the parading of 'the Austrian example' but also in the dramatic reconciliation with Yugoslavia, and in the reversion of the military base at Porkkala to Finland. This was the only Soviet military base outside the Soviet bloc, and its relinquishment was probably intended to strengthen demands for the withdrawal of American bases from Europe. Certainly, Soviet leaders and publicists[84] began to give unprecedented and seemingly unconditional approval to neutralism at this stage of world affairs. The 1954 edition of the *Great Soviet Encyclopaedia* slightly revised the 1939 section on neutrality to read that the Soviet Union "used the institution of neutrality as a means of strengthening its own as well as the world's security".[85] By 1956 the term 'neutralism' had emerged in Soviet vocabulary, and was used synonymously with 'neutrality'. The most important Soviet pronouncement concerning the neutralist states was Mr Khrushchov's first speech at the 20th Party Congress when he adroitly adopted the uncommitted countries of Asia as his friends, describing them as part of "a peace camp" allied to the "socialist" one, with "fraternal Yugoslavia" hovering ambiguously between the two, and with Finland, Austria and other non-aligned countries distinguished from America's allies.[86]

In fact, the vital, though naturally unpublicized, reservation to Soviet approval of neutralism was that it was only to be encouraged outside the

---

[83] See R.I.I.A., *Survey for 1955-6*, pp. 48-50, 54, and *Docs. for 1955*, pp. 193-8. The Treaty of Friendship, Co-operation and Mutual Assistance (the Warsaw Treaty) was signed by Albania, Bulgaria, Hungary, the German Democratic Republic, Poland, Rumania, the Soviet Union and Czechoslovakia. Article 11 of the Treaty said that the treaty was to remain in force for twenty years, or could lapse before in the event of a general European treaty of collective security coming into being. It was announced on 14 May 1955 that a joint command of the forces of the Warsaw Treaty States would be set up.

[84] See D. Melnikov, "Neutrality and the Current Situation", *International Affairs* (Moscow, 1956), pp. 74-81, and L. Modjoryan, "Neutrality", in *New Times* (Moscow, Feb. 1956), pp. 12-15, while Paul de Groot wrote in the Moscow journal *Kommunist* (1957, No. 2, p. 63): "For a state over which America rules at present, neutrality guaranteed by both camps would constitute a step forward toward national independence. For a socialist state neutrality constitutes a step backward, toward the subjugation to American imperialism and its sphere of influence".

[85] I am indebted to my colleague, Mr Maurice Hookham, for this translation, and for much help with Soviet materials. Cf. p. 26 above.

[86] See R.I.I.A., *Survey for 1955-6*, pp. 222-9, and *Soviet News Booklet*, No. 4 (Feb. 1956).

Soviet bloc. This had, perhaps, been implicit in the abortive rising in East Berlin in June 1953 and in the carefully qualified "liberalization" in Poland in the middle months of 1956,[87] but it was brutally demonstrated in October 1956 when Soviet troops crushed the attempts of the Hungarians to defect from the year-old Warsaw Pact and to work out their own variant of neutralism. Parallel with events in Hungary, and quite apart from the palpable inability of the Western powers to intervene on behalf of the Hungarians, came the swift cooling of Soviet-Yugoslav relations and the imponderable but undoubted intrusion of China into east European affairs during 1956. After the Hungarian revolution[88] had been quietened, Soviet efforts were concentrated on repairing rifts in the Communist camp. This repair work seemed to be complete by the time of the Moscow meeting of the ruling Communist parties in October 1957, which time seemed also to mark the undoubted emergence of Mr Khrushchov as the pre-eminent leader in the Soviet Union.[89]

In the Middle East during these years there were four dominant trends. Firstly, Egypt under Nasser's leadership began to emerge clearly as the leading and most ambitious Middle Eastern neutralist state. There was a rapid deterioration in British-Egyptian relations, paralleled by a deterioration in Franco-Egyptian relations (especially as the Egyptian government gave open support to the Algerian 'rebels' soon after the Algerian 'War of Independence' began in late 1954).[90] These tensions converged and culminated in the Anglo-French-Israeli attack on Egypt in October 1956.[91] Secondly, there was the formation of the Baghdad Pact in 1955, bringing together Britain, Turkey, Pakistan, Iran and Egypt's greatest rival for leadership of the Arab world—Iraq, though leaving the United States in the ambiguous position of silent partner and not a formal member.[92] Egypt and her close associates regarded the rejection of membership in the Baghdad Pact as a necessary act of "positive

---

[87] See Hugh Seton-Watson, *The Pattern of Communist Revolution*, pp. 357-76, and his *Neither War Nor Peace* (London, 1960), pp. 338-46.

[88] See George Mikes, *The Hungarian Revolution* (London, 1957); also Imre Nagy *on Communism. In Defence of the New Course* (London, 1957). Nagy was the Hungarian Communist Prime Minister who tried to adopt a neutralist course in early Oct. 1956. This tract was written during his forced retirement in 1955-6 and reveals some of his neutralist ideas; see esp. chapter 3, also Seton-Watson's introduction to this English translation.

[89] See Seton-Watson, *The Pattern of Communist Revolution*, p. 359.

[90] See Edward Behr, *The Algerian Problem* (Penguin Books, 1961), esp. pp. 76, 80, 84.

[91] See Campbell, *op. cit.*, chapters 4-9, and *Full Circle, The Memoirs of Sir Anthony Eden* (London, 1960), Book 3, chapters 1-9.

[92] See Campbell, *op. cit.*, chapter 5. For *en clair* diplomatic correspondence, memoranda etc. see R.I.I.A., *Docs. for 1955*, pp. 284-312.

neutrality". Hence, these developments re-emphasized pre-existing divisions in the Middle East and provoked strenuous responses, not only
from Egypt, but also from Syria and Saudi Arabia, and, for different
reasons, from Israel. Thirdly, there was the dramatic renewal of active
Soviet interest in the region and signs of a growing association between
the Soviets and Egypt and Syria.[93] Fourthly, throughout the years
1954-6, American policy tried to reconcile the irreconcilable, by seeking
to build up Western defences in the area while at the same time trying
to cultivate good relations with Arab neutralist states. Such a vacillating
policy found its nemesis when in January 1957 the Eisenhower Doctrine
—offering military and economic assistance to any Middle Eastern state
that asked for help against "armed aggression from any country controlled by international Communism"—met with strong opposition from
most states, and only tepid enthusiasm from a few, throughout the
whole region.[94]

It was at this high tide of Anglo-American pact-making that the
Communist powers began actively to preach and promote their gospel
of "peaceful co-existence" between states with differing social systems.
The Chinese led the way by appearing to settle their differences with
India over Tibet. The Sino-Indian agreement was signed in August
1954, and a preamble to the treaty proclaimed the Five Principles of
Peaceful Co-existence* for the first time in an international context.

The Soviets also soon sought actively to popularize the notion of
peaceful co-existence, presenting it as a revival of a true Leninist principle. It is recorded[95] that Lenin first used the phrase in February 1920
but it is clear that he regarded "peaceful co-existence" as a tactic, a
temporary expedient before the eventual and inevitable triumph of
'socialism' over 'capitalism'. Stalin, too, periodically asserted his belief
in the temporary possibility of co-existence. But it was a notable revision
of Leninist principles when, in February 1956, Mr Khrushchov, speaking
at the Soviet 20th Party Congress on the subject of 'deStalinization',
recommended "peaceful co-existence" as the best form of class struggle
on a world scale and denied that war between the 'socialist' and
'capitalist' powers was fatalistically inevitable. At this time the Chinese
did not publicly disagree with these theories, and it seemed that a new

[93] See Walter Z. Laqueur, *The Soviet Union and the Middle East* (London,
1959), esp. pp. 211-28, 247-63.
[94] See Campbell, *op. cit.*, chapters 4-9, 17.
[95] In an interview with the *New York Evening Journal* of 18 Feb. 1920 Lenin
said, "Our plans in Asia? The same as in Europe: peaceful coexistence with the
peoples, with the workers and peasants of all nations"—quoted in R. N. Carew-
Hunt, *ibid.*, p. 27. The whole article, pp. 26-33, is a brief and penetrating discussion
of coexistence.
* See below, pp. 66 and 124.

Communist flexibility of doctrine might match the newly developing flexibility of policy.

Such Soviet acts as the retrocession of Port Arthur to the Chinese in May 1955, and the official "visits of friendship"[96] by Bulganin and Khrushchov, in late 1955, to India, Burma and Afghanistan (the latter marked by the ceremonious prolongation of the Soviet-Afghan treaty of neutrality and non-aggression, which originated in 1926) were all part and parcel of Moscow's new line of encouraging and co-operating with most of the neutralist nations of the world. Support for Afghanistan's irredentist claims against Pakistan, and the Indian position with regard to Kashmir and Goa, and offers of aid and trade were further instances of this new trend.[97]

In the rest of Asia, American attempts to build up defence arrangements against possible Communist attack further alienated neutralist opinion, and official American spokesmen openly regarded most forms of neutralism with suspicion and dislike.[98] The conclusion of the South East Asian Defence Treaty in September 1954[99] linked the security interests of the Philippines, Thailand, Australia and New Zealand (each of which was already linked in some way with the United States) with Britain, France and Pakistan in a comprehensive agreement—S.E.A.T.O. Three of the four and newly independent successor states of former French Indo-China, South Vietnam, Laos and Cambodia (the fourth was Communist North Vietnam) were declared to be under the 'protection' of the S.E.A.T.O. treaty members, though they did not become full members themselves. The United States' adhesion to the treaty was qualified in a protocol which made clear the American preoccupation with Communist aggression, thus appearing to regard other forms of aggression as less reprehensible. Formosa was excluded from S.E.A.T.O., but, under pressure from Chiang Kai-Shek, the United States felt it necessary to conclude with Formosa a bilateral defence agreement. This was signed on 1 December 1954,[100] and completed the list of America's formal defence commitments in the Far East.

[96] On Port Arthur see R.I.I.A., *Survey for 1955-6*, pp. 53, 126. For full texts of Bulganin and Khrushchov speeches in India, Burma and Afghanistan, see supplement in *New Times* (Moscow, 22 Dec. 1955).

[97] It is to be remembered that Soviet trade and/or aid offers were also made about this time to Turkey, Pakistan, Iceland, Great Britain, among others.

[98] Thus, President Eisenhower in his 1954 Christmas message: "The times are so critical and the differences between these world systems so vital that grave doubt is cast on the validity of neutralistic argument". See also the speech of American Deputy Under-Secretary Murphy on 16 Nov. 1954, printed in D.S.B., 29 Nov. 1954, pp. 799-803; also R.I.I.A., *Survey for 1954*, "The Politics of Neutralism", pp. 283-9.

[99] For a full account see *Collective Defence in South East Asia*, A Report by a Chatham House (R.I.I.A.) Study Group (London, 1956).

[100] See R.I.I.A., *Survey for 1955-6*, pp. 7, 10-14.

In the aftermath of the Korean and Indo-China wars, American concentration on military arrangements seemed to be rather backward-
looking as the Soviets' rapid development of trade and aid programmes
to neutralist states added a new dimension to Cold War rivalries. Previously, the Western powers had been the sole, and rather parsimonious,
suppliers to neutralist nations. The first Soviet loan to a non-Communist
country was made to Afghanistan in January 1954 for the sum of
$3·5 million. In that first year, the total aid from the Soviet Union and
other Communist countries to non-Communist countries was $10·6
million. For 1955 it was $305 million, for 1956 nearly $1,100 million,
and for 1957 over $1,900 million.[101] In total volume U.S. aid greatly
exceeded Soviet aid, but U.S. aid priorities seemed to be with Israel,
Libya, South Korea, South Vietnam, Laos and Formosa, whereas the
main Soviet efforts were concentrated on Syria, Yugoslavia, Afghanistan,
India, Egypt, Cambodia, Ceylon, Indonesia and Nepal.[102] Communist
China, too (still ostensibly the Soviet Union's close ally) began her own
aid programmes to non-aligned states, starting with a grant to Cambodia
in 1956 and then with a sizeable loan to Egypt in August 1956. But, all
in all, it is notoriously difficult to compare aid programmes even in
economic terms, let alone assess their political effects,[103] though certainly, foreign aid first became a serious matter of Cold War rivalry in
these years. The Soviets began with a number of advantages[104] over their
Western rivals: the novelty of their aid programmes, the prevailing
Afro-Asian anti-imperialist image of the U.S.S.R., the apparent absence
of political or military 'strings', the procedural advantages of absolutist
governments in operating foreign aid programmes,[105] and the fact that
Soviet bloc aid was growing at a more rapid annual rate than Western
aid. The novel experience of being actively courted by Communist states
proffering 'unconditional' aid was not only attractive in itself to
neutralist nations, but it afforded opportunities for provoking the
United States to increase, or initiate, its own programmes, whatever the
misgivings of many Americans about such moves. During June and July

[101] See U.S. Dept. of State, *The Sino-Soviet Economic Offensive in the less
Developed Countries* (Washington, U.S.G.P.O. 1958).
[102] *Ibid.*; and V. K. R. V. Rao, *International Aid for Economic Development*
(Leeds, 1960), esp. pp. 11-13, and Joseph S. Berliner, *Soviet Economic Aid* (New
York, 1958).
[103] See Berliner, *ibid.*, esp. chapters 2 and 4. For Communist China's efforts
see Victor Purcell, *China* (London, 1962), chapters 21-3, esp. p. 260. See also
A. Nove and D. Matko, "The Pattern of Soviet Foreign Trade" in *Three Banks
Review*, March 1962, pp. 18-35.
[104] See Berliner, *loc. cit.*
[105] E.g. a report in *The Times*, 4 Jan. 1958, showing the main direction of Communist trade and aid, pointed out that "the scale of foreign aid is being withheld
from the Russian people".

NEUTRALISM, SUPERPOWERS AND COLD WAR

1956 U.S. spokesmen made a spate of contradictory pronouncements,[106] approving or disapproving of neutralism in general terms—including Mr Dulles' notorious phrase that "except under very exceptional circumstances" neutrality is an "immoral and short-sighted conception".[107] All these pronouncements should be seen in the context of the Eisenhower administration's difficulties in attempting simultaneously: to increase American foreign aid programmes in the face of strong opposition from neo-isolationists at home with Presidential elections being due in the autumn;[108] to placate the anxieties of those allies who feared a reduction of their aid from the United States, and to take increasing account of the needs of neutralist nations.[109] By the middle of 1957 there was evidence of a far more balanced estimate than hitherto in influential American thought about neutralism.[110]

The Afro-Asian Conference held at Bandung, Indonesia, in April 1955[111] was a dramatic illustration of trends which were increasingly cutting across strict Cold War rivalries. Delegates came from twenty-three Asian and from six African countries to what was primarily a gathering of leaders who were anxious, above all, to keep out of Cold War quarrels and yet aware, as President Sukarno said, that "the affairs of the world are our affairs, and our future depends on the solution found to all international problems, however far or distant they may seem".[112] It would be wrong to convey the impression that the Bandung Conference was wholly a neutralist meeting, for the views of aligned states were

[106] There is a collection of the major speeches, with commentaries in *Foreign Policy Bulletin* (New York) for 15 Aug. 1956, and 15 Feb. 1957. For full texts, see D.S.B., 18 June 1956, pp. 999-1004; D.S.B., 25 June 1956, pp. 1043-7, and pp. 1063-5; D.S.B., 16 July 1956, pp. 91-5. See also D.S.B., 17 Dec. 1956, pp. 943-8 and *ibid.*, 9 July 1957, p. 49; also R.I.I.A., *Survey for 1955-6*, pp. 200-2. For a Soviet comment on these American pronouncements, see "Washington and the Neutrality Problem", *New Times* (Moscow), July 1956, pp. 3-7.

[107] See D.S.B., 18 June 1956, pp. 999-1004.

[108] See Norman A. Graebner, *The New Isolationism. A Study in Politics and Foreign Policy since 1950* (New York, 1956); also his "Foreign Aid and American Policy" in *Current History*, 1956, pp. 212-17.

[109] See *The Economist*, 16 June 1956, p. 1076, for a balanced assessment of the American leaders' predicament. The Prime Minister of Burma, U Nu, made a state visit to the U.S. in 1955 and Mr Nehru and President Sukarno also did so during 1956. These visits may have had an educative effect on American opinion.

[110] See the analysis of neutralism in the *Report on Foreign Policy and Mutual Security*, House of Representatives 85th Congress, 11 June 1957 (Washington, 1957), esp. pp. 56R-61R.

[111] See R.I.I.A., *Survey 1955-6*, chapter 5; *Documents for 1955*, pp. 397-438; Mary Knatchbull Keynes, "The Bandung Conference", in *International Relations*, Oct. 1957, pp. 362-76; G. M. Kahin, *The Asian-African Conference* (Cornell U.P., 1956); and Triska and Koch, "The Asian African Nations and International Organization", *Review of Politics*, April 1959, pp. 417-56.

[112] Kahin, *op. cit.*, pp. 46-7.

fully ventilated (with Chou En-lai skilfully plying China's current policy of ostensible peace and friendship with Afro-Asian neutralists), and anti-colonialism in its various manifestations was another important theme. However, neutralism was becoming a vital strand in the Afro-Asian movement, though by no means fully synonymous with it, as neutralists began to shed some of their former defensiveness and to move more surely internationally, encouraged by accords with fellow neutralists.[113] It was probably in such matters as increasing contacts and seeing the advantages of an international platform that Bandung was most beneficial to neutralists. The conference met at a time when Cold War deadlocks had prevented for more than five years any expansion in the membership of the United Nations—a fact much regretted by all neutralists and especially by the still 'unenfranchised' states. However, with the so-called U.S.-U.S.S.R. "horse-trading deal"[114] of December 1955, by which the United Nations immediately gained sixteen new members,[115] and became open to further increases in membership,[116] that organization seemed to gain a new relevance and vitality in world affairs, whilst greatly augmenting the number of neutralist votes and voices.

Though the rivalries between the U.S. and the U.S.S.R. quickened, became more varied in scope and, on the whole, slightly less venomous in their verbal interchanges, direct contacts between the two superpowers were virtually as rare and unproductive as in the Stalin-Truman era. Mr Dulles quickly withdrew from participation in the 1954 Geneva Conference on Indo-China, leaving Mr Eden and Mr Molotov to attempt a compromise settlement.[117] Both the Geneva Summit Conference of July 1955[118] and the follow-up Conference of Foreign Secretaries in October-

[113] Mrs Keynes, op. cit., p. 375, says that there were nine confirmed neutralists at Bandung—Afghanistan, Burma, Cambodia, India, Indonesia, Laos, Nepal, Syria and Yemen. The positions of Egypt, Ethiopia and Saudi Arabia were not fully clear but were at times neutralist. There were two Communist states—China and North Vietnam, and fifteen anti-Communists—Ceylon, Gold Coast, Iran, Iraq, Japan, Jordan, Lebanon, Liberia, Libya, Pakistan, Philippines, Sudan, Thailand, Turkey and South Vietnam.
[114] See Goodwin, op. cit., pp. 224-6.
[115] These were Albania, Austria, Bulgaria, Cambodia, Ceylon, Finland, Hungary, Ireland, Italy, Jordan, Laos, Libya, Nepal, Portugal, Roumania and Spain. Cambodia, Ceylon, Laos and Libya were all new states created since 1945.
[116] Sudan, Morocco and Tunisia—all new states—became members in Nov. 1956; Japan in Dec. 1956; Ghana, a new state, in March 1957; and Malaya, another new state, in Sept. 1957.
[117] See R.I.I.A., Survey for 1954, pp. 42-73; and The Memoirs of Sir Anthony Eden. Full Circle (London, 1960), chapter 6. Eden writes (p. 123): "This was the first international meeting at which I was sharply conscious of the deterrent power of the hydrogen bomb. I was grateful for it."
[118] See R.I.I.A., Survey for 1955-6, pp. 155-60.

November 1955[119] were unproductive, though there was much superficial talk then and for some time afterwards about a vague but new,
welcome and all pervasive "Geneva spirit". As both superpowers
developed their nuclear capacities (and the facts or rumours of other
emergent nuclear powers became publicized), the need to avoid thermonuclear war and agree on some form of "peaceful co-existence" was
recognized on all sides. The outstanding problem was to establish a basis
on which the two Cold War camps could agree to co-exist. This problem
was no nearer solution than it had ever been when the successful
launching of the Soviet Sputnik in October 1957 encouraged Mr Krush-
chov to claim that this event had altered the power balance in the world.
In a sense, this was no doubt true; but other more gradual changes were
increasingly affecting the nature of Cold War rivalries. The Soviet
Union and the United States were still predominant, but both thence-
forward had to give greater attention to independent forces, both within
and outside their own alliances.

(4) VARIABLE WEATHER, 1957-DECEMBER 1962

The chief characteristics of this fourth phase of the Cold War, which
for present purposes takes us up to the end of 1962, seem to be: the
developing global character of Cold War struggles (as Africa and Latin
America now become areas of active Cold War rivalry, too); the greater
number of direct contacts between the two superpowers, the rapid
growth in numbers and self-confidence of neutralist states, and the
increasing complexities facing each of the superpowers in their dealings
both with their alliance partners and with neutralist states.

Following the Soviet success in launching the first satellite (Sputnik)
it seemed that Soviet leadership had gained fresh confidence and that
the Soviet state, now militarily stronger and industrially more powerful
than ever before, began to extend the scale of its international operations. However much of this was due to the undoubted emergence of
Mr Khrushchov[120] as the first man in Russia—expressing his immediate
attempts to achieve a greater flexibility and revolutionary élan in the
policies of both the Soviet Union and the international Communist
movement[121]—a more important reason probably was that a new state
of 'mutual deterrence' between the two superpowers had been ushered

---

[119] Ibid., pp. 167-74.

[120] In July 1957 it was reported that Molotov, Kaganovich and Malenkov were
expelled from the Praesidium of the Central Committee of the Communist Party
of the Soviet Union. Shepilov was demoted, too, and these changes were widely
interpreted as marking the further emergence of Mr Khrushchov; see The Times,
4 July 1957.

[121] See Richard Lowenthal, "Schism Among the Faithful", in Problems of Communism, Jan.-Feb. 1962, pp. 1-14.

D

in, now that Russian capacity to launch intercontinental missiles had marked the end of the territorial invulnerability of the American homeland. In such a situation, the advantages accruing from Communist inspired local aggression were likely to increase, not only because the threat of American nuclear retaliation was now less credible as a deterrent to local attack on her minor allies, but also because further developments in America's own weaponry were reducing her dependence on large numbers of fixed overseas bases and might even reduce the military value of small, exposed allies in her eyes. But the Soviets soon came to moderate their ardour for stimulating situations thought to be fraught with 'revolutionary' potentialities when it became evident that China was anxious to act as the pacemaker in these endeavours and yet was far less careful than her senior partner of the danger of thermonuclear war. None of this, of course, reduced the chances of local wars, and between October 1957 and December 1962 there was a succession of skirmishes, limited wars, or at least war scares, over Syria, Lebanon, Jordan, Iraq, Formosa, Laos, South Vietnam, Congo, Berlin, the Sino-Indian frontiers, and Cuba.

Another feature of this post-Sputnik phase was the considerable growth in the number of direct contacts between the citizens and leaders of the two superpowers. This process began formally with a two-year agreement on cultural, technical and educational exchanges signed in January 1958, was followed by the official visits of Mikoyan, Kozlov and Khrushchov (the latter in September 1959) to the United States, and by the meeting between Kennedy and Khrushchov in Vienna in June 1961. Even so it is doubtful if the superficial cordiality which was becoming customary in these new encounters appreciably lessened the distrust and mutual irritation which marked the fundamental relations between the two governments. In terms of U.S. - U.S.S.R. relations the abortive Paris summit conference of May 1960 was a revealing example of deep-rooted incompatibilities. The Vienna meeting of June 1961 clearly underlined the point that any substantial settlement of Soviet-American issues was highly unlikely, as the two leaders disagreed sharply over Germany and Berlin, the stalemated disarmament talks and a treaty to ban nuclear testing. Sino-American relations remained unrelentingly hostile.

The rivalry between the two superpowers was now increasingly complicated by incipient stresses and strains within their respective alliance systems, as well as by the growing number of new states which were emerging and pursuing neutralist courses. The days when American leaders acted as energetic recruiting officers gathering more members for military alliances, and when Soviet leaders openly and consistently denigrated all neutralists, had gone. Many neutralists were proselytizers themselves now, and the very new neutralist state did not find itself in a world where it was expected to apologize for its neutralist stance, but in a world where it could point to many notable exemplars and precedents. A new and looser international system, more flexible and multilateral, was in being, and formal ties now seemed far less significant than hitherto. Within both Cold War camps it became increasingly clear that military alliances now prescribed far less exclusive and comprehensive bonds than ever before. And as so many states were not members of Cold War alliances, less importance now attached to the mere fact of being outside certain military alliances and more to matters of general diplomatic relations and standing — securing invitations to neutralist conferences and being recognized as "one of us" by other neutralists.

Stresses and strains were certainly evident throughout America's alliances.

The defection of Iraq from the Baghdad Pact, following regicide and revolution, called forth a reconstruction of that alliance with the United States assuming a much more active rôle in what became called the Central Treaty Organization (C.E.N.T.O.)[122] with its new headquarters in Turkey. Iran was thus left as the most vulnerable of all America's formal allies to direct Soviet pressure. Unlike its two neighbouring C.E.N.T.O. partners, Turkey and Pakistan, Iran[123] lacked the collateral coverage which these states enjoyed in virtue of their membership of N.A.T.O. and S.E.A.T.O. respectively. And though she rebuffed both threatening diplomatic notes (in 1958) and overtures for a non-aggression pact (in 1959) from the Soviet Union, Iran's position is an uncomfortable one and the temptations of a return to the traditional (and largely unsuccessful) diplomacy of manoeuvre between the great powers may well eventually entice Iran out of C.E.N.T.O. The Iranian cabinet resigned in July 1962, ostensibly because of the insufficiency of American aid. Mr Khrushchov has said that the Shah's system of government is bound to collapse in time. Though Iran has a long common frontier with the Soviet Union no doubt the prospect of turmoil in Iran does not daunt the Soviet leader. Iran remains one of the latent trouble spots in the Cold War.

Throughout 1960-2 there were reports[124] that both Iran and Pakistan

[122] For a brief account of the Iraq revolt, see U.S.W.A., 1958, pp. 201-3, and for C.E.N.T.O. see Daily Telegraph, 24 May 1960 and 26 Apr. 1961, and Economist, 6 May 1961, p. 556.
[123] For Persia see Economist, 18 Apr. 1959, pp. 241-2, and 5 Aug. 1961, p. 557—"Check for Neutralists". The Shah said, in March 1961, that Persia had had about £320 m. from America in the previous ten years, the equivalent of about a third of Persia's present income from oil. See Daily Telegraph, 7 Mar. 1961. Later the Shah reaffirmed his policy of remaining in defensive alliances and recalled how Iranian neutrality had been violated during two world wars; see The Times, 21 Aug. 1961.
[124] See Daily Telegraph, 8 June 1961; Economist, 1 Apr. 1961, pp. 10-12 and

were complaining of what seemed to them the sympathetic treatment
extended to the United Arab Republic by the United States, and were
discussing again whether it was better to be non-aligned to get foreign
aid. Certainly there were indications from 1957 onwards that the United
States was anxious to establish permanently good relations with Egypt,
an Egypt which became joined with Syria in a single "United Arab
Republic", proclaimed in Cairo in February 1958 as a first step towards
the unification of the Arab peoples. Though this particular union lasted
only three and a half years, being dissolved in fact though not in name by
the secession of Syria at the end of September 1961, Nasser's Egypt had by
December 1962 undoubtedly achieved a considerable ascendancy throughout the Arab lands and was one of the world's leading neutralist powers.

Within S.E.A.T.O. deteriorating situations in the two 'protected'
states of Laos and South Vietnam revealed a lack of any concerted
alliance policy. After civil war, foreign intervention, tedious negotiations and internal political squabbles Laos was eventually neutralized
by international agreement in July 1962. South Vietnam, subject to
complex internal convulsions ever since 1954, despite massive amounts
of American aid, was still wracked by guerrilla warfare throughout 1962.
And although American disillusionment with Diem's government was
by now patent, American troops were committed to guerrilla operations
in South Vietnam, purportedly to resist Communist subversion. Further,
there were a number of reports that the Philippines and Thailand were
disillusioned about the alleged advantages of membership in American-
led alliances and that they were actively seeking other, unspecified,
means of ensuring their security. Thailand, like Persia, had traditionally
practised a policy of manoeuvre between the great powers, and in
November 1960 it was announced that she had for the first time
accepted Soviet offers of economic assistance.[125] Pakistan began, shortly
after General Ayub's seizure of power in 1958, to test and re-appraise
the value of her alliance commitments. And although in December 1962
Pakistan was still a full member of both C.E.N.T.O. and S.E.A.T.O.
there were indications that she now attached much less importance to
these alliances and was gravitating towards a neutralist course.[126]

20 May 1961, pp. 791-2; C.S.M., 5 Apr. 1960, and New York Times, 4 Sept. 1960,
and The Times, 19 July 1962.

[125] See C.S.M., 5 Nov. 1960. A report from Bangkok mentioned America's current
balance-of-payments difficulties and the shock to Thais of hearing about an
American mission to Bonn "begging for money . . . the image of a shockproof
American economy was until this year about as firmly lodged in the Asian mind
as perhaps the myth of Asian military inferiority to Europe before 1905". See
Guardian, 21 Dec. 1960.

[126] See The Times, 17 Feb. 1961 and 4 Mar. 1961, and Daily Telegraph, 14 July
1961; and B. C. Rastogi, "Alignment and Non-alignment in Pakistan's Foreign
Policy 1947-60" in International Studies (New Delhi), Oct. 1961, pp. 159-80.

Though in January 1960 the U.S. signed a thoroughly revised and re-drafted version of the 1951 defence treaty with Japan, political stresses and riots in Tokyo compelled the cancellation of President Eisenhower's official visit to Japan in June 1960 even though American ratification of the treaty was not held up. By October 1960 a prominent member of the U.S. Senate Foreign Relations Committee was warning his fellow members of the popular appeal of neutralism in Japan, and the likelihood that this would increase.[127]

In Latin America[128] the cumulative effect of the overthrow of pro-American military dictatorships in a number of countries—Peru (1956), Columbia (1957), Venezuela (1958), Cuba (1959)—and growing Russian and Chinese interest in this region prompted the United States to pay greater attention to Latin American affairs and to increase economic assistance to Latin American countries. The status of the Latin American states in the Cold War was becoming more and more ambiguous, and it was far from clear what significance Soviet, or even American, leaders attached to membership of the Organization of American States or the signature of the treaties of Rio and Chapultecec. Such matters as Brazil and Mexico's association with the other so-called 'neutral' nations in the U.N. seventeen-nation disarmament conference in 1962, Venezuela's association with other oil-producing states from 1958 onwards and the emergence of the new states of Jamaica and Trinidad and Tobago (and with the impending arrival of the new state of Guyana from the former British Guiana) were all signs of a growing Latin American involvement in world affairs generally. Yet, by December 1962, only Cuba (following the accession of Fidel Castro to power in January 1959) had openly repudiated all ties with the United States. And when in January 1963, at American instigation Cuba was accused of being aligned with the 'Communist bloc' and expelled[129] from the Organization of American States one of the legal instruments cited in justification of the expulsion was the Rio pact.

By January 1963 N.A.T.O. of all America's alliances seemed least threatened by the corrosive effects of "creeping neutralism" from within the alliance, or the enticements of already neutralist leaders from without. But if none of the N.A.T.O. states had shown a marked disposition to secede from the alliance trade rivalries between member states,

[127] See *Letter of Transmittal by Senator Mike Mansfield* to Senate Committee on Foreign Relations, 21 Oct. 1960, p. 7; and I. I. Morris, "Japanese Foreign Policy and Neutralism", in *International Affairs* (R.I.I.A.), Jan. 1960, pp. 7-20.

[128] See three articles entitled "Coexistence, Communism and Latin America" in *Problems of Communism*, Jan.-Feb. 1961; *Economist*, "Latin American Tribune", 22 Apr. 1961, pp. 319-40; "Peking vs. Moscow in Latin America", in *Problems of Communism*, Jan.-Feb. 1963.

[129] See *The Times*, 1 Feb. 1962.

the growing self-confidence and assertiveness of France under President de Gaulle (who came to power in June 1958) and Soviet pressure (from November 1958 onwards) on the Western powers to reach "a permanent solution" of the Berlin question, all added to America's task of reconciliation and leadership. The launching of the six-nation European Economic Community (E.E.C.) in January 1958 and the considerable economic progress achieved in its first three years had at least three important immediate effects. In August 1961 Britain made a formal application for full membership of the Community, the non-aligned states of Europe were each faced with difficult and urgent problems of how best to reconcile their economic and politico-strategic interests,[130] and America began to find more resistance to its views among its N.A.T.O. allies. By January 1963 British attempts to join the E.E.C. had failed, principally because of French opposition. France under de Gaulle's leadership, now that Algerian independence had been granted, seemed bent on asserting French ascendancy in European affairs and on reducing American influence in Europe—perhaps with the eventual hope of creating a "third force" in Europe, a "third force" disengaged from either of the two superpowers. Though throughout the years 1957 to 1962 intra-N.A.T.O. debates still centred on the tasks the alliance should assume in common, in retrospect it may be that these years may come to be considered a time when the close post-war identity of interests between western European powers and America finally began to dissolve.

In some respects the Soviet Union as the leader of the Communist camp seemed to be experiencing similar difficulties to those of its main Cold War opponent. The meeting of the ruling Communist parties in Moscow in November 1957 marked the definite failure of Khrushchov's three-year-old attempts to woo Yugoslavia completely back into the Communist camp. Subsequent to the November 1957 Moscow meeting and throughout the period under consideration here, there was considerable evidence of Sino-Soviet disagreement.[131] Whatever the full reasons for Sino-Soviet tensions in these five years, Chinese dissatisfaction with the way that Mr Khrushchov was dealing with Yugoslav type "revisionism" and promoting good relations especially with India but also with Indonesia (even to the extent of neglecting to support China's interests in her quarrels with these two countries) were undoubtedly among the imme-

---

[130] See J. R. Lambert, "The Neutrals and the Common Market", *The World Today*, Oct. 1962, pp. 444-52.

[131] See *The Sino-Soviet Dispute*. Documents and Analysis by G. F. Hudson, Richard Lowenthal and Roderick MacFarquhar (published by *China Quarterly*, London 1961); Richard Lowenthal, "Schism Among the Faithful", in *Problems of Communism*, Jan.-Feb. 1962, pp. 1-14; and Donald Zagoria, *The Sino-Soviet Dispute, 1956-61* (O.U.P., London, 1962).

diate causes. Though China was, and still is, Russia's formal ally Soviet financial assistance to China has been surprisingly modest, and between 1960 and 1962 all forms of Soviet assistance to China dwindled to a trickle. From 1957 onwards China certainly took the initiative in the offensive against Tito, and in the developing conflict between Yugoslavia's neighbour Albania and the Soviet Union, Albania found succour in Chinese support. Throughout these years China showed a greater militancy and aggressiveness internationally than did the Soviet Union and the official Chinese attitude to neutralism[132] was, in general, much less friendly than that of her senior partner,[133] though both powers preferred to distinguish between neutralists they approved of and those who, for various reasons, met with their disapproval.[134]

Instead of being faced by an apparently monolithic bloc controlled from Moscow the Western Powers increasingly found themselves faced with a series of Communist states, displaying different degrees of hostility, and 'polycentric',[135] or at least 'bicentric', rather than monolithic. By December 1962 the Communist World appeared as a political spectrum stretching from Poland—which had concluded trade and aid agreements with the United States in 1957 and continued to deal with the Americans thereafter — through the Soviet Union and her thoroughly 'reliable' satellites to Albania and China, and, possibly, to Cuba. International Communism had clearly become a complicating factor in Soviet foreign policy rather than an undoubted source of support available to Soviet diplomacy whenever wanted.

One of the most striking developments in these five years was the considerable increase in the number of new states, and with their

[132] See A. M. Halpern, "The Chinese Communist Line on Neutralism", in *China Quarterly*, Jan.-Mar. 1961, pp. 90-115. This article surveys Chinese statements on neutralism between Nov. 1957 and Dec. 1960.

[133] Though in March 1958 a leading Soviet publicist again made clear that neutralism was only to be welcomed outside the Soviet bloc—"a system of collective security [i.e. any Soviet alliance] serves as a barrier to aggression and is, hence, a higher form of struggle for peace than the policy of neutrality. That is why a retreat from collective security in favour of neutrality would be a step backward, not forward, in international relations". Quoted from E. Korovin, "The Problem of Neutrality Today" in *International Affairs* (Moscow), Mar. 1958, p. 6. The bracketed interpretation is mine, but this meaning is clear in the context of the whole article.

[134] In the Nov. 1960 Moscow Manifesto the neutralist states approved of by the Communist powers (including China) were generally, and thus conveniently, styled "independent national democracies". See Hudson, Lowenthal and MacFarquhar, *op. cit.*, pp. 192-6, esp. pp. 194-5. The statement made clear that to secure Communist approval a neutralist must "fight" against all forms of "imperialism".

[135] In this context the term 'polycentrism' was first coined by the Italian Communist leader Togliatti in June 1956. For a discussion of the theoretical and practical significance of this term see the special number of *Survey*, June 1962, entitled "Polycentrism".

emergence—they were mostly African states—sub-tropical Africa at last became drawn into the mainstreams of international politics. Indeed, more than twenty newly independent states were born, seventeen in Africa between January 1958 and October 1960—all of them free of the entanglements of Cold War alliances, and thus neutralist, and all of them soon becoming members of the United Nations.*

This large increase in the numbers of neutralist nations not only gave new impetus and strength to neutralist currents but increasingly there were signs of a desire on the part of a large number of neutralist leaders to try to concert together on issues of common concern. This latter trend was clearly evident in the autumn 1960 session of the U.N. General Assembly[136] and was dramatically illustrated by the summoning of a neutralist 'Summit' in Belgrade in September 1961,† the largest and most important neutralist conference so far; also by the Cairo economic conference of the non-aligned, which met in July 1962, ostensibly because of adverse terms of trade and consolidating trade blocs from which they were excluded.

The Belgrade conference of the non-aligned states was interesting for at least three reasons. Firstly, because the responsibility for calling and arranging the conference was largely Tito's and Nasser's, though it soon became clear that they were anxious to associate Nehru with their scheme, so that these three neutralist leaders should be seen to be agreed and working together. Secondly, the composition of the conference marked Nasser's and possibly Fidel Castro's triumph. For although Nehru had wished the convenors to invite a wide range of, what were in India's eyes at least, non-aligned states from Europe and Latin America, as well as from Asia and Africa, this Indian wish was not satisfied. By comparison with the Bandung conference of 1955 the Belgrade conference was less different in its composition, preoccupations and tone than changes since 1955 might have led one to expect. It is true that, unlike Bandung, no Communist states were represented and that the presence of Cuba (with observers being sent by Brazil and Bolivia) seemed to mark the association of Latin-American non-aligned states with their fellows in Africa and Asia. But, in fact, Cuba arrogated to itself the right to pronounce on the 'true' non-alignment of fellow American states, and this had the effect of restricting the size of the Belgrade gathering. Of Africa's then twenty-eight independent states only ten went to Belgrade, and six of these were the associates of the United Arab Republic in the Casablanca grouping.[137] The fact that

[136] See Tom Little, "Mr Krushchev and the Neutrals at the U.N.", in World Today, Dec. 1960.

[137] See Colin Legum, Pan-Africanism (Pall Mall Press, 1962) for a brief and clear account of the rapidly-changing configurations of African alignments and of African neutralism in that context, and below pp. 180 and 183.

*See table on pp. 202-4 below.   † See chapter vi.   ‡See below, pp. 137-8 and 148.

only Yugoslavia and Cyprus, of the European non-aligned states, were present at Belgrade underlined the point that the conference did not mark an unrestricted expansiveness on the part of the non-aligned and did not show a clear willingness by all those at Belgrade to agree on how precisely they would widen their ranks and contacts. Thirdly, while the Belgrade conference attracted much attention at the time its actual immediate achievements were slight; and the very fact that the leading neutralist states were far from being fully agreed as to which states should 'properly' be described as non-aligned, quite apart from the question of securing common neutralist policies, was probably not without an educative influence on participants and aligned states alike.

But if the Belgrade conference provided educative opportunities for those anxious to learn about neutralism the two most dramatic crises of 1962 offered more. These crises were the Chinese invasion of India in October 1962, and the Soviet - American brink-of-war situation over Cuba, also in October 1962.

On 20th October the Chinese attacked in strength on India's north-east frontier and in the Ladakh area of Kashmir. Shortly afterwards Chinese troops entered Assam. There had been frontier skirmishes between India and China ever since 1959 but this situation prompted Mr Nehru to declare a state of national emergency, though not formally of war against China. Three days later India accepted military assistance from the United States and then from Britain, Canada and Australia. This no doubt confirmed for China her previous claims that India was in fact linked with the 'imperialist' powers, though the Soviet Union was remarkably unwilling to endorse the Chinese claims. Chinese action showed clearly that Cold War non-alignment was of itself no guarantee of a state's territorial integrity. Different, and mostly tepid, neutralist responses to India's plight marked the flimsiness (one might say the fictitious character) of much talk about neutralist solidarity.

After some months of rumours and reports of growing Soviet-Cuban collaboration President Kennedy announced on 22nd October that the Russians were building missile bases in Cuba. He ordered a partial blockade of Cuba and from the 22nd until the 28th October, when Mr Khrushchov agreed to dismantle and remove the Russian missiles, the world's two greatest powers hovered on the brink of war. At the height of the Cuban crisis, 24th October, the delegates of a group of forty-five non-aligned states[138] met at the United Nations to urge the United States and the Soviet Union to open serious negotiations. Though both sides did take the case to the Security Council it is doubt-ful if the discussions there or the pressures of neutralist opinion had any significant influence at all. Essentially the question was settled by

[138] See *Guardian*, 25 Oct. 1962, and below pp. 117-18.

direct dealing between President Kennedy and Mr Khrushchov, and Fidel Castro thus learnt that he could not count on unhesitating Soviet support in every contingency, certainly not if there was a real risk of precipitating thermonuclear war between the two superpowers.

For the superpowers the difficulties of trying simultaneously to please both allies and 'friendly' neutralists whilst also pursuing their own interests, were now familiar predicaments. The results of such endeavours varied, and will vary, with the issues at stake, the attitudes and policies of individual neutralists, and their own actions, expectations and aims.

CHAPTER III

NEUTRALISM AS INTERNATIONAL DOCTRINE

"The spread of neutralist doctrine in an ever-widening circle from Bandung outwards is perhaps the clearest evidence of a new constellation in international affairs."

Professor Geoffrey Barraclough in 'Confluence', Fall, 1957.

"We have to do our own thinking, profiting by the example of others, but essentially trying to find a path for ourselves suited to our own conditions."

Jawaharlal Nehru, The Basic Approach, 1959.

ANYONE who begins to think about neutralist doctrine must regard the words of Professor Barraclough, quoted above, as being somewhat ironic. For it certainly requires some temerity to write of a doctrine which seems to have no canonical works, no authoritative exegesis, and not yet even a convenient collection of representative neutralist pronouncements.[1] It may help to understand some of the characteristics of such an apparently insubstantial doctrine when we remember who the leading neutralist 'ideologues' are, what rôles they perform, what aims and aspirations they have in common.

Most people would almost certainly want to describe Mr Nehru as an exponent of neutralist doctrine, and would probably agree to dub him as the world's foremost neutralist. It has even been suggested that neutralism is a peculiarly Indian invention, and that the spread of neutralist doctrine is a process whereby Mr Nehru's old arguments become the world's commonplaces.[2] But this is surely to exaggerate Mr Nehru's influence and the novelty of his pronouncements. For it has become common to consider Nehru, Tito and Nasser together as 'the high priests' of the doctrine of neutralism,[3] and to regard the writings and speeches of all three men as significant expressions of neutralist holy writ. Though the importance of some other figures who come to mind—President Sukarno, U Nu, Prince Sihanouk, the late Solomon

[1] I have made a collection of representative statements of neutralist doctrine which, together with an introductory essay and full biographical and bibliographical notes, is to be published as A Primer of Neutralism by Frank Cass & Co. (London).
[2] "Neutralism . . . imparts an aura of high moral purpose; it is theoretical and Brahminical." Economist, 29 Oct. 1955, p. 377; see also Economist, 21 Sept. 1957, pp. 948-9.
[3] See, e.g. The Times, first leader of 26 Oct. 1959, "Neutralism".

Bandaranaike, Kwame Nkrumah—might arouse more controversy, there is little doubt that the list of prominent and representative neutralist 'ideologues' could be added to without great difficulty.

While it would be wrong to discount the uniquely personal[4] elements shaping individual expressions of neutralist doctrine, it is more significant for present purposes that most of the leading neutralist 'ideologues' share a wide range of strikingly similar national and personal problems, that they are facing these problems at approximately the same time, and that these similarities tend to give something of a common character, even an international aspect to neutralist doctrine. For these 'ideologues' are not only prominent figures in international politics, they nearly all spring from the Western-educated intelligentsia[5] of their countries. They are all, in a sense, both producers and consumers of anti-colonial and nationalist revolution, and have to act as the chief spokesmen—at home and abroad—for their generally new, poor, ex-colonial states. At home they may, or may not, be demagogues; they will almost certainly have to act as pedagogues, the prime political educators of their largely illiterate populaces. Abroad, they need to justify their policies and to enlist support. Just as the leaders of each superpower champion views about what are the true principles of social and political life in all states, so in this self-consciously ideological age, with the Cold War touching so many matters to which it does not seem germane, there is much need to fasten on to some generally acceptable criteria in terms of which a neutralist case can usually be made.

All neutralists begin by rejecting emphatically the notion that they should view the world from within the 'confines' of a Cold War alliance. Thereafter, having avoided, in their own view, the prevailing East-West stereotypes, they are liable to accept some other attractive but deceptively simple views of the inter-state system—the big versus the small, the old versus the new, the colonialist versus the anti-colonialist, the rich versus the poor, are four favourites. Such dichotomies, which cut across and divide Cold War solidarities, can suggest to many neutralists a spectrum of common sympathies and antipathies, and these become powerful influences shaping their world outlook.

Even so, ambiguities inevitably arise within various versions of the doctrine—mainly from the conjunction of influences which are not always similarly and simultaneously present—and it is by remembering

[4] The Belgrade Conference Report gives brief biographies of the heads of delegations at the conference.
[5] There are valuable discussions of this theme in: Edward Shils, "The Intellectuals in the Political Development of the New States", *World Politics*, Apr. 1960, pp. 329-68; Harry J. Benda, "Non-Western Intelligentsias as Political Elites", *Australian Journal of Politics and History*, Nov. 1960, pp. 205-18; and Hugh Seton-Watson, *Neither War Nor Peace* (London, 1960), chapter 6, esp. pp. 182-8.

their deep emotional well-springs that one can begin to see why neutralist doctrine reflects such a variety of often contradictory views. Why it is sometimes doctrinaire, and yet more often extremely pragmatist. Why its exponents sometimes make exaggerated claims for the novelty of their proposals. Why it unmistakably bears the mark of its time and contains matter which is wholly ephemeral. Also, why there is much evidence of *ex-parte* statement—for all neutralist doctrine is, in some respects at least, an essay in advocacy adapted to the urgencies of Cold War situations. Yet, what is perhaps most surprising about contemporary neutralist doctrine is not the nationalist colourings and the partisan pleading in which it is undoubtedly invested, but its markedly international tinge, and the degree to which it presents, in part at least, an explicitly general view of international relations.

It is in Africa and Asia that the leading neutralist 'philosopher-kings' reside.[6] For it was in the Afro-Asian world, during the third phase of the Cold War, that neutralism began to crystallize as an international doctrine; and it is still in Asia and Africa that the most comprehensive expressions of neutralist doctrine can be found. This is not to subscribe to the belief sometimes propounded by Asian and African neutralists that neutralist doctrine is 'intrinsically' and/or distinctively Afro-Asian. For reasons already outlined it is suggested that, in ideological matters, emotional affinities are more important than geographical propinquities. Up to the time of writing there has been since 1945 no Latin American neutralist 'ideologue' of international significance, though since 1958 Fidel Castro seems to be aspiring to this rôle. In Europe neutralist doctrine is generally either not strongly couched in international terms, or its proponents lack significant political influence. Even exceptionally where official neutralist pronouncements chime with those from Africa and Asia, this seems to be mostly coincidental, as in the case of some Swedish statements, or carefully contrived, as with Yugoslav neutralism. French neutralist pronouncements are also excluded from consideration here. For French neutralism, though often expressed by men of great intellectual distinction and displaying a bewildering variety of articulate opinion, has, so far, lacked effective political influence in France, and has never enjoyed an international platform. Like many French intellectual movements, it is characterized by a defiant ethnocentrism, is an affair of coteries, and is best studied solely as a French phenomenon.[7] And, for similar reasons, British

[6] For the way in which this Platonic notion is relevant to modern nationalism, see Elie Kedourie, *Nationalism* (London, 1960), pp. 49-50.

[7] To date, French neutralism has attracted a surprising amount of scholarly attention, considering its insignificance internationally. John T. Marcus's book *Neutralism and Nationalism in France* (New York, 1958) is a thorough study of the available sources and has a good bibliography. Marcus repeatedly stresses

neutralism[8] can be ignored here.

It is assumed, then, that for present purposes we must look not to philosophers but to rulers for authoritative, influential, expositions of neutralist doctrine; that to be internationally significant the protagonists of neutralism need the nourishment of political power; and that neutralist doctrine is more likely to be learned at the press conference or from the public platform than in the study or seminar. And if public forums are the academies of neutralism, it must be expected that neutralist doctrine will at best present not a corpus of knowledge, an integrated body of theory, but rather a constellation of concepts—and these will be shrouded in a confusing medley of supporting argument.

Yet, despite these difficulties of interpretation, it does seem possible to detect five main threads in the tangled skein of neutralist argument. These are:

(1) that Cold War conditions can be mitigated and perhaps removed altogether;
(2) that neutralism is morally justifiable;
(3) that neutralists must pursue an 'independent' foreign policy;
(4) that all forms of colonialism must be eradicated;
(5) that foreign aid must be given without strings.

It is not pretended that all neutralists would willingly subscribe to the above list, nor that any of these propositions are necessarily exclusive to them. All that is claimed is that these five affirmations suggest what are the central concerns of virtually all neutralists. In actual discourse all five points habitually run together and become enmeshed—certainly, point number (3) should be considered as primary, and points (4) and (5) as common corollaries of it. They are separated out here in order to provide some fixed points round which ideas that often recur can be examined in order to show their main supporting arguments, the degree of novelty present, and reveal their underlying assumptions, affinities and incongruities.

I

Fear of 'hot' war and irritation at the continuation of the Cold War are constant themes in neutralist rhetoric. Yet it is not this that distintinguishes neutralists, but rather the diagnoses, and, especially, the

---

(though he is too immersed in detail to demonstrate this clearly) the close connection between neutralism and nationalism in France.

[8] There is as yet no satisfactory study of British neutralism. Two partially helpful references are Leon Epstein, *Britain, Uneasy Ally* (Chicago, 1954); and John Strachey, *The Pursuit of Peace* (Fabian Tract 329, London, Dec. 1960). Constantine Fitzgibbon's novel, *When the Kissing had to Stop* (London, 1960), is a fable designed to show the dangers of British neutralism. See also many articles since 1957 in the *Tribune* and in the *New Left Review*.

prognoses they offer of this common predicament. Neutralists tend to place great stress on the rôle of fear[9] as a tension-breeding factor, and with this often goes the implication that many fears are unwarranted and, hence, removable. They maintain that the mutual fears of the Cold War antagonists create a war-like atmosphere which discourages any possibility of lessening tension and unfreezing the Cold War. It seems almost as if many neutralists believe that there is a *Zeitgeist* and that they understand it better, and so can think more purposefully, than can any non-neutralist.[10] Such a view necessarily lays great trust in the therapeutic power of neutralist advice and lays stress on the moral suasive power of "independent" example and "the healing touch" [11] of the man of peace.[12]

The view that general war is entered into as a deliberate act of policy is seldom heard today, and the classic isolationist case for non-involvement—that, for the isolationist, participation in war can, in fact, be avoided—now represents a relatively minor part of neutralist argument. Though the emotional attitudes of present day neutralists and pre-1939 isolationists may be similar, the situations faced by each are different enough to elicit quite different responses. No neutralist

[9] See, e.g. Nehru in Lok Sabha, 20 Nov. 1956: "Now, I claim this as a virtue for us, for our country, for this Parliament and for our people. We are not obsessed by fear. We are not obsessed by hatred of any country. We are not obsessed even by the dislike of any other country. Our minds are a little more receptive than those of others—Communists, anti-Communists or Socialists. I do think that is a virtue in us and it is in the good democratic tradition. When that goes, it is bad for the world." *Jawaharlal Nehru's Speeches*, vol. iii (Delhi, 1958), p. 46.

[10] See, e.g. Nehru's speech at the Asian Legal Consultative Committee meeting, Delhi, 18 Apr. 1957, *ibid.*, p. 513; and U Nu's speech in Burma's Chamber of Deputies on 27 Sept. 1957 (English translation issued by the Burmese Embassy in London), p. 321.

[11] See below Section II also. These optimistic assumptions, and the parallel one that ignorance of each other's ways greatly aggravates fears and increases tensions, are part of the common currency of Anglo-American liberalism, and are enshrined in the Preamble to the Constitution of U.N.E.S.C.O. In this respect many present-day neutralists seem to re-echo Gladstone and Woodrow Wilson. E.g. Woodrow Wilson: "The example of America must be a special example . . . not merely of peace because it will not fight, but of peace because peace is the healing and elevating influence of the world and strife is not." See *The Public Papers of Woodrow Wilson*, ed. by Baker and Dodd, vol. 1, p. 321. Cf. particularly the speeches of Nehru and U Nu.

[12] It is a widely held view that men from the Hindu-Buddhist world of South and South East Asia are peculiarly well fitted to be neutralists and men of peace. This is usually maintained by people favourably disposed towards neutralists, and is a contemporary version of the well-known maxim *ex oriente lux*. But it is notoriously difficult to trace definite connections between 'cultural patterns' and political behaviour. This theory is more plausible at the level of doctrine than of policy, and needs much more investigation than it has yet enjoyed.

today can confidently assert, as did a leading Canadian isolationist in the 1920s, that he lives in a 'fireproof house';[13] he does not even claim that his Cold War neutralism necessarily means that his own country would not become involved in a general 'hot' war. The present defence of neutralism is, substantially, that it can help to *prevent* war.

There are three popular variants of this argument in neutralist circles.

The first is that neutralists should play a 'third' rôle in world affairs. In its strongest form this view sees neutralists acting together as a 'Third Force', holding a position that can save the world from self destruction. Very few neutralists, however, now see any practical possibility in the idea of a Third Force, though there are hints of such thinking in their most optimistic expressions. Strong neutralist advocacy of Third Force views is usually connected with ardent support for some particular scheme—the Commonwealth, European Union, the Afro-Asian bloc, Pan-Africa, the Asian Socialist Conference, are some examples. The past achievements and future prospects of such schemes are viewed by their proponents with greater respect than their actual impact on world affairs would seem to warrant, and their common neutralist character is always exaggerated. The weaker, and more common, form of this 'third rôle' argument is to see neutralists as creators and spreaders of areas of disengagement[14] from Cold War struggles— "areas of peace" is Mr Nehru's favourite description of these disengaged regions.[15] By themselves refusing to take sides in the Cold War struggle, neutralists claim to slow down the drift towards a bipolar world, in which international tensions would be raised to an intolerable pitch and war would become an immediate and ever present danger. Though neutralists dislike talking about 'balancing power', their implicit assumption is that a multilateral balance can be substituted for the present bi-lateral, or near bi-lateral, balance and that this would make for peace. At the very least, the existence of, and the need to woo, unaligned states is conceived of as exercising a form of restraint on the Cold War combatants.

The second variant of the argument that neutralists can be valuable peace-makers concerns 'bridgemanship'. For neutralists often assert that

---

[13] Senator Dandurand in 1924 to the League of Nations, see P. N. S. Mansergh, *Survey of British Commonwealth Affairs, Problems of External Policy 1931-1939* (London, 1952), p. 95.

[14] Disengagement is a term which has already been stretched to cover many different plans. Captain Hinterhoff's encyclopaedic book *Disengagement* (London, 1959), though devoted mainly to Europe, lists 174 different projects. Clearly, one does not have to be a neutralist to advocate disengagement, but if one is a neutralist, then, logically, one must be prepared to include one's own country in some kind of disengagement scheme.

[15] See e.g. Nehru's speech in Lok Sabha during a debate on the President's Address, 25 Feb. 1955; *Nehru's Speeches, op. cit.*, p. 285.

they offer the best remaining hope for ultimately bridging the gap between the Communist powers and the Western world.[16] They claim that their middle position enables them to provide acceptable channels of communication across Cold War barriers. Here again, the neutralist sees his rôle as one which facilitates understanding and breaks down the mutual ignorance Cold War contestants have of each other's views.[17] This view necessarily presupposes that the Cold War contestants are willing to accept neutralist intermediaries, and this is not always the case. (Canadian policy since 1945[18] provides at least some refutations of the claim that only neutralist states can act as mediators, moderators, purveyors of compromise formulae.) Neutralists stress, then, that they can undertake with some hope of success to act as friendly mediators. Their proposals for the settlement of outstanding disputes are (in their view) more likely to get a respectful hearing from both Cold War camps than those advanced by the partisans of a particular side; and in present circumstances they regard their availability for service on armistice, observation and other comparable commissions as invaluable. Even though it is admitted that such activities are seldom spectacular, it is claimed that by slow and patient conciliation a firmer base for international co-operation may eventually be secured. Neutralists and non-neutralists alike agree that negotiation and peaceful settlement are not panaceas for all the problems of international politics, but neutralists claim that they encourage a greater use than might otherwise be possible of these sometimes valuable solvents. The neutralist thus sees himself acting as a prophylactic; seeking to prevent tension by removing its causes, calming the atmosphere by keeping calm himself, evoking goodwill by showing it.

The third, and most ambitious, variant of the view that neutralism aids international peace conceives of the neutralist rôle in even larger terms. It proposes that neutralism can make a more effective contribution to the containment of Communist expansion, and the amelioration of Cold War difficulties, than can any Western sponsored regional defence arrangement. This argument maintains that the neutralists by deliberately adopting a non-aligned posture in the face of Western warnings, by declining to join in any measures of a hostile character aimed at Communist states and by placing *public* faith in Communist

[16] E.g. Mr Bandaranaike's address to the U.N. General Assembly, 22 Nov. 1956, in *The Foreign Policy of Ceylon* (Ceylon Government Press, 1957), pp. 3-7.

[17] E.g. Mr Nehru: "The rôle of India is a sort of catalyst. We are the uncommitted people. That is why we try to steer a middle course between two camps, so that both will trust us . . . we are in a position to break down mutual prejudice." *Lok Sabha Debs.*, 17 Mar. 1953, vol. ii, No. 7:2147.

[18] One can only mention here Canada's initiatives over Suez in 1956, her policy towards Indo-China, and in disarmament negotiations. But this theme deserves fuller treatment than it yet seems to have received.

E

intentions, have thereby produced earnests of Communist good behaviour. If a Communist power were to attack one of the neutralist countries, it would, according to this theory, irretrievably destroy its political credit throughout the uncommitted world. This seems to be the rationale underlying most neutralist faith in Panch Sheel type agreements.

Panch Sheel, or "the five principles of peaceful co-existence", were formally enunciated in the preamble to the Sino-Indian treaty on trade and communications with Tibet of 29th April 1954. The principles are (1) mutual respect for each other's territorial integrity and sovereignty; (2) non-aggression; (3) non-interference in each other's internal affairs; (4) equality and mutual benefit; and (5) peaceful co-existence. Though neutralists in general, and at that time Mr Nehru in particular, seemed to regard these principles as being a special contribution to world politics, they were not at all original, were repetitious, and really boiled down to the edict that a state's independence should not be infringed.[19] Of course, the whole argument about their efficacy hinges on the assumption that Communist states making such public pledges[20] will go to great lengths to avoid offending neutralist opinion, and it seems to exaggerate the extent to which neutralist states might regard a hostile act against one neutralist state as being a hostile act against the whole neutralist world.

It is ironic that the practical efficacy of Panch Sheel agreements should first be called into question seriously as a result of rapid deterioration in the relations between the two original promoters, India and China. Actually, many Panch Sheel agreements between neutralist and Communist states are unlikely to be subject to similar strains, if only because the direct clash of interests is less likely where there is geographical separation of the signatory states. For it is important to remember that all the foregoing arguments have been concerned with international peace and security rather than national security. While it does not necessarily follow that without international security there can be no national security, neutralists seldom make this distinction openly. Appeals to history—quite apart from the argument about the degree of novelty inherent in Cold War situations in the presence of thermo-nuclear weapons—are inevitably inconclusive. For, in the past,

[19] There seems to be no need to seek deep philosophical sources for such an unremarkable point, but such searches persist. See e.g. *Panch Sheel : Its Meaning and History* (Lok Sabha Secretariat, New Delhi, 1955) and the discussion reported in *The Indian Journal of Political Science*, Jan. - Mar. 1956.

[20] E.g. Nehru: "It is not a question of believing the other party's word; it is a question of creating conditions where the other party cannot break its word, or if I may say so, where it finds it difficult to break its word." If it did, it was "likely to find itself in a much worse quandary". *Lok Sabha Debs*, 29 Sept. 1954, vol. vii, part 2, col. 3687. See also cols. 3692-3.

neither alliance nor non-alliance policies have proved to be infallible recipes for preventing, or even avoiding, war.

II

One of the most vital elements in neutralist doctrine is the resistance that is put up to claims that either Cold War camp commands an exclusive monopoly of rectitude. Neutralist resistance to American policies was probably heightened by some of Mr Dulles' more notorious phrases—"massive retaliation", "the brink of war", "neutrality is an immoral and shortsighted conception", "agonizing re-appraisal", are some which immediately come to mind. What many neutralists say is that they themselves have no messianic mission, they do not think in terms of moral absolutes and they quite genuinely do not see everything in the Cold War as an incident in a drama where the 'good' forces of one bloc must confound the 'evil' forces of the other bloc.[21] They refuse to see the East-West struggle in terms of a conflict between 'right' and 'wrong', and, hence, to be drawn into a crusade to extirpate evil on either side. This is an effective counter to some of the more extravagant or hypocritical moral claims advanced by the committed in the Cold War and is a pertinent reminder of the values of humility and sincerity in politics.

But humility is not the only moral attitude of neutralists. For some of them assert a moral neutralism, an indifference, with regard to the two Cold War camps because they consider that both sides in the Cold War are basically at the same moral level. The extreme negative and positive poles of this view are summed up in the phrases 'a plague on both your houses'[22] and 'I am holier than thou'. No matter whether the negative or the positive variant is dominant in a particular argument, all expressions of moral neutralism rest on a loose identification of the Soviet and Western systems with values from which the neutralist feels equidistant,[23] and on loose analogies between Soviet and Western policies with scant regard for their vital differences.[24]

The negative attitude of 'a plague on both your houses' expresses a

[21] E.g. see K. M. Panikkar, *Common Sense About India* (London, 1960), p. 148.

[22] Thus Mr Nehru: "If there is a Cold War today, certainly we are neutral. It does not matter who is right and who is wrong. We will not join in this exhibition of mutual abuse." *Lok Sabha Debs.*, 12 June 1952, vol. ii (1), p. 1662.

[23] Thus President Sukarno in an unsolicited letter to the *New Statesman* (London), 28 June 1958, p. 828: "It is past time for the West, Communist and anti-Communist alike (sic) to draw back from the edge of complete moral bankruptcy . . . There can be no question of the West giving moral leadership to Asia. Your moral leadership has, for us, meant first colonialism and now the philosophical, moral, political and social bankruptcy of a nuclear arms race." The whole letter is a fascinating statement by a leading neutralist.

[24] I owe this point to Denis Healey, *Neutralism* (London, 1955), p. 20.

desire to 'think neutralism' and thus to assert an impartiality of mind towards the moral issues involved in the Cold War. In its most defensive position this negative mood finds refuge in *tu quoque* argument—for which, of course, in politics there are endless opportunities. Righteous indignation at Indian 'appeasement' of Communist aggression in Tibet, for example, tempts those who are scolded to cite the record of Teheran, Yalta and Potsdam—the attempted 'appeasement' of Soviet dictatorship by the 'surrender' of the liberties of Poland and Czechoslovakia. Invariably, the Suez and Hungary episodes of 1956 get dragged into these inevitably inconclusive arguments. But a more aggressive defence of this negative moral neutralism is to assert that there are no *moral* issues involved in the Cold War struggle. In fact, those who take such a stand are driven to adopt, at least implicitly, a double standard of judgment—an exacting one for the parliamentary democracies and a complaisant one for the totalitarian dictatorships.

In a sense, of course, double standards are always being applied in international politics; this is mainly because the moral agents in international relations are not individuals only but governments, and governments are far more intimately concerned with issues that seem to involve the national interest, and are often indifferent to others that do not. But any responsible moral comparison between the two rival Cold War groupings must surely take into account respective responsibilities for the development of the Cold War, and the behaviour of the parties in this struggle towards allies, opponents and neutralists. If, after such analysis, the neutralist still *publicly* insists that the behaviour of both Cold War camps is morally identical, protagonists of either side in the Cold War would, no doubt, immediately reply that such a judgment amounts to refusing to distinguish between light grey and dark black—an ironic reply to indefatigable moralists who constantly claim to 'decide each issue on its merits'. Privately, it may be that the neutralist makes use of the facile back-handed compliment that he expects higher standards of probity from the Western than the Communist camp, or admits that people under Communist rule are too well sealed off to be open to much neutralist persuasion.

Perhaps the neutralist *penchant* for deciding each issue on its merits is best shown in the working distinction observed by all those neutralists —Nehru and Nasser are two notable examples—who refuse to be anti-Communist in foreign policy though actively anti-Communist in their domestic policy. And, perhaps, a useful touchstone of state morality is to see to what extent a distinction is preserved between public policy and private attitude. For it is arguable that the degree to which a state permits its own citizens to criticize government policies is one rough indicator of the probity to be expected from it in its international dealings. There is no common neutralist standard here, though.

Furthermore, there is a persistent tendency for some neutralists to act as if verbal pronouncements, without any subsequent substantive policy on their own part, are sufficient to 'decide' complex issues in international politics, without assuming any responsibility for seeing that a verbal 'decision' is carried out. In fact, for most neutralists staying non-aligned must often seem more important than the issues involved in a particular dispute—unless they are themselves a contending party—because both their concept of their own proper rôle in world affairs and their bargaining position depend on remaining non-aligned.

The claim that the non-aligned states present judgments and suggestions that are impartial and objective is often questionable. It is likely to be questionable for at least two reasons. Firstly, to seek, let alone to attain, informed judgments on any important international matter requires a rigorous, unremitting attention to detail, something like the kind of earnest application that Dag Hammarskjöld (replying to Khrushchov's charge that "while there are neutral states there are no neutral men") said was of the essence of the professional, diplomatically neutral, international civil servant.[25] And what was most significant about Hammarskjöld's reply was that he stressed integrity and professionalism far more than any idea of neutrality. To have informed judgment one must presuppose some expertize, and experts are so often what neutralist states lack.[26] The second major objection to neutralist claims about disengaged 'objectivity' is that there is far more truth than is today conceded in Bismarck's claim that in international matters partiality, involvement in a dispute, is a necessary condition for understanding the issues at stake and for pronouncing on the merits of a case. Not to be partial is often to be ill-informed and perhaps indifferent too. The moral claims of neutralists to participate in discussions and decision taking about complex problems of economic development and nuclear testing do not stem from their possession of Olympian wisdom, or from

[25] See Dag Hammarskjold, *The International Civil Servant in Law and in Fact* (Oxford, 1961), esp. p. 27. Mr Khrushchov's assertion that while there were "neutral countries there were no neutral men" was made to the American columnist, Mr Walter Lippmann, and reported by him in the *New York Herald Tribune* on 17, 18, 19 Apr. 1961.

[26] Two examples might illustrate these themes of expertize and objectivity: (1) At the seventeen-nation Geneva discussions on disarmament and nuclear testing in 1962 only two—India and Sweden—of the eight 'neutral' states appear to have had technical advisers. Yet, undoubtedly, there were grave technical as well as political problems involved. (2) Speaking at a ceremony to launch a new supervisory board for the official Indonesian news agency, President Sukarno said its task was to present news which favoured and credited the revolution. There was a notion among Indonesian journalists that news reporting should be objective, he said. This was not correct because no revolution was objective. See *The Guardian*, 19 Dec. 1962.

any intrinsic quality of detachment or objectivity. Their most impressive moral claim is, or could be, that they *are* affected, interested and involved in matters of this kind. In this respect, to be interested is to have a moral commitment.

Though the claim that 'I am holier than thou' is rarely voiced explicitly,[27] such claims to moral superiority as are implicit in some neutralist rhetoric are immediately open to the objection mentioned earlier about moral chauvinism. For there seems to be no logical reason to deny oneself the very humility which is urged on the Cold War rivals. Even so, many speeches at the Belgrade Neutralist Conference in September 1961 clearly implied that non-alignment was morally superior to Cold War alliance policies; and this was surely implied in Sukarno's opening speech at the Bandung Conference when he claimed that "we the peoples of Asia and Africa . . . can mobilize the Moral Violence of Nations in favour of peace". To cite such examples is not, of course, to deny that there may be powerful historical-emotional reasons why some neutralists assume their own moral superiority. Many of the most prominent contemporary neutralists, while leading 'independence' movements in the days of colonial rule, claimed as against their rulers a superior morality. They also claimed that they had the support of 'the people' of their country and that the colonial rulers did not. Such attitudes, once adopted, die hard and probably influence thinking in post-independence days.

Indeed, it seems almost customary now for neutralists to regard themselves as in some way custodians of a notional 'world opinion' (which by means of an unexplained equation sometimes seems to become a kind of 'world conscience'), and to talk as if voting majorities in the United Nations General Assembly[28] were proximate expressions of 'world opinion'. This view may stem from a vague and implicit populism[29]—some parallels lie in: appeals to the people, conspiracy theories of history, militant reformism, nationalism and anti-imperialism —crudely applied to international politics. Just as nationalist leadership by its nature involves an appeal to, or, at least, a reference to, 'the people', so heroic leaders, such as Presidents Sukarno, Nkrumah and

[27] Though occasionally one comes across such remarks as "Independence is not synonymous with stylishness or pomp. There is no merit in hiding our poverty. India's status in the world depends upon her moral supremacy." Mahatma Gandhi's *Delhi Diary*, 22 Jan. 1947, p. 370.

[28] See Alistair Cooke's instructive article, "A Letter from the United Nations", *Listener*, 6 Oct. 1960, pp. 549-50; and Robert Stephens, "Neutralists Take the Offensive", *Observer*, 2 Oct. 1960. The attractions of the U.N. for neutralists are briefly discussed above, p. 000.

[29] For the international outlook of populism, see Shils and Hugh Seton-Watson (both cited in n. 5). Cf. also Richard Hofstadter, *The Age of Reform* (New York, 1955), chapter 2, "The Folklore of Populism", esp. section 3.

Nasser, claim not only to be the spokesmen for one state in an international organization made up of states, but also for the whole of their large populations—and such a rôle often encourages the speaker to remind his listeners of the many 'uncommitted' people in the world[30] and perhaps to quote, with high approval, the opening words of the Preamble to the United Nations Charter—"We the Peoples of the United Nations . . . " Even the neutralist from a country with a small population can derive satisfaction from dramatically reminding his listeners that his country is part of this large neutralist world.

The customary language of the Cold War neutralist is significantly different in emphasis from that usually to be expected from a neutral in time of war. The neutral will tend to stress that there is a legal right of states to be neutral and that if international law is respected neutrality will be respected. The neutralist tends rather to stress that it is morally right for any state to be neutralist, and that 'world opinion' endorses the rightness of neutralist policies or wishes. The neutral tends to talk of law more than of morality. The neutralist tends to talk of morality more than of law. Admittedly, this is only a difference of emphasis, for it is not pretended that it is an especially neutralist characteristic to be neglectful of international law; but differences of emphasis can be significant. Many neutralists do feel that whilst the established legal rules of international society certainly need strengthening, these rules have hitherto been too 'Western' in character and now need to have a larger 'Afro-Asian' content.[31] Furthermore, it is often felt that international law favours the *status quo* powers, and whereas pre-1939 neutrals were, generally speaking, satisfied states territorially, the present day neutralist often has a piece of 'unfinished business',[32] the completion of which it is thought 'world opinion' may approve of, or at least condone, while existing international law may more likely serve as an obstruction. 'World opinion', like 'non-intervention' as enshrined in the Panch Sheel principles, is thus regarded as a permissive or protective, never as a prohibitive, force.

Even if it can be granted that a rough and ready measure of 'world opinion' on a particular issue is to be found by the size of the majority in favour of the motion in the U.N. General Assembly—and this is

[30] This is a theme to be found in many speeches delivered at the Bandung and Belgrade conferences and in U.N. General Assembly meetings, especially since 1955.

[31] See e.g. Mr Nehru's speech at the Asian Legal Consultative Committee Meeting; *Nehru's Speeches* (n. 9, above), pp. 508-13.

[32] This applies to all the irredentist claims of neutralists; the list is too long to set out here. Of course, it would be wrong to assume that only neutralist states have irredenta. The word, and much actual irredentism, originated in Italy. Italy from 1861 to 1941 provides some interesting analogies with present day neutralists.

often dubious—it may seem difficult to know what moral significance[33] to attach to such political arithmetic. But this is not a prime concern for the student of politics. For there is no necessary and inevitable relationship between morality and the number of votes cast for a resolution, any more than there is between morality and the strength, or size, or age, of a state. Arguments which bring such categories together more often serve to confuse than to clarify political appraisals. For with states, as with individuals, one should not judge behaviour primarily by reference to physical attributes but by reference to behaviour. As Burke said, conduct is the only language that rarely lies.

III

A dominant strand in all neutralist assertion is the claim to pursue an 'independent' foreign policy. In fact, of course, all states seek to conduct an independent foreign policy, but the type of independence sought will be strongly influenced by past experiences as well as by present predilections and power considerations. 'Independence' is naturally attractive to the newly independent, and as most neutralists come from newly independent countries and are the heirs of nationalist and anti-colonial revolution, they tend to be sensitively aware of their newness in international society, suspicious of their former colonial rulers, and fearful of the direction great power policies may take in the future. Indeed, the whole of neutralist doctrine could be described as a quest for distinctive, intellectual expression of independence, and starts from the assumption of a given independent statehood.

Neutralists fear that formal alignment with either Cold War bloc would impair their newly acquired independence.[34] For most of them the Cold War struggle pre-dates their own independence, and they feel that the issues involved are not central to their own concerns. About a half of the one hundred and ten members of the United Nations on 1st January 1963 were new states, independent since 1945, and virtually all of these were neutralist inasmuch as they were not members of any Cold War military alliance. Probably the leaders of all these neutralist states suspect that if their states were to become aligned they would

---

[33] This is not to deny that such votes can have considerable political significance. For two penetrating discussions of this problem, see F. S. Northedge, "The Authority of the U.N. General Assembly", *International Relations*, Oct. 1957, pp. 349-61, 376; and Vernon Aspaturian, "The Metamorphosis of the U.N." in *Yale Review*, Summer 1957; see also below, p. 111 n. 56.

[34] These currents are all especially strong in Arab neutralism (see e.g. Gamal Abdel Nasser, "The Egyptian Revolution", in *Foreign Affairs*, Jan. 1955, 199-211.) This may in part be due to significantly different experiences of colonial rule—as Henry A. Kissinger suggests in his *Nuclear Weapons and Foreign Policy* (New York, 1957), p. 257.

quickly sink to the level of neglected junior partners in a large alliance. No longer would they be 'honest brokers', 'bridges of peace' between competing coalitions. No longer would they be wooed by the great powers. They fear they would be taken for granted, and instead of taking vital foreign policy decisions themselves, they feel that these would be decided for them by their older, stronger and richer partners.

It is here that the popular analogy between early American isolationists and present day neutralists is most suggestive. For instance, with very little alteration many of the themes and language of George Washington's *Farewell Address of 1796* could be usefully borrowed by today's neutralists. Washington said: "Europe has a set of primary interests which to us have none, or a very remote relation . . . Why . . . entangle our peace and prosperity in the toils of European ambitions, rivalship, interest or caprice?" What is often forgotten is that Washington also stressed that America enjoyed a favourable geographical position and that 'neutrality' was neither an absolute good nor of itself always an adequate means of national defence. Otherwise, if one substitutes the superpowers for Europe and the newly freed colonies for the United States, Washington's words might well have been spoken by Nehru, Nasser or Nkrumah. Some other themes—the need to clarify the national interest, the need for national unity, the dangers of party strife, for example—are easily and equally susceptible to similar treatment.

National unity and national independence are among the greatest of neutralist preoccupations. For though nationalist[35] claims have in most cases helped to bring independent statehood, 'the nation' legitimatizing the state, national unity is often precarious and its roots shallow. National unity thus has to be strengthened and consolidated, and it is thought that a truly 'independent' foreign policy will facilitate this.[36] The acquisition of statehood brings with it the realization that state boundaries are important points of discontinuity with the rest of the world, and that there is a real need to discover, to articulate and to safeguard and strengthen one's own national interests in the world. Two crucial touchstones here are: freedom from external control, and

[35] Thus, President Sukarno: "For us nationalism is everything. Though nationalism in the West may be an out-of-date doctrine for many, for us in Asia and Africa it is the mainspring of our efforts", quoted from his address to the Congress of the United States on 17 May 1956. And President Nasser: "Positive neutrality is in itself a protection for independence, and independence is, in its turn, a protection for Arab nationalism", quoted in *The Times*, 26 Oct. 1959.
[36] See e.g. James Barrington's article, "The Concept of Neutralism. What Lies Behind Burma's Foreign Policy", in the special Burma Supplement of the *Atlantic Monthly* in 1958, pp. 28-30. Barrington, an Anglo-Burman, is the leading Burmese career diplomat.

the desire for status[37]—for acceptance, as of right, in the eyes of the outside world. Such preoccupations often give rise to two common dilemmas. Firstly, whether insistence on 'complete' national sovereignty can be reconciled with the simultaneous pursuit of a wide range of international friendships, full international co-operation and world peace. Secondly, there is an uncertainty whether domestic matters should take precedence over foreign policy, or whether neutralists, too, should accept Ranke's principle of 'the primacy of foreign policy'.

The first dilemma is often resolved by professions of faith in the United Nations, and by asserting the need for its universality of membership. Nor is it surprising that men who have probably grown up diplomatically with the United Nations, who regard their state's membership of this organization as the most tangible expression of their enfranchizement in international society, and who see their state enjoying formal equality with the other states participating in United Nations activities, should attach great importance to United Nations happenings. At the very least, membership of the United Nations helps a state to avoid diplomatic isolation without involving that attachment to power blocs which, in Mr Nehru's view,[38] inhibits national freedom and is said to be detrimental to the growth of 'true democracy' on an international plane. (Strictly, democracy is a form of government and not just a general approval word. Not surprisingly, each neutralist cherishes his own version of 'democracy', and there is no common neutralist brand. Many hint that their concept of democracy embraces a synthesis of what is 'best' in the East and West.[39]) Besides encouraging 'true democracy' and relishing the rôle of 'floating voter' in United Nations assemblies, the neutralist generally regards his membership also as important in the pursuit of a much professed neutralist ideal of

[37] Thus, M. Senghor of Senegal: "We intend to show our independence by claiming all the attributes of sovereignty, even if that sovereignty is bound to be partly theoretical", quoted in *C.S.M.*, 15 Sept. 1959. One remembers, too, the ringing motto of Dr Nkrumah's party in the days before Ghanaian independence: "Seek ye first the political kingdom and all else will be added unto you." See *Ghana. The Autobiography of Kwame Nkrumah* (Nelson ed., Edinburgh, 1957), p. 135. The search for status often becomes confusingly mingled with freedom —individual and national—as Isaiah Berlin warns us in his *Two Concepts of Liberty* (Oxford, 1958), pp. 39-47.

[38] Nehru: "Alignment means regimentation. I object to Communist regimentation of individuals and countries as I object equally to non-Communist regimentation because both are opposed to democracy", reported in the *Daily Telegraph*, 7 July 1956. A common corollary of this view is that the aligned should show more respect for the neutralist position. Ironically, this plea seldom admits a reciprocal obligation on the part of the neutralist to respect the position of the aligned.

[39] There is a temperate and wise discussion of the relations between democracy and Afro-Asian nationalism in Rupert Emerson, *From Empire to Nation. The Rise to Self-Assertion of Asian and African Peoples* (Harvard, 1960), esp. part 3.

'equal friendship'[40] with all, regardless of ideological and political differences. But 'equal friendship' is an easy precept, difficult to practise. In reality, no state, nor any individual, is, or can be, friendly with all. And too much can be claimed for the mere fact of being formally uninvolved in Cold War alignments. For alliances are not the only, nor necessarily the most compelling, way of forging diplomatic friendships, and the world pattern of diplomatic friendships and enmities at any particular time is not sufficiently explained* in terms of the aligned and non-aligned.

At first glance it may seem that the second dilemma is entirely theoretical. For no statesman today can pursue either a domestic or foreign policy to the exclusion of the other. Clearly, the task of statesmanship is to work out one's scale of national priorities and to concert both foreign and domestic policies. But for a number of neutralist leaders, faced with an acute shortage of highly trained administrators, diplomats, or technicians, the allocation of scarce, skilled manpower resources between the competing claims of pressing domestic and foreign policy tasks, may make them talk as if the vital question was one of opting for either a foreign or a domestic policy.

In one mood the neutralist is inclined to say that he and his compatriots have been conquered, exploited, and fought over quite enough in the past, and now they want just to be left alone. They do not want to be fenced in by the formal constrictions of alignment. Theirs are transitional societies, their cultures are in disarray,[41] their own problems are overwhelming, they want only to rebuild in peace, to discover and give expression to their 'true national'[42] or, at most, their 'continental' personalities. Yet pan-continental enthusiasms[43] relate to neutralism only because some neutralists claim that the 'true' Asian or African character is neutralist and because some of them have asserted Monroe Doctrines for their continent. It is undeniable that there is nowadays, more than ever before, both considerable talk and striving for continental solidarities, especially in Africa. But such striving is neither wholly novel nor remarkably successful. The compatibility and desirability of both nationalism and pan-continentalism was one of Mazzini's

[40] President Tito, in particular, strongly professes "equal friendship" with all.
[41] An interesting discussion of some of these problems is reported by Edward Shils, "Old Societies, New States", in Encounter, Mar. 1959, pp. 32-41.
[42] Some outstanding literary examples of this kind of quest are: Jawaharlal Nehru, The Discovery of India (London, 1946); K. M. Panikkar, Asia and Western Dominance (London, 1953); G. A. Nasser, The Philosophy of the Revolution (Economica Books, Buffalo, U.S.A., 1959); Kwame Nkrumah's Autobiography: Ghana (London, 1957).
[43] See further P. H. Lyon, "The Pan-Continental Movements of Asia and Africa, 1947-58", Australian Outlook, June 1959, pp. 100-11; and Colin Legum, Pan-Africanism, op. cit.
* See below, chapters iv-vi.

favourite themes; West Indians have for a long time played an active part in promoting pan-Africanism; and the continents still remain cartographic conventions rather than political units. G. K. Chesterton's observation on Cecil Rhodes now has a contemporary relevance. 'It is just as easy to think in continents as to think in cobblestones', Chesterton said. 'The difficulty comes when we seek to learn the substance of either of them.'

In a contrasting mood the neutralist is often inclined to escape, temporarily, from seemingly intractable domestic problems, where each action has its political price, to the more dramatic and possibly less demanding task of suggesting 'solutions' to hitherto intractable world problems — disarmament is a favourite theme — where on an international tour, or in the congenial atmosphere of some international arena, the kind of admirable general principles which so often resist easy translation into practice at home, now meet with widespread applause and acclamation. Nevertheless, this seeming readiness, on occasions, to abandon a national for a world rôle is more apparent than real. Though self-respect may demand the giving of advice as well as the taking of aid, many neutralist statesmen do often succeed in suggesting some remarkable coincidences between what would be globally beneficial to all and yet nationally advantageous to themselves; especially stressing the desirability of great powers spending less on armaments and giving more 'unconditional' aid to the poor and newly independent states, or the need for concerted efforts to remove all remaining vestiges of 'colonialism'. Thus, the paradox of strengthening both 'independence' and 'inter-dependence'[44] simultaneously is resolved.

IV

"We talk about the crisis of our time and many people view it in different ways. Probably in the U.S.A. the crisis of the time is supposed to be Communism versus anti-Communism. It may be so to some extent. But the crisis of the time in Asia is colonialism versus anti-colonialism, let us be quite clear about it."[45]

It was Mr Nehru who said this in August 1954, and although by 1962 there was plenty of evidence that he seemed inclined to stress 'world peace' more than 'colonialism v. anti-colonialism', this was a change of priorities not an abandonment of concern for 'anti-colonial' issues. Although there are substantial differences of emphasis, all

[44] See, for instance, James Barrington's article cited in n. 36, and Sékou Touré, "Africa's Future and the World", *Foreign Affairs*, Oct. 1962, pp. 141-51, esp. 151. In 1848 Marx and Engels wrote: "In place of the old local and national seclusion and self sufficiency we have intercourse in every direction, universal interdependence of nations." See *Communist Manifesto* (edited and introduced by Harold Laski, 1948), p. 124.

[45] Mr Nehru quoted in *The Times of India*, 27 Aug. 1954.

neutralists are agreed that it is important to end all forms of 'colonialism'[46] and 'imperialism'—in contemporary polemic the two words are virtually exact synonyms. Just as an 'independent' foreign policy is considered to be an essential corollary of national independence, a consequence of being freed from the shackles of imperial rule, so virtually all neutralists deem it obligatory to help remove the remaining vestiges of 'colonialist power' wherever they may be. By 1962 African expressions of anti-colonialism were generally much stronger than Asian because there were so many more 'vestiges' of (Western) 'colonialism' in Africa. Furthermore, this task of combating 'colonialism' is often considered to be preventive as well as curative: an alert eye has to be kept open for 'neo-colonialism' which it is felt may come in more subtle forms than did the older colonialism. Besides, to have a common external enemy is one way of discovering common internal interests.

Not surprisingly, the problem of identifying 'colonialism' in 'all its forms' is highly controversial, and produces a spate of tendentious working definitions. In effect, the colonial problem cuts across Cold War issues, mostly to the advantage of the Communist powers.

The greater sensitivity of most neutralists to Western rather than Communist colonialism is perhaps surprising in view of Communist expansion and the large-scale contraction of Western colonial empires since 1945. Yet such a bias is probably to be explained largely in terms of the slowness with which certain ideas and experiences disappear from men's minds and others take hold.

For one should not underrate the importance and influence in ex-colonialist states of Hobson-Leninist theories of imperialism. Hobson's and Lenin's books on imperialism were two highly influential examples of a species of demonology, masquerading as accurate history. In current international politics it apparently matters little that much subsequent criticism and research[47] has shown their, rather different, arguments to have been frail or false. In fact, both Hobson's and Lenin's tracts were polemics and it is as polemic that their arguments still live today. It is

[46] The whole debate about colonial rule and self-government is, of course, much wider and more complicated than will appear from this brief treatment which is concerned only with the relation to neutralist argument. John Plamenatz's book *On Alien Rule and Self-Government* (London, 1960) is an extraordinarily lucid exposition and criticism of the central arguments in the colonialism debate. See also Denis Healey, *op. cit.*, pp. 20-8.

[47] Sir George Paish showed the statistical weaknesses of Hobson's study in the *Journal of the Royal Statistical Society*, Sept. 1909 and Jan. 1911. I believe that each of the following studies contains substantial criticisms either explicit or implicit, of Hobson and Lenin: Robinson, Gallacher and Denny, *Africa and the Victorians. The Official Mind of Imperialism* (London, 1961); C. D. Cowan, *Nineteenth Century Malaya: The Origins of British Political Control* (London, 1961); H. S. Ferns, *Britain and Argentina in the Nineteenth Century* (Oxford, 1960); and H. Feis, *Europe the World's Banker, 1870-1914* (New Haven, 1930).

not that their books are now widely read, but that some of the arguments, and assertions, they employed are widely echoed. It is conveniently forgotten that Hobson was not against all forms of
'imperialism' but approved of the idea of a genuinely beneficent
'civilized' rule of 'backward' peoples by trusteeship. It is for his fulmina-
tions against the actual colonial regimes of the nineteenth century and
as a source for Lenin to pillage that Hobson's book is most remembered
today. Lenin's notion of the imperialist powers keeping themselves going
by milking their overseas territories in order to provide surplus value to
appease their own proletariats[48] is a congenial and superficially convincing explanation for many Asians and Africans. Lenin also disposed
of 'capitalist' claims to have granted former colonial territories political
independence by asserting a theory of 'neo-colonialism' — the continuance of economic control despite the granting of formal independence—which is often simply taken over by many neutralist leaders
without acknowledgement.[49]

Indeed, some version of Marxism[50]—though probably in syncretistic
and highly idiosyncratic forms—is almost bound to be popular in ex-
colonial countries, since it can offer, as well as idealism[51] and apocalyptic
visions, a rationale and justification for present fears, suspicions and
resentments felt towards former colonial masters. This often makes
possible a coincidence of neutralist and Communist demands which is
unlikely to occur where either emancipation from colonial rule is not
so recent, or where the temptations to make glib verbal connections
between "capitalism" and "colonialism" are less alluring. It is one of

[48] See V. I. Lenin, *Imperialism. The Highest Stage of Capitalism*, 1916 (Little
Lenin Library, vol. xv, London, 1948), esp. p. 132.

[49] Thus, President Nkrumah speaks of "clientele-sovereignty"; which arises, he
claims, from "the practice of granting a sort of independence by the metropolitan
power, with the concealed intention of making the liberated country a client-
state and controlling it effectively by means other than political ones". See
Kwame Nkrumah, *I Speak of Freedom* (London, 1961), p. 265.

[50] This theme is dealt with in detail: for South and South-East Asia by Saul
Rose, *Socialism in Southern Asia* (London, 1959); J. H. Brimmell, *Communism in
South East Asia* (London, 1959); and Frank N. Trager (ed.), *Marxism in South
East Asia* (Stanford, 1960); for the Middle East by Walter Z. Laquer, *Communism
and Nationalism in the Middle East* (London, 1956); and for Africa, briefly, by
Thomas Hodgkin, "A Note on the Language of African Nationalism" in *St.
Antony's Papers*, No. 10, *African Affairs*, No. 1 (London, 1961), pp. 22-40. See
also the articles in *Survey. A Journal of Soviet and East European Studies*, Aug.
1962, when the whole issue was devoted to the theme of "National Communism
and the Uncommitted Nations". Robert A. Scalapino, "Neutralism in Asia",
A.P.S.R., Mar. 1954, pp. 49-62, suggests that Marxism is attractive to neutralists
for domestic and for international reasons.

[51] Thus, Harold Laski, *Communism* (London, 1927): "Communism has made its
way by its idealism and not its realism, by its spiritual promise, not its materialis-
tic prospect" (p. 250). See also J. Nehru, *Autobiography* (New York, 1936), p. 592.

the ironies of the appeal that some version of Marxism seems to have for most Asian and African neutralists that it is the *dirigisme*, the rôle and importance attached to economic planning and to state controls, that is probably the most satisfying element. It is ironic because this appeal must be drawn from the practice of Communist regimes—most notably either from Russia or China—and not from the canonical writings of Marxism. For though as a creed Marxism promises the eventual "withering away of the State" this famous and notably unelaborated aspect of Communist doctrine does not seem to find much realization in the current practices of Communist states. In Communist vocabulary a Communist government cannot, by definition, commit "colonialism", which is a practice of "imperialist - capitalist" powers. This has a convenience in Communist dealing with the neutralists, for though Americans may talk of the 'free' and 'unfree' parts of the world, in terms of whether a state has a Communist government or not, the neutralist much prefers to distinguish between colonial status and 'freedom' from it.[52]

So, while neutralists have experienced Western rule and memories of it are still strong, there seems to be small awareness of the extent or finality with which 'Western colonialism' has receded, and continues to recede.[53] The facts of Communist colonialism[54] may not yet have sunk in or appear so immediate — save, perhaps, since 1957, to the neutralist states bordering China : India, Nepal, Bhutan, Burma, Sikkim and Laos; and all these, apart from India, have, so far, seen more of Chinese 'carrots' than of Chinese 'sticks'. Furthermore, it is worthwhile remembering that there is at present still no new state formed from the Soviet 'empire', willing and able to testify to Communist colonialism in, say, U.N. forums. It seems that there is still a widespread acceptance of 'the salt water fallacy'[55] about colonialism—the supposition that

---

[52] For some time after 1949 much of Asian neutralist approval for Mao's, as opposed to Chiang Kai-Shek's, China seems to have been based on some such incompletely descriptive definition of freedom. See further C. P. Fitzgerald, *Revolution in China* (London, 1952), p. 214. See also Alec Nove, "The Soviet model and underdeveloped countries" in *International Affairs* (Jan. 1961), pp. 29-38.

[53] This view would be strongly repudiated by many Arab neutralists who would cite Western landings in Egypt 1956, in Jordan and Lebanon 1958, and in Kuwait 1961; besides mentioning the tenacity with which Britain holds on to her Persian Gulf interests, and the Western powers' attempts to safeguard their oil interests.

[54] See Walter Kolarz, *Russia and Her Colonies* (London, 1952); and Hugh Seton-Watson, *The New Imperialism* (London, 1961).

[55] The phrase "salt water fallacy", and the notion underlying it, seems to have been first developed in public by Sir Hilton Poynton in a speech to the 4th Committee of the General Assembly of the United Nations on 3 Oct. 1947, and published in "Information on Non-Self-Governing Territories", *Colonial Office*

only if salt water lies between the metropolitan power and 'the colony' can the relationship of colonialism be said to exist. By this device Western overseas territories, holdings, bases and transmarine alliances can all be dubbed as 'colonialism', or 'neo-colonialism', while the policies of Communist governments can usually escape such opprobrium.

But it should not be forgotten that many of the new Asian and African nations, many of these with a history of armed revolt, have been aided (in varying degree, actively or passively) by the Soviets in achieving their independence. Whatever the misdeeds of the Russians in eastern Europe, and whatever their ultimate goals may be, for many political leaders in Asia and Africa the existence of a powerful state as a counterfoil to their colonial masters enlarged their ability to achieve independence and they took advantage of it. The history of post-war national independence conflicts shows many instances of direct aid from the Russians, appeals for such aid, or threats to make such appeals as a means of wresting concessions from the European colonial powers.

When neutralists voice fears of the re-imposition of Western rule, these fears may seem ridiculously exaggerated to Westerners virtuously conscious of their own reformed characters, but this does not seem so to neutralists. After all, the neutralist view of Western alliance and bases in Asia and Africa (which is, not surprisingly, voiced by the Communists, too) as 'imperialist' arrangements is understandable within their frame of reference where the word 'imperialist' is associated with the defence and promotion of Western interests. For the defence and promotion of Western interests is at least *one* of the main purposes of having such alliances and bases. Of course, from a Western point of view the word 'imperialist' has overtones connoting an active expansionist, probably annexationist, policy, and it seems absurd to apply it to instruments so clearly intended to prevent Communist expansionism. However, the identification of Western interests overseas with states at loggerheads with their neutralist neighbours gives the neutralist an added concern. For not only is it complained that this 'brings the Cold War' into regions where it has no relevance, but it is suspected that Pakistan or Thailand's membership of S.E.A.T.O., for example, is not merely a result of a dedication to anti-Communist causes, but is mainly a means of gaining powerful support for the furtherance of more immediate, local rivalries.

The notion that Western imperialism is still a strong and potentially dangerous force is reinforced by the tendency of most Asian and African neutralists not only to identify themselves with territories which are still Western dependencies, but with non-European peoples anywhere

No. 228 (1948). I am grateful to Mr Gretton of the B.B.C. for supplying this information, and to Sir Hilton Poynton for confirming it and telling me of the background to his thinking on that occasion.

in conflict with European ones. The revolt against colonial status thus merges with the revolt against the old European ascendancy, and the demand for equality becomes racial as well as political, economic and diplomatic.[56] The West is embarrassed, not only by the practices of the past, but by the remnants of discrimination that a good many non-Europeans still encounter from Europeans. White Americans, too, share in this obloquy, not only by reason of their close political and diplomatic ties with Europe—a kind of 'guilt by association'—but also because of their own 'Negro problem', and the greater publicity that unsavoury aspects of United States politics receive in the world at large by comparison with the Soviet Union. So the colour question, too, cuts across the Cold War struggle to the propaganda advantage of the Communist bloc, in as much as Communist China is non-white and because the Soviet Union has skilfully, and with some success, propagated the idea that she is politically and racially 'colour-blind'.[57]

Though anti-colonialist clamour today reaches a larger audience and probably commands more support than ever before, its arguments are not novel. For they were common currency in Western 'leftist' circles in the 'thirties; indeed, the arguments of many of today's neutralists merely repeat views current in the publications of European Left Book clubs, the kind of literature that Louis Fischer once aptly described as 'Laskiology'.[58] Whatever the significance of these echoes of earlier controversies, it seems undeniable that neutralist identification with anti-colonialism[59] is apt to have a confusing effect on their judgment of what could otherwise be regarded as fairly straightforward political or strategic issues—for neutralist opposition to Western pacts and bases in Asia and Africa is wholly explicable without the anti-colonialist arguments which are persistently dragged into it. Geography and politics have compelled the Western powers to rely on methods of defence which neutralists automatically dislike. The Communist powers have placed less reliance on formal alliances, for they have far more compul-

---

[56] Thus Mr Nehru, talking of those who attended the Bandung Conference: "The common factor was rather against Western domination. Everybody agreed about that . . . They were levellers in the political sense, as between Europe, America, and Asia or Africa. That was the dominant feeling and most of them were levellers, both patient and impatient, in the social sense." Tibor Mende, *Conversations with Mr Nehru* (London, 1956), p. 62.

[57] See Plamenatz, *op. cit.*, pp. 186-97.

[58] In chapter xvii, pp. 220-36, of *The Great Challenge* (London, 1947).

[59] There is much to be said for Richard Lowenthal's contention that "the real line of division that emerges from a study of the facts is not between true nationalists and neo-colonial stooges, or between progressives and traditionalists, or even between revolutionaries and reformists—it is simply one between states that are territorially satisfied and those with programmes of nationalist expansion". See *Encounter* (Mar. 1961), p. 64. N.B., too, Mr Nehru's distinction (see above, n. 56) between the patient and the impatient.

F

sive bonds. Again, the geographical situation of the United States has
made the alliances of which it is the core embarrassingly dependent on
a system of farflung bases, more vulnerable to nationalist pressure than
the compact, interior forces of the Communist powers, and perhaps more
dependent on the development of nuclear weapons to counterbalance the
huge standing armies which the Communist powers could quickly deploy
in 'conventional' warfare in Europe or Asia. And it is alliances, foreign
bases and nuclear explosions that particularly scandalize the neutralists.

V

Another plane of contrasts which the neutralist commonly asserts as
being more important than that between the aligned and the non-
aligned is that of the 'rich' and the 'poor', the 'have' and the 'have-
nots',[60] the developed and the under-developed,[61] nations. This assertion
tends to be strengthened rather than weakened by the claim that the
anti-colonial campaign deserves more attention than the Cold War
struggle, as both sets of inequalities are quite often attributed to the
same general source—'colonialism'.[62] Marxism may seem to have an
oblique relevance here, too. For even if Marx's prophecy of increasing
inequalities, in respect of internal class divisions within states, has not
been fulfilled, it has been unexpectedly realized in the field of national
divisions between states.[63] Furthermore, most neutralists undoubtedly
see great pertinence in the Leninist *cliché* that economic subordination
to a foreign power can be just as crippling to national independence as
can overt political control.[64]

[60] The phrase "have-not powers" seems to have been first used by A. T. Mahan
in *Some Neglected Aspects of War* (1907), pp. 69-70. And for a book which
examines many of the fallacies now, by analogy, commonplace in neutralist
argument, see Norman Angell, *This Have and Have-Not Business. Political
Fantasy and Economic Fact* (London, Hamish Hamilton, 1936).

[61] Thus Sékou Touré of Guinea: "For us the division of the world does not
consist of two blocks, East and West, but of two wholes clearly distinguished by
the obvious fact that one is developed and the other underdeveloped"—quoted
in the *Guardian*, 4 May 1960.

[62] And Nasser, addressing the Indian Parliament, said that the Arabs must be
ready to face "the monopoly of science, imperialism's new style"—quoted in
The Times, 1 Mar. 1960.

[63] See Emerson, *op. cit.*, p. 181, who describes how Lenin "sidled up" to the
theory of rich bourgeois nations versus poor proletarian nations. Reviewing
Emerson, Martin Wight writes: "It was by the ex-socialist journalist Mussolini
that the theory was at last espoused, to become standard Fascist doctrine echoed
at the Bandung Conference." See R.I.I.A., *International Affairs* (July 1961),
pp. 343-4. One thinks particularly of Sukarno and Nasser in this connection.

[64] E.g. Mr Nehru talking of economic control: "They will be called self-
governing countries, but will in reality be under the control of this small
minority from Europe or from America . . . Yes, this is what is called Latin
Americanization in South East Asia . . . but it is really worse in Africa because

There is no doubt that the notion of 'economic independence' is widely attractive among neutralists. This does not, however, give the notion precise content and it is easier to say what the notion does not mean than what exactly it does mean. It does not mean autarky, which is seen to be impossible and undesirable, nor does the notion portray some generally recognizable plateau of achievement in terms of *per capita* income or some other economic standard of measurement. In fact, the concept of 'economic independence' is mostly used as a powerful emotion-evoking slogan to claim a reduction of economic dependence on former colonial powers, and often to justify acts of appropriation, sequestration and nationalization of foreign property.

It seems almost as if an industrialization programme is regarded as one of the hallmarks of civilization. It certainly seems to be regarded as a visible sign of growing economic independence. The same attitude is partly responsible for the importance attached to prestige projects, often great hydro-electric power schemes like the Aswan or Volta Dam projects. And while the need for prime movers is an urgent matter in underdeveloped countries, it is at least open to question whether too large a proportion of national energy and the limited capital available is not being sunk in these schemes and whether it would not be wiser at this stage to concentrate on agrarian improvements. Rostow's[65] concept of a "take-off" — into a (perpetual?) period of self-sustaining economic growth—may be alluring for these far from affluent societies, but for all Asian and African neutralists the concept states an aspiration rather than suggests a precise programme of action.

Undeniably, it is difficult to avoid all the snares of alien economic control when every neutralist leader wants his country to have an industrialized, technically efficient, 'rich', national economy, to augment national power and national welfare. Whatever the real limitations to such national plans are—and, of course, these differ widely—it is universally believed that much can be done. The desired changes and required growth in the national economy are not conceived of as aims to be achieved in a remote future, but as immediate goals to be achieved as speedily as possible.[66] With the requirement of urgency comes the

---

of the racialism, the segregation and all that"—Tibor Mende, *Conversations with Mr Nehru* (London, 1956), p. 134.

[65] The reference is to the American economic historian, now a personal adviser to President Kennedy, Walt W. Rostow, who popularized the notion of "take-off" in his *Stages of Economic Growth. A Non-Communist Manifesto* (Cambridge, 1960), see esp. pp. 7-9. Rostow's analysis was subjected to some substantial criticisms by Cairncross in the *Economic History Review*, vol. viii, no. 3, 1961.

[66] E.g. President Nkrumah's statement to the National Assembly of Ghana on 14 July 1958, as reported in the *Daily Graphic* (Accra), 16 July 1958; and James Barrington, "The Concept of Neutralism", in the Special Burma Supplement of the *Atlantic Monthly* in 1958, pp. 28-30.

realization, however unwelcome, that outside capital and technicians are essential if rapid development is to begin, let alone to be sustained. But it is insisted that this aid must be obtained in such ways as not to compromise national independence. Hence the common neutralist insistence that the way in which aid is proffered is as important as the quality and quantity of the aid itself. A wide range[67] of opportunist and high-minded appeals are produced to buttress the plea for aid without 'strings', but, basically, four main sets of justifications are offered, and what all four have in common is the priority which political considerations take over economic. Briefly, these pleas for aid use the language of retribution, common humanity, mutual interest or blackmail.

The claim that aid ought to be given in order to expiate for past misdeeds was heard of mostly in the years before 1954—that is, before the Communist bloc had embarked on foreign aid programmes to neutralists, when the Western powers were the sole source that neutralists could appeal to, and when, in fact, the Western powers were not giving substantial aid to neutralists. It is certain that such pleas did not move Western governments much, though they may have caused unease to some individuals. Even if a government were to accept responsibility to pay retribution for 'colonialist sins', which is highly unlikely, the vexed question of who has to decide the manner and scale of retribution remains. However, from 1954 onwards, as foreign aid issues became a matter of Cold War rivalry, little has been heard of the retribution plea and it tends to be resurrected only occasionally as a rhetorical reminder by a speaker who disclaims its appropriateness himself.[68]

It might be expected that claims for aid on grounds of common humanity, in the absence of any political allegiances, would consist of appeals to the highmindedness of the potential donor, pointing to the obvious needs of the neutralist, and asking for aid to be given in a spirit of undemanding generosity. It would be wrong to say that appeals of this kind are never made, but it is more often the case that the neutralist suggests that rich states show their disinterested desire to help by channelling more aid through international institutions. It is felt

[67] The literature on foreign aid is already immense and growing fast. To my knowledge, there is no single study which concentrates on neutralism and foreign aid. Three useful recent works are: George Liska, *The New Statecraft. Foreign Aid in American Foreign Policy* (Chicago, 1960); Joseph Berliner, *Soviet Economic Aid* (New York, 1958); and F. Benham, *Economic Aid to Underdeveloped Countries* (London, 1961).

[68] E.g. see President Sukarno's address at the Opening Meeting of the Colombo Plan Countries in Jogjakarta (Central Java), 11 Nov. 1958 (published in *Indonesian Information*, Summer - Autumn, 1959). Cf. the speech by the Cuban delegate at the Belgrade Neutralist Conference 1961, see B.C.R., p. 121.

that the best interests of the recipient country are more likely to be served in this way, and even if international bodies do attach conditions to their aid, these seem far more innocuous than any strings which may be attached to the bi-lateral aid which is feared as a calculated method of drawing neutralists into Cold War conflicts. It, apparently, matters less that the greater part of international aid comes originally from American funds than that it is to be channelled through agencies thought to be less directly contaminated by Cold War considerations. Unhappily for neutralists, international aid of this sort represents but a small proportion of foreign aid, and there is very little prospect of this proportion being substantially increased.

The claim that the granting of foreign aid is in the interest of the donor as well as the recipient neutralist, even though the latter is unwilling to accept any 'strings', rests on some dubious assumptions about the relation of prosperity to 'peace', of peace being brought nearer by a progressive reduction of the gap in the standard of living of 'have' and 'have-not' countries.[69] It has yet to be proved that there is a *necessary* connection between peace and prosperity. The simple fact is that all neutralist countries today want material improvement. Some neutralists — the Indians most notably (until the Chinese attack in 1962)—try to give an earnest of their real priorities by insisting that the aid they receive shall be economic only and not military; but this is by no means a widespread urge, for many neutralists regard being aided in the procurement of 'essential' weapons for self-defence as important as other forms of aid. Be this as it may, it is doubtful if there is any simple connection between 'peace' and political viability, or economic advance and the incidence of foreign aid.[70] It is certain that the underdeveloped countries would benefit far more from the stabilization of the prices of primary products at levels satisfying to buyers and sellers alike than from any amount of aid likely to be forthcoming. The value of foreign aid to an underdeveloped country is not that it relieves the recipient of the need for saving and investing (indeed, if it does encourage this belief aid may do more harm than good) but that it provides foreign exchange. Soviet barter deals and American sales of surplus foodstuffs for local currencies are both devices to avoid adding to a country's foreign exchange difficulties; both devices are necessarily only stop-gap solutions and do not of themselves strengthen the economies of the underdeveloped country. The problem of fluctuating and unpredictable terms of trade means that the underdeveloped, primary producing, neutralist countries face not only immediate restrictions of

[69] See Emerson's discussion of this point in *Empire to Nation, op. cit.*, esp. chapter ix.
[70] Note the lack of economic advance in Laos and South Vietnam despite substantial U.S. aid since 1955.

foreign purchasing power when the terms of trade are unfavourable, but the very unpredictability of the terms of trade makes it impossible to know how to invest so as to be able to increase foreign earnings in the future. All donors of aid would like to impose some strings though they may not feel it politic to insist on this, and a potential donor is not easily persuaded that it is as much in his interest as in the neutralists' that he should make aid freely available, although no strings are to be attached.

Fourthly, there are quite often hints of blackmail in statements about neutralist need of foreign aid, and this is most evident where the neutralist is obviously aware and eager to take advantage of the possibilities for playing off one side in the Cold War against another. Such hints can take many forms. It can be implied that if one bloc were to withdraw, or substantially reduce, its aid, then the neutralist would thereby lose its freedom of action—that is, its neutralism—and would, therefore, probably end up in the opposite Cold War camp.[71] It can be said that if certain kinds of 'essential' aid, particularly military aid, are refused by one bloc, then the neutralist has no alternative but to seek satisfaction from the other side, with all the attendant risks that such unbalanced dependence implies. President Nasser's justification of his Czech arms deal in 1955 was that the Western Powers were refusing arms to Egypt whilst supplying them to Israel.[72] Also, it can be implied that unless one bloc gives as much aid as the other bloc, then there is a real danger that the neutralist will fall under the undue influence of the more generous. A clear expression of such thinking appeared in a speech of President Nkrumah when he claimed that as there were now 3,000 Ghanaian students studying in Soviet bloc countries, as well as 3,000 already studying in the Western world, this was "a practical demonstration of the Ghana philosophy of positive neutralism and non-alignment".[73] A more blatant admission was that of President Nasser: "Tito is a great man. He showed me how to get help from both sides—without joining either."[74]

The four types of claim outlined above are seldom stated in the stark way that they have been sketched here, but one or more is present, mostly in a muddled or disguised way, in every neutralist argument about foreign aid.

[71] E.g. Prince Sihanouk: "If the U.S.A. withdraws its aid as a reaction against Communist aid . . . our neutrality will have to be compromised . . . but what would the U.S.A. gain by seeing our country completely integrated with the Communist bloc?" See Norodom Sihanouk, *Analyse de la Conférence du Prince Norodom Sihanauk à Kampot, 6 avril, 1956* (Phnom Penh, 1956?), pp. 6, 15.

[72] See Keith Wheelock, *Nasser's New Egypt* (London, 1960), pp. 228-31.

[73] Nkrumah's speech was quoted in the *Daily Graphic* (Accra), 12 Dec. 1960.

[74] Nasser's words were quoted in the *New York Times*, 3 Mar. 1958.

Neutralists' insistence on aid without strings openly draws attention to their thin-skinned sensitivity about potential encroachments on their sovereignty. Yet such misgivings are not peculiar to neutralists. All states find difficulty today in demonstrating, preserving and increasing the traditional attributes of national sovereignty at a time when these have shrunk, and when it is certain that there are no longer satisfying solutions for pressing national problems within the confines of isolationism and national self-sufficiency.

*   *   *

It might be appropriate to end this chapter with an excerpt from one of the speeches of the late Prime Minister of Ceylon, Mr Bandaranaike, for it is a terse and frank statement of neutralist doctrine:

"We have to build up a new society for ourselves, as I have said, which best suits the genius of our country. We should like to get some ideas and some principles from this side, and some from the other, until a coherent form of society is made up that suits our own people in the context of the changing world of today. That is why we do not range ourselves on the side of this Power-bloc or that Power-bloc. That is the philosophy of neutralism. It is not something dishonest. It is not a matter of sitting on the fence to see whether we can get the best of both worlds. It is a position that is inexorably thrust upon us by the circumstances of the case. It is a position that will be of great help in the world situation today, for we do provide a bridge over the gulf between the two opposing factions."[75]

It is obvious from this statement by a leading neutralist and, perhaps, from this chapter's survey of some common neutralist assumptions and arguments, that neutralist doctrine is not very sophisticated and is frankly pragmatist and eclectic. There are a number of possible reasons for this. An oblique one may be the inherent difficulty of theorizing about international politics[76] in view of the changing multi-dimensional complexity of international politics. More direct reasons certainly stem, as was suggested earlier, from the rôles played by leading neutralists. For it is not a major aim of active political leaders to be profound and subtle political theorists, even though they may often make important pronouncements. Certainly, there is nothing very original in neutralist ideas. Most of them can be found earlier in the controversies of Europe or North America.

Considered by rigorous philosophical standards, neutralism appears

[75] Address to the U.N. General Assembly, 22 Nov. 1956, quoted in *The Foreign Policy of Ceylon* (Ceylon Government Press), p. 5.
[76] This theme has been discussed recently with great penetration by Martin Wight: "Why is there no International Theory?", *International Relations*, vol. ii, no. 1, Apr. 1960, pp. 35-48.

to do little more than invoke pious generalities, ill-substantiated assertions and loosely connected propositions. It may even be contended that
neutralism is in no way either a coherent or an international doctrine
and that the only useful exercise is to try to uncover the distinctive
characteristics of various versions of neutralist affirmation. Certainly,
this would be useful and would call for a great deal more exploration
than was attempted here, but it would be wrong to deny it any international character. For not only does neutralist doctrine express the felt
needs, the apparent interests and the dominant prejudices of its
proponents, but there seems to be a sufficiently common predicament,
sufficient similarity in certain pressing problems to be faced, to elicit
similar ways of thinking about the Cold War and the problems raised
by it, and these similarities often encourage neutralists to stress their
likenesses rather than their differences. It is 'international' also in the
sense that its central concerns are about international rather than
domestic problems.

Furthermore, to admit that the doctrine is superficial in its arguments
is not to deny its importance, appeal, or influence. Its importance stems
directly from the very fact that the leading proponents *are* nationalist
leaders articulating and transmitting national hopes and fears to the
world at large. Their main precepts have widespread appeal because
they express in slogans some of the dominant fears and hopes of large
masses of people throughout the world, and particularly in Asia and
Africa. Finally, it is not paradoxical to suggest that these new national
movements are, in a sense, international movements, too. For not only
can new national leaders meet together easily and often, should they
want to, but changes in the means of communication have also meant
that infections of fear, hatred and sympathy can pass rapidly across
continents to create new and larger areas of shared loyalties and
enmities. Though the connection between neutralist emotions and
neutralist policies will vary with each particular case, the ideas and
feelings that men have about events in which their lives are engaged
are a dimension of the events themselves. The things neutralists think
and feel most strongly about are ingredients in the very Cold War
struggle in which they are unwillingly embroiled.

CHAPTER IV

NEUTRALISM AS STATE POLICY — AN
OVERALL VIEW

"The situation of each country on the operational map makes its
neutrality improbable or probable in advance."
Raymond Aron, *The Century of Total War.*

"It is one thing to have one's own peculiar way of interpreting one's
commitments (and all states tend to do that): it is another thing
to deny, or to repudiate out of hand those commitments (and this
states will seldom or never be known to do).
C. A. W. Manning, *The Nature of International Society.*

THERE is a problem in defining the major differences between the
neutralist and the aligned states. At first glance the task may
seem easy—the neutralists are simply those states that are not
members of the major military alliances of either Cold War camp. On
1st January 1963 forty-five of the then one hundred and ten members
of the United Nations were members of one or more of the Cold War
multilateral military alliances (see table on pages below) and so were
aligned in virtue of being members of N.A.T.O., S.E.A.T.O., C.E.N.T.O.,
the Rio or Warsaw Pacts. Three more states—Formosa China, Japan,
and Spain—had close bilateral military relations with the United States,
and were thereby not neutralist. And membership of a military alliance
is not the only way to be aligned. Three U.N. members—Byelorussia,
Ukraine, and Mongolia — were Soviet satellites and thereby not
neutralist. Clearly, a formal distinction between the aligned and non-
aligned—resting on the existence of certain known treaties—may of
itself not reveal all, and may perhaps reveal little about the nature and
significance of neutralism as state policy. For the factual situation, and
contemporary reading of it at any particular time, is, of course, much
more complicated and controversial than the obvious forms of alignment and non-alignment would indicate. An ostensibly neutralist state
may, in fact, be more fettered than some aligned states; and many
neutralists, even when they do their best to achieve freedom from international entanglements, are so vulnerable to the play of international
politics, so needful of foreign aid, that they cannot help being caught in
the very entanglements they seek to avoid. The determination of a
superpower to treat a state merely as a client or satellite of its rival may
have the effect of restricting it, however unwillingly, to that rôle. The
agreement of a number of neutralist states to recognize, or not to recog-

nize, another state as a fellow neutralist can be vital in determining what kind of foreign policy can be pursued. Furthermore, the global pattern of alignment and non-alignment changes (as was shown in Chapter 2); a neutralist may become aligned (as Pakistan did in 1954), or an aligned state may revoke alliance commitments and adopt a neutralist policy instead (as Iraq did after 1958).

Ever since 1945 it has been widely recognized, both by students of neutralism and in diplomatic practice, that no member of a Cold War multilateral security pact can be a neutralist state. But the fact of having a bilateral pact or a military base agreement with one of the Cold War camps, which used to preclude neutralism, has ceased since 1957 to be a necessary disqualification—certainly in the eyes of the leading self-avowed neutralists, as the Belgrade Neutralist Summit showed. It may be in the future that it will be possible for a state to be regarded as a full, formal member of a Cold War multilateral security pact and yet neutralist. In terms of direct involvement in Cold War matters, the Rio Pact of 1947 has certainly played a lesser rôle than any of the other American multilateral security treaties. As it is, the present position of a number of Latin American states makes it clear that the Rio Pact cannot be regarded as a Cold War commitment at all comparable in its main features and functions with, say, N.A.T.O. or S.E.A.T.O. And increasingly since 1957 United States policies towards Latin American states seem to have been shaped very much as if these states were like Asian and African states in their need of economic as well as military aid; in their poverty; and in their anti-colonialism.[1] Undoubtedly, striking similarities do exist. Yet, apart from a brief mention of Cuba, Latin American states[2] are excluded from this study. This exclusion, on the grounds that they are all members of the Rio Pact, is a matter of convenience rather than of conviction, for there are many analogues for the present policies of Afro-Asian neutralists in the past and present policies of Latin American states. Yet, though there are bonds of sympathy, actual diplomatic contacts between Afro-Asian and Latin American states have so far been few and minor.

Clearly, the substance and significance of a neutralist foreign policy

[1] Four powers—Great Britain, the U.S., France and Holland, still control territories in Latin America or off its shores. Lenin regarded Latin America as exemplifying "economic imperialism": "countries which, officially, are politically independent, but which are, in fact, enmeshed in the net of financial and diplomatic dependence". V. I. Lenin, *Imperialism. The Highest Stage of Capitalism* (London 1948, Little Lenin Library), vol. xv, p. 104; see also p. 116.

[2] Neither Ecuador nor Nicaragua was a signatory of the Rio Pact in 1947 because of domestic upheavals—see R.I.I.A., *Survey for 1947-8*, pp. 469-71. Both joined the Pact at a later stage. Regarding U.S. security policies in Latin America in 1960, see M.S.P. *Fiscal Year 1961* (Dept. of State, Washington, Mar. 1960), pp. 103-10.

cannot simply be known from the mere fact of not being a member of certain military alliances. While all the evidence suggests that states neither enter nor leave alliances lightly, it must be remembered that alliances are one way, and not perhaps the most compelling way, of forging international friendships and alignments.

With all these preliminary cautions in mind, six types of neutralist policy may be usefully distinguished. A neutralist policy may be practised by:

(1) a neutralized state,
(2) a traditional neutral,
(3) a buffer or former buffer,
(4) an erstwhile isolationist,
(5) a pioneer neutralist,
(6) a new state neutralist.

This classification serves a two-fold purpose: it is a convenient way of drawing attention to certain major aspects of neutralism as state policy; and at the same time it helps to explain why the policies of certain states have been singled out for more detailed attention in the next chapter.

(1) Neutralization

Before 1955 neutralization[3]—the institution of a status of permanent neutrality—had seemed obsolete. It was a device recognized in nineteenth-century international law by which great powers brought about a change in the status of small states, in an endeavour to remove small but strategically important territories outside the active sphere of international rivalries. It was also a way of indicating that the great powers, by making this neutralization agreement, intended to respect the independence of the neutralized state. Both motives were probably at work when the Russians brought about Austria's* neutralization in 1955.

Legally, neutralization requires an international agreement between interested great powers and the state concerned, whereby the former guarantee individually and/or collectively the independence and integrity of the latter, which must agree to abstain from any hostile action or any international connections likely to involve it in hostility. There is no marked uniformity of practice here; the terms prescribing a neutralized status for Switzerland, Belgium and Luxembourg were each defined somewhat differently in the nineteenth century.[4]

Neutralization definitely involves some form of international tutelage, and this is probably why states are more ready to recommend it for

---

[3] See Oppenheim-Lauterpacht, op. cit., vol. ii, p. 244; and C. R. M. F. Cruttwell, A History of Peaceful Change in the Modern World (London, 1937), pp. 183-92.
[4] Ibid., pp. 112-16 and 183-92.
* See below, pp. 164-76.

others than to adopt it themselves. At the Geneva Conference on Laos in 1961 Prince Norodom Sihanouk was recommending "an Austrian style neutrality" for Laos,[5] though it was Cambodian representatives, at the Geneva Conference of 1954, who succeeded by pertinacious diplomacy[6] in avoiding the imposition of a neutralized status on Cambodia. Contrary to popular opinion, none of the successor states of former French Indo-China was formally neutralized by the 1954 Geneva agreements. This has been ably demonstrated by J. A. Modelski,[7] in an analysis of the ambiguously worded tangle of documents issuing from this conference; though his further point that these states are not precluded from full membership in S.E.A.T.O. has, to date, more significance legally than politically. For none of them has shown a strong desire to become a full member of S.E.A.T.O. Instead, Cambodia swiftly and Laos more slowly came to repudiate any notion of being under the 'protection' of S.E.A.T.O. Uncertainty about the exact orientation of Laos, between 1954 and 1961, was aptly illustrated in the following cryptic remark, made by the Laotian Prime Minister in September 1956: "Our country has no intention of joining any bloc, even the neutralist bloc . . . Neutrality is more neutral than neutralism." This primitive landlocked state[8] was eventually neutralized in July 1962,[9] one year after leaders of the three main factions had agreed in principle on neutralization for their country, though without agreeing who was to head the government. When, by July 1962, Prince Souvanna Phouma, the leading Laotian 'neutralist', (which in Laotian politics merely meant someone who was not strongly and openly either pro-American or pro-Communist), was generally accepted as the head of a coalition government to effect the neutralization of Laos, it was patent that this was a hastily improvised agreement merely papering over cracks. The international status and continued existence of a neutralized Laos is far more precariously poised even than that of Austria.

The successful maintenance of neutralization depends on the continuance of the balance of power which produced it, and/or upon the determination and ability of the neutralized state to resist encroachments on its status. To enumerate these conditions is to admit that neutralization is far from being a universal panacea. In Cold War con-

[5] See Guardian, 17 May 1961.

[6] See Fifield, op. cit., pp. 370-4; and Ellen J. Hammer, The Struggle for Indo-China Continues. Geneva to Bandung (Stanford, 1955), esp. p. 8.

[7] J. A. Modelski, "Indo-China and S.E.A.T.O." in Australian Outlook, Mar. 1959, pp. 27-54.

[8] See two articles by E. H. S. Simmonds, "A Cycle of Political Events in Laos" in The World Today, Feb. 1961, and "Power Politics in Laos" in The World Today, Dec. 1962.

[9] See Cmnd. 1828 (1962) for a brief résumé of the main events affecting Laos 1954-62, and for a useful collection of documents.

ditions it is perhaps best seen as an alternative to occupation and partition. It is only in this restricted sense that one should speak of the
'Austrian example'.

(2) Traditional Neutrality

Sweden and Switzerland are together a class apart. They are distinguished from all other non-aligned states in two ways. They are the
only states to have successfully practised from the nineteenth century
to today policies of complete abstention from military alliances,
neutrality in wartime, and non-alignment in the Cold War. Their
policies reflect standards of success and prosperity which may be envied
or admired but are widely recognized as distinctive. However attractive
Swiss or Swedish 'models' may seem to other countries, their own
nationals rightly regard their country's foreign policy as matured
national traditions which cannot be transplanted abroad, nor be easily
restored once lost.

Much of what non-alignment has meant in the past, as well as what
it means and rests on in the contemporary Cold War, is reflected in
the contrasting historical experiences of these two states. The study
below* is an analysis of problems arising within two different national
traditions of non-attachment, showing how these traditions fare in
changing situations.

(3) Buffer or Former Buffer Status

In international politics a buffer is a small state interposed between
two or more greater states. Buffer states can be roughly divided into
neutrals and protectorates. Neutral buffer states are states without an
active foreign policy at all; a buffer protectorate is a state whose foreign
policy is, in fact, controlled by another power.[10] A territorially satisfied
power usually prefers to surround its frontiers with neutral buffers or
allies. A territorially expansionist power usually prefers to surround its
frontiers with buffer protectorates or satellites.

Neutral buffer status is best preserved where a small, landlocked
state is kept in being by the reciprocal enmities of two or more roughly
equal powers around its frontiers. A multi-balance of power is more
beneficial to the buffer than is a bi-lateral balance, as the latter always
contains the threat of one of the two powers securing hegemony and
turning the neutral buffer into a protectorate or even a satellite.

---

[10] Russo-British imperial rivalries in Southern-Central Asia, during the latter
half of the nineteenth century, produced classic examples of the creation and
preservation of buffer states in the interests of great powers. See the excllent
article, "Buffer States. Their Historic Service to Peace" in Round Table, vol. xlv,
pp. 334-45.
* See pp. 151-64.

Alternatively, they might agree together to dismember the intermediary state—as has been Poland's fate at least three times in the past. Switzerland was more secure from invasion between 1815 and 1871 when she was the still centre of a multi-balance of power system, than she was in the eighteenth century when France was the preponderant neighbour. In the nineteenth century neutral protectorates, though subordinate internationally to the 'protecting' power, maintained and valued highly their internal freedom, and this was the main principle secured by the buffer concept in practice.[11]

Because of the geographical separation of the Soviet Union and the United States, and the American adoption of a 'containment' thesis, Cold War buffers have hitherto existed only along the frontiers of the Sino-Soviet bloc. There are other buffer states—Outer Mongolia is one obvious one—but it is only where the Soviet and American alliance systems meet, or nearly meet, that buffer status has so far been of significance in Cold War terms.

Afghanistan is the oldest of the Asian buffers. When the term was first adopted into international politics at the end of the nineteenth century,[12] buffers were created between British power in India and an expanding Tsarist Russia.[13] Until 1919 Afghanistan was under British tutelage, and for exactly one hundred and ten years British policy vacillated between treating her as a neutral or as a 'protected' buffer. After 1919, following regicide and war with Britain, Afghanistan began to develop her own foreign relations, concentrating on building up friendly terms with neighbouring states and, on the whole, leaning more heavily towards Russia than towards Britain.[14] Neutral throughout the Second World War,[15] as she had been throughout the First World War, she became a member of the United Nations in November 1946. Since 1946 she has endeavoured to carefully balance much needed trade and diplomatic friendships, not only with the superpowers, but also with those close neighbours with whom she has historic ties. This has been a difficult policy to practise and was especially so during the third phase of the Cold War. Soviet aid to non-aligned states began with a small programme of aid to Afghanistan in 1954. In 1955 Afghanistan rejected Turkey's invitation to join the Baghdad Pact and welcomed Soviet endorsement of her irredentist claims against Pakistan

[11] Ibid., pp. 344-5.

[12] Ibid., p. 334; Lenczowski, op. cit., pp. 207-9.

[13] In 1840 a Captain Arthur Connolly described Anglo-Russian rivalries, especially around Afghanistan, as "the Great Game". See Guardian, 28, 29 June, 4 July 1960.

[14] See Afghanistan (Reference Division, Central Office of Information, London, Apr. 1960). See esp. p. 11 regarding Russo-Afghan pacts of "neutrality and non-agression" of 1926 and 1931.

[15] See Lenczowski, op. cit., pp. 219-21.

—the so-called 'Pakhtunistan' issue.[16] Geography and recent quests to modernize what is still one of the most backward of all the United Nations' members impose salutary checks on Afghanistan. With no trade outlets, save through Pakistan or through Russia, and with the need to seek foreign aid, non-alignment is the only tenable international posture. By 1960 Soviet economic aid probably exceeded Western aid in the country.[17] No doubt, Afghan leaders intend their country to stay independent; association with other African and Asian states in such meetings as the Bandung and Belgrade conferences indicates the international identity Afghan leaders have preferred since 1955. The vital question is whether Afghanistan can avoid slipping into the Soviet orbit in view of the opportunities for infiltration afforded by the multifarious Soviet activities within her territory. After all, Afghanistan is geographically to the Soviet Union as Mexico is to the United States. And locational factors must always be numbered among a state's most important constraints.

Concern with the creation and preservation of buffer protectorates is not restricted to the 'committed' powers in the Cold War. India inherited and carried on, however unwillingly, Britain's buffer state system along her Himalayan frontiers. A dynamic situation only developed after 1950 with Chinese Communist occupation of Tibet. Subsequently, the Himalayan rivalry of India and China has been shaped by political and strategic, and perhaps ideological, considerations, most of them of long standing. It is in Nepal that we can see the afflictions that 'the age of the common man' is bringing to the rulers of a buffer state. Nepal[18] is a country approximately 500 miles long from east to west, and 100 miles wide from north to south, between Chinese Tibet and India's Gangetic plain. This land of mountains and jungle is the home of about nine million people, including the famous Gurkha soldiers. For more than a hundred years up to 1950 Nepal was governed by the sprawling hierarchical clan system of the Ranas which provided hereditary ruling Prime Ministers. This was a system of autocratic feudal rule, stable and unprogressive, and, apart from the activities of Gurkha mercenaries, Nepal was virtually a closed country. In 1951, with Indian help, this system was replaced by a form of constitutional monarchy. But subsequent governments have found it a difficult task

[16] See the letter by the Afghanistan ambassador in Washington in *C.S.M.*, 14 Dec. 1960. Also *The Times*, 15 Mar., 6, 7 Sept. 1961.
[17] See Peter G. Franck, *Afghanistan, between East and West. The Economics of Competitive Coexistence* (National Planning Association, Washington, D.C., May 1960).
[18] My account is mostly based on Werner Levi, "Nepal in World Politics" in *Pacific Affairs*, Summer 1957; and Saul Rose, *Socialism in Southern Asia* (London, 1959), chapter 5.

to try to institute orderly administration and material improvements within an independent Nepal. No ministry since 1951 has brought internal stability to the country (there is no lack of political 'parties', with many Nepalese politicians soliciting either Indian or Chinese support) and, in December 1960, King Mahendra dissolved Parliament, banned all political parties, put his ministers in gaol and said Nepal would now have "basic democracy". Only since King Mahendra's succession to the throne in March 1955 has Nepal, for the first time, begun to practice an active foreign policy—as an avowed non-aligned state. This has been made evident through Nepal's representation at the Bandung and Belgrade conferences, through her declaratory policies in the United Nations ever since she became a member in December 1955, and by seeking economic aid abroad.[19] Since 1947 India has sought (often without much regard for Nepalese susceptibilities) to inherit and continue Britain's traditional 'protective' rôle towards Nepal, an ambition which has become onerous with the development of open Sino-Indian rivalry. Several times since 1957 official Indian spokesmen have declared publicly that "any attack on Nepal will be treated as an attack on India herself". Nepalese spokesmen have retorted sharply that Nepal's defence treaty with India in no way provides for any automatic military assistance. Nepal has to ask for it first. So far, Communist China has practised a more subtle and sensitive diplomacy towards Nepal. This fact, and the temptation to lean towards the stronger party had, by the end of 1962, apparently improved Sino-Nepalese relations, while friction between India and Nepal was growing.[20] A still primitive country, experiencing considerable internal tumult, Nepal is now not isolated nor passive but is little more than a pawn in active Sino-Indian rivalry.

The positions of Bhutan and Sikkim are, to date, similar to that of their larger neighbour, Nepal. Bhutan, legally an independent state, is obliged by a treaty of August 1949 to accept Indian 'guidance' in

[19] "Now Katmandu is knee-deep in some of the most bizarre economic aid missions the cold war has yet produced. Americans—and the Indians, despite their own poverty—top the list of benefactors, but there are Russians building cigarette factories, Chinese putting up paper mills, United Nations teams surveying hydro-electric schemes to rival the Grand Coulee, and even a Swiss group energetically teaching non-cheese eating Nepalis to make Gruyere from yak's milk." See Stephen Barber, "Tangled Politics over Nepal" in Daily Telegraph, 9 Mar. 1962.
[20] See George N. Patterson, "Recent Chinese Policies in Tibet and towards the Himalayan Border States" in China Quarterly, Oct.-Dec. 1962, pp. 191-202, esp. pp. 195-7. See also the papers by W. Levi, Y. P. Pant and Gopal Singh Nepali in United Asia, vol. xii, No. 4 (1960)—which also includes the texts of three documents relating to the Sino-Nepalese boundary question and an economic aid agreement signed by China and Nepal, 21 Mar. 1960.

foreign affairs, including defence. Sikkim, a much smaller though more open and better known country, formerly a British protectorate, was declared an Indian protectorate in June 1949. Though both[21] are too small to apply for United Nations membership, as long as Sino-Indian tensions persist there is little chance of either sinking into the internationally inconsequential rôle of vestigial buffer states—Asian counterparts of Andorra, Monaco, San Marino and Liechtenstein.[22]

Since 1945 Finland has been a buffer protectorate of the Soviet Union in a double sense. It is widely believed that if Finland was absorbed as a Soviet satellite Sweden would join N.A.T.O.; and the Soviets also regard Finnish neutrality as a form of re-insurance for themselves against future German attack. A further vital condition of Finland's precarious independence is the defiant strength of Finnish nationalism, as the unwavering hostility of Finns to Soviet encroachments in two Finno-Soviet wars between 1939 and 1944 showed.[23] After Finland's second capitulation in 1944 Russia took one-twelfth of her territory, on which about one-tenth of her population lived (these all emigrated to what was left of Finland rather than accept Soviet rule) and imposed reparations which the Finns could meet only with dollar aid from the United States. The legal basis of Finland's circumscribed brand of 'neutrality'[24] is a single phrase in the preamble to the Defence Treaty signed with Russia in April 1948. This mentions Finland's wish "to remain outside the conflict of interests of the Great Powers".[25] Ironically enough, the Treaty immediately goes on to destroy that neutrality, at least in the event of war affecting Finland's territory. For under Article 1, Finland is bound to oppose Germany, or any ally of Germany, attacking either Finland, or Russia through Finland, "with the assistance in case of necessity of the Soviet Union". In 1955 the Soviet Union secured a twenty-year extension of this 1948 agreement, in return for handing

[21] See Werner Levi, "Bhutan and Sikkim: Two Buffer States" in *The World Today*, Dec. 1959, pp. 492-500; and Patterson, cited in the preceding note.

[22] For these four European Lilliputian states, see Martin Wight, *The World in March 1939*, p. 152, n. 1. Curiously, though, during 1962 San Marino, the world's smallest republic (area 38 sq. miles, population 15,000), began to establish diplomatic relations for the first time with Asian, African and South American countries. See *Daily Telegraph*, 4 Jan. 1962.

[23] See further Anatole G. Mazour, *Finland between East and West* (New York, 1956).

[24] The common Finnish word for neutrality is *puoluettomuus*, which translates literally as "impartiality".

[25] See *U.N. Treaty Series*, vol. xlviii, pp. 149-61. A Finnish statesman who helped to negotiate the original Moscow agreement later told a British reporter (see *Daily Telegraph*, 2 July 1959) that the then Soviet Foreign Minister, Vyshinsky, objected violently to even this watery legal recognition of Finnish neutrality. Though he eventually conceded this, it was not until after 1955 that Soviet spokesmen referred publicly to Finland's "neutrality".

back to Finland the Soviet-occupied Porkkala base. And though the bilateral defence pact still binds Finland to Russia in a hot war, since 1955 Soviet spokesmen have abandoned their reticence about Finno-Soviet relations and have widely advertised the Paasikivi line as a model of what relations between the Soviet Union and a 'neutral' state could and should be. The 'Paasikivi line'—so called after its late author, the Prime Minister (1944-6) and President (1946-56) of Finland—assumes that her independence depends on maintaining good relations with the U.S.S.R., by keeping outside the conflicts between the great powers and by avoiding suspicion in any quarter.[26] In fact, since 1955 Soviet policy has been characterized by alternate use of 'the carrot and the stick'—the carrot in such measures as permitting Finland's full membership of the Nordic Council and, after much hard bargaining, agreeing to her associate status with E.F.T.A. in March 1961.[27] The stick was much used in 1958 when by withdrawing the Soviet ambassador, by suspending purchases from Finland,[28] and by other pressures,[29] she secured a change of government[30] and its replacement by a cabinet more acceptable to Moscow. By the end of 1962 Britain and Russia, at least, seemed confident of Finland's ability to maintain her present position outside N.A.T.O. and the Warsaw Pact. Both agreed to supply Finland with guided missiles, although the 1948 Finnish peace treaty, of which they were the main signatories, forbade Finland to have such weapons. Clearly, Finland is neither a Soviet satellite nor wholly dependent on Western support but genuinely non-aligned, even though there is no doubt that all major foreign policy moves must secure at least tacit Soviet approval.

[26] See further Allan A. Kuusisto, "The Paasikivi Line in Finland's Foreign Policy" in *Western Political Quarterly*, Mar. 1959, part 1, pp. 37-49. For a Soviet view, see the review article of Paasikivi's published speeches by P. Krynov and E. Lavnov, "The Paasikivi Policy", *International Affairs* (Moscow), Sept. 1957, pp. 160-4. This policy has been carried on by Paasikivi's successor as President, Dr. Kekkonen, and is now sometimes called the "Paasikivi-Kekkonen line".

[27] See *Guardian*, 28 Mar. 1961.

[28] Only about 20% of Finland's foreign trade is with Russia. Her principal trading partner is Britain, and her biggest supplier of manufactured goods is W. Germany; but she is dependent for all her basic imports—coal, steel, fertilizers, cereals, cotton and crude oil—on Russia, and this dependence is buttressed by a most-favoured-nation clause in the Soviet-Finnish trade treaty.

[29] See Kent Forster, "The Finnish-Soviet Crisis of 1958-9", *International Journal*, Spring 1960, pp. 147-50.

[30] The conventions and inevitable manoeuvrings of Finland's multi-party system provide opportunities for intervention by Russia to further her interests. By July 1961 Finland had had forty-six cabinets in forty-three years of independence. For internal Finnish politics, see A. Kuusisto, "Parliamentary Crises and Presidential Governments in Finland" in *Parliamentary Affairs*, Summer 1958. Though the Communists are the second largest of the eight parties in Parliament, no Communist has been in the Cabinet since 1948

In general, it seems that buffer status is becoming less and less possible or popular in this atomic and Cold War age. There are two main reasons for this. Firstly, buffer status was a device more clearly appropriate to an age when fighting had to be by close contact. Today, small buffer states are less able to act as barriers separating combatants when hostile powers can wage war using high-speed aircraft, rockets and missiles, and the so-called buffer can now be easily overflown, or overshot, if not overrun. Secondly, while the term 'buffer state' suggests something inert and passive, compared with the powers adjoining it, passivity has now gone. Neutralist doctrine now seems to be the natural creed of the former buffer. Certainly, their neutralist leaders are nowadays numbered among the world's assiduous travellers and seekers of foreign aid and trade.

(4) Erstwhile Isolationism

Isolationism as a state policy rests essentially on two conditions: the determination of those in charge of their country's affairs to eschew an active involvement in international affairs, and geographical or military conditions favourable to ensure this. The history of isolationism has been one of the progressive undermining of both of these conditions in the face of an increasingly interwoven network of international contacts, and developing military technology.

Strictly, isolationism implies no foreign policy at all, but in general it has been regarded much more loosely and relatively. Both China and Japan successfully practised strict isolationism from the seventeenth to the nineteenth centuries.[31] The prime reasons for their failure to maintain this was the superior military strength of Western powers determined to have dealings with them. Neither American isolationism,[32] nor Britain's so called "splendid isolation" — or "policy of the free hand"[33] — was ever a policy of complete abstention from all international affairs. Indeed, both would have been more accurately designated by the term 'unilateralism'—though this is not an established usage in this context. And though the avoidance of permanent military commitments was a persistent and popular tradition in both countries,

[31] A minor qualification to this picture of complete isolation is necessary in each case. China permitted a restricted foreign trade through Canton; while, similarly, Japan permitted a limited trade through the single port of Nagasaki. See G. F. Hudson, *The Far East in World Affairs* (London, 1939), chapter 2, pp. 12-26.
[32] See above, pp. 23-4. See also Molotov's and Cordell Hull's mutual badinage, at the Moscow Conference in 1943, about the ending of their respective country's isolationism, in *The Memoirs of Cordell Hull* (London, 1948), vol. ii, pp. 1297 and 1310.
[33] See description in *British Security* (A Report by a Chatham House Study Group, London, 1946), chapter 3, pp. 37-46.

though obviously in different ways and for different reasons, both have abandoned this in the post-1945 world.

Apart from the freedom for independent manoeuvre cherished by the large isolationist power, many small states have in the past sought in isolationism security through self-effacement, or complete non-involvement in international matters. Switzerland long practised this policy successfully, though her military reputation and mountainous topography probably counted for more than diplomatic skill; today she is best regarded as a traditional or unique neutral.* The fate of Tibet since 1950 shows that mere willingness to remain inactive internationally is not sufficient to ensure isolationism.

Because isolationism implies aloofness or indifference to world affairs and a reluctance to engage in widespread diplomatic relations, it is an unpopular term today, thought to describe a policy incompatible with membership of the United Nations and to be an admission of national backwardness diplomatically. Five states in particular — Ethiopia, Liberia, Saudi Arabia, the Yemen and Ireland—illustrate different ways in which erstwhile isolationists can evolve into neutralist states.

Ethiopia and Liberia were two of the four independent states of Africa in 1945—the Union of South Africa and Egypt were the other two. Of all the five states briefly considered here, Liberia[34] so far. has done least to modify her former isolationism. Though she has been an independent republic since 1847, and was an original member of both the League of Nations and the United Nations, she is still notorious for her general backwardness. Described by one historian as "that poor and neglected African step-child of the United States",[35] Liberia was created as a land for freed American slaves. The United States has on occasions acted to restore order in Liberian affairs, and ever since 1923 the American Firestone Estates Company has played a large part in her economy. Liberia allowed the United States to construct airports on her territory during the Second World War, though all American forces left after the war. Liberia's economy is still based on the American dollar and she has a defence agreement with the United States, providing for "consultation in the event of aggression", and for economic aid and limited military assistance. The recent discovery of large deposits of rich iron ore near her borders with Guinea has already resulted in an iron ore exporting trade. The government, though providing none of the development capital, has a half share in Lamco, the operating consortium, in which the other shares are Swedish, West German and

[34] See R. L. Buell, *Liberia: A Century of Survival, 1847-1947* (Philadelphia, 1947), and E. J. Yancy, *The Republic of Liberia* (London, 1959).

[35] See F. P. Walters, A *History of the League of Nations* (London, 1952), p. 568. See esp. pp. 568-71.

* See below, pp. 151-64.

British, as well as American. Despite her historic connections with America and her reputation in U.N. circles as a pro-Western state, there are plenty of signs that Liberia will not escape the pressures and dilemmas of present day African politics. Indeed, it is only since the emergence of three new states—Guinea, Ivory Coast and Sierra Leone—around Liberia's land frontiers, as successors to British and French colonial power, that President Tubman (continuously in command of the state since 1943) has had to show an active interest in the world outside his country. He acted as host to a conference[36] of 'moderate' independent African states in June 1961, though it was reported that "prestige in African eyes might have remained greater had the realities of Liberia's domestic situation not been brought home to so many African leaders".[37] Clearly, Liberia is only just beginning to develop her foreign relations.

Ethiopia[38] has the longest record of independence of any African state in modern times; and, apart from Italian occupation from 1936 to 1941, has not otherwise been under foreign domination throughout her known history. For almost three thousand years prior to the Italian air, sea and land invasion in 1935, Ethiopia was too inaccessible, too mountainous and impregnable to large-scale attack. Indeed, the Ethiopian defeat of Italian forces at Adowa in 1895 was as important an event in African history as Japan's defeat of Russia in 1905 was in Asian annals, and Mussolini vowed revenge for this Italian 'national' humiliation, just as in 1945 Stalin claimed retribution for the defeat of 1905. Ethiopia is a benevolent despotism, ruled by Emperor Haile Selassie ever since 1930. It is Haile Selassie who has closely identified Ethiopia with other African and Asian neutralist states since 1955. The country has considerable economic potential, and yet has perhaps so far achieved proportionately the least actual development of potential, in the whole of Africa. But in attempts to speed up development, Haile Selasssie has been an assiduous world traveller on behalf of his country's interests; paying state visits to the United States and to most west European countries, including Yugoslavia in 1954, and visiting Moscow in June 1959 whence he returned home with promises of substantial Soviet aid. India, Sweden, and Israel each provide technicians and teachers to forward the Emperor's development plans. The Americans have a radio and monitoring station at Radio Marina, Asmara, in Eritrea,[39] and

[36] See "The Monrovia Conference" in *The British Survey*, June 1961 (Main Series, No. 147), pp. 20-2.
[37] See Hella Pick, "Liberia's Poor Showing Among Africans" in *Guardian*, 28 June 1961.
[38] See Edward Ullendorff, *The Ethiopians* (London, 1960); "Ethiopia", *The British Survey*, June 1961 (Main Series, No. 147), pp. 1-19; and Edward Ullendorff, "Haile Selassie's Empire Today", in *Listener*, 6 Dec. 1962, pp. 950-2.
[39] The former Italian colony of Eritrea became in 1952 "an autonomous state

provide various forms of technical aid, including equipment and training for Ethiopia's armed forces.[40] Not only did Ethiopia send a delegation to the Bandung Conference in 1955 and to the Belgrade Neutralist
Conference in September 1961, but her capital city, Addis Ababa, has
been the venue for several all-Africa conferences recently and has
become the permanent headquarters of the U.N. Economic Commission
for Africa, founded in 1960. With Sudan becoming independent in
1956, with the emergence of a new republic of Somalia in 1960 keen
to promote irredentist claims against Ethiopia, and with Kenya about
to become an independent state too, Ethiopia will soon have mainly new
nation-states and not European 'imperialist' powers as her neighbours.
There was an abortive revolt against Haile Selassie's rule while he was
away in Brazil (he is one of the few African leaders who have yet
visited Latin America) in December 1960. One authority[41] on Ethiopia
believes that the background to the revolt has probably to be sought on
the "heady wine" of the sudden strengthening of contacts with newly
independent African states. Even so, the Emperor seems to have concluded that he and his countrymen must try more of this wine rather
than attempt to do without it altogether. For in February 1962 Ethiopia
joined the Pan-African Freedom Movement for East and Central
Africa. By December 1962 Ethiopia had clearly moved from an
apparently pro-Western position, held at the time of her participation
in the Korean War, to a position of undoubted moderate neutralism in
the Cold War, while seeking to accommodate herself to new forces at
work in Africa.

Ethiopia's two near neighbours across the Red Sea, the Yemen,[42] and
Saudi Arabia,[43] are both states which are now to be numbered among
the neutralists. Both were isolationist states prior to the Second World
War, the Yemen even more so than Saudi Arabia. They were two of
the four independent states of the inter-war period who never applied
for membership of the League of Nations (the other two were the U.S.A.
and Nepal). Both are still feudal monarchies, still mostly absorbed in
Arab quarrels and parochial concerns, but are now less determined and
less able to insulate their countries from outside influences. Both have
sought to come to terms with Nasser's Egypt and to stay neutralist in
the Cold War, though they have attempted to do this in different ways.

Saudi Arabia has had close ties with the United States—unofficially,

federated with Ethiopia", and consequently Ethiopia acquired a seaboard. See
G. K. N. Trevaskis, *Eritrea. A Colony in Transition, 1941-52* (London, 1960).
    [40] See M.S.P. 1961, p. 80.
    [41] Edward Ullendorff in *Listener* (see n. 38 above), p. 952.
    [42] See Lenczowski, chapter 13, pp. 455-66; *The Middle East*, pp. 94-102; and
Campbell, *passim*.
    [43] See Lenczowski, chapter 12, pp. 431-54; *The Middle East*, pp. 75-94; and
Campbell, *passim*.

through the American oil companies' development of Saudi Arabian oilfields since the 1930s, and, officially, since the Second World War with the establishment of a large American air base at Dhahran. This air base agreement has been renewed roughly every five years since the war, but in March 1961[44] Saudi Arabia notified Washington that she would not renew the agreement when it expired on 1st April 1962— probably because of nationalist pressures within the Arab world. Saudi relations with Britain have been strained, particularly since 1952, over the disputed Buraimi Oasis, on the border between Muscat and Trucial Oman; while relations with the Communist powers have been virtually non-existent. Saudi relations with Egypt (a vital aspect of Saudi politics) have fluctuated considerably—reaching low points in March 1958 when King Saud was implicated in abortive attempts to stage a military coup in Syria, secure the murder of Nasser, and prise apart the new United Arab Republic; and in the last quarter of 1962 when, reputedly, Egypt was seeking the overthrow of the Saudi royal dynasty.

Yemen's foreign policy is dominated by the quest to realize irredentist claims against Aden, though otherwise, and even before she effected her purely nominal 'union' with the United Arab Republic in 1958, she had followed the Egyptian line in her foreign policy. In April 1956 she concluded a tripartite agreement with Egypt (who had already agreed to supply aircraft, guns and tanks) and with Saudi Arabia. The hitherto almost meaningless 1927 Treaty of Friendship with the U.S.S.R. expired in 1954, but in 1955 it was decided to renew it and to strengthen economic relations with the U.S.S.R. China began aid programmes to Yemen in 1958; at the same time encouraging her to harass British interests in Aden. By the last quarter of 1962 there was civil war in Yemen, ostensibly between republicans and monarchists, with Egyptian troops openly fighting with the republicans.

The ruling dynasties in Saudi Arabia and the Yemen are finding it increasingly difficult to square the circle of token support for radical Arab nationalism outside their frontiers while yet preserving mildly progressive, feudal monarchical systems at home.

It is strange to have to include Ireland among the erstwhile isola- tionists because for at least ten years after becoming an independent state in 1921 she proclaimed policies[45] which were in their anti- colonialism, championship of the rights of small nations, expressions of pride in her membership of the League of Nations, opposition to British bases on her soil, insistence on the need for economic development, and obsessive irredentist claims (against the six 'lost' counties of Ulster),

[44] See *The Times*, 18 Mar. 1961; and *Daily Telegraph*, 20 Mar. 1961.
[45] See W. K. Hancock, *Survey of British Commonwealth Affairs: Problems of Nationality, 1918-1936* (London, 1937), chapters 3 and 6; and N. Mansergh, *Problems of External Policy, 1931-1939* (London, 1952), chapter 8, and pp. 400-7.

very like the avowed policies of so many new state neutralists today. Then, during 1935 and 1936—that is, during the time of the Italian conquest of Ethiopia, and the Anglo-Irish treaty of 1936 whereby Britain evacuated her treaty ports in South West Ireland—she relapsed into isolationism. This was intensified by her neutrality throughout the Second World War,[46] and this isolationism, in effect, lasted until she gained admission to the United Nations in December 1955—the Soviet Union having vetoed her application for United Nations membership in 1945. Her refusal to join N.A.T.O. in April 1949 (principally for the avowed reason that the national territory was still divided) and her decision to leave the Commonwealth in the same year underlined her isolationism; and, apart from her participation in the relatively insignificant activities of the Council of Europe, Ireland was virtually without a foreign policy between 1949 and 1955. Her active involvement in a wide range of international issues since joining the United Nations[47] —she sent troops to serve in the United Nations observer corps in Lebanon in 1958 and a large contingent to the Congo in 1960, she has supported Indian moves to consider the admission of Communist China to the United Nations, and has proposed disengagement schemes for central Europe—is a dramatic example of how membership of the United Nations can lead to a radical alteration in the policies of an erstwhile isolationist. Ireland's application for full membership of the E.E.C., in August 1961, implied a willingness to abandon her non-alignment, demonstrated the closeness of her economic ties with Britain and showed that the issue of partition was now of greatly diminished significance in Irish domestic politics. This decision to apply to join the E.E.C. was preceded by and subsequently evoked surprisingly little public discussion, let alone opposition. Though Ireland's application was not made conditional upon British entry, there is little doubt that Britain's failure to join the E.E.C. will mean that Ireland will not join at this time either. But it seems that Irish foreign policy is now increasingly governed by economic considerations rather than by sensitive nationalist issues.

While it has been the aim here to indicate different ways in which some states have come to modify their former isolationism, it is not, of course, implied that all erstwhile isolationist states become neutralist. Spain, isolationist at least from 1937 to 1953, ended her isolationism by allying with the United States; and it is arguable that the policies of such small island states as Iceland and Haiti are still fundamentally isolationist, despite their Cold War alignments and United Nations

[46] See *The War and the Neutrals* (R.I.I.A., 1956), pp. 230-56.
[47] There is, as yet, no study of Ireland's post-1949 foreign policy comparable with those of Hancock and Mansergh for the period when Ireland was a member of the Commonwealth.

membership, and even if their isolationism is less pronounced than formerly. South Africa, despite leaving the Commonwealth in 1961, has retained her loose defence arrangement of 1955 with Great Britain,[48] which guarantees the maintenance of the Simonstown naval base by South Africa and its use by Britain and her allies in time of war whether South Africa herself were neutral or not. But she differs from all other states in that she has tended to become more and more isolationist: because of her government's determination to press on with *apartheid* policies and the growing hostility and opposition with which these policies are regarded by other states. At present her isolationism is aided by the fact that all her land frontiers are with colonial territories. So far, it seems, no one inside or outside South Africa thinks of her as a neutralist.

(5) Pioneer Neutralism

The reason for considering India, Yugoslavia and the United Arab Republic together and apart from other neutralist states is that they are the three leading neutralist states today, and each of them has initiated certain policies which are now widely regarded as being 'neutralist' in character. In asserting that these states have been pioneers it is not necessarily claimed that many other neutralist states have become neutralist by deliberately imitating them — indeed, this is unlikely. What is claimed is that these three states were, in their different ways, the first to practise in Cold War conditions certain policies which many neutralist states now practise, or seek to practise.

India spread, by advocacy and example, the idea that neutralism could be a respectable and responsible policy, and that a neutralist state could usefully act as a mediator in international disputes—and she did this at a time when all forms of neutralism were regarded with great suspicion by both Cold War camps. Indian leaders stressed that their preoccupations in managing a newly independent state were with preserving and consolidating national independence, with industrializing, or at least 'modernising', the state, and in staying out of avoidable international conflict.

Yugoslavia showed that a neutralist state could resist strong pressures from one superpower without having to become a formal member of the other Cold War camp. She also showed that it was possible to receive aid from both of the Cold War camps without becoming beholden to either.

Egypt (in the years before she joined with Syria in the United Arab

[48] See *Cmd.* 9520 of 1955. For the significance of this Anglo-S. African "Exchanges of Letters on Defence Matters" see W. C. B. Tunstall, *The Commonwealth and Regional Defence* (University of London Institute of Commonwealth Studies, Commonwealth Papers No. VI, 1959).

Republic) showed that it was possible to persuade a Western power to evacuate an important military base, and also led the way in pursuing an 'active' neutralist policy of simultaneous dalliance with both Cold War camps. In so doing, Egypt showed that an 'active' neutralist policy requires very quick reactions to the moves of the superpowers; positions held too long can become compromising if a wholesale dependence on one Cold War camp seems to be developing. She has shown that this policy, if it is to succeed, must exhibit qualities of flexibility, some would say inconsistency, similar to those with which — in rather different circumstances—'Perfidious Albion' was accused from the time of Cardinal Wolsey onwards.

These points are illustrated in their context in Chapter V.* There are other ways in which these three states are of significance in the history of neutralism, but these, too, are mentioned in the case study.

(6) New State Neutralism

On 1st January 1963 forty-one of the neutralist states were newly independent states.† That is to say that they had all acquired their independence since 1945, and none of them was a member of a Cold War multilateral alliance, though they were all members of the United Nations. Two of these forty-one are here regarded as special cases: India is described as a 'pioneer neutralist', and Laos is the only new state of the post-war world to be neutralized. So, strictly, this present class of new state neutralists had thirty-nine members on 1st January 1963. It is arguable that some of these thirty-nine new states are not really neutralist, but the doubtful cases will be referred to in the course of this chapter. It is also arguable that some states, formally independent before 1945, become 'new', as it were, by coup d'état or by revolution. For instance, Egypt after 1952, Iraq after 1958, or Cuba after 1959, could all be cited in support of this argument. But such claims raise many controversial issues about the degree of continuity and discontinuity in foreign policy after a coup or revolution, and distract attention from a central contention of this study: that international relations are still principally relations between ostensibly sovereign states and the fact of becoming an independent state after being a dependency is of major importance for the territory and people concerned. Under the heading of new state neutralists we are here concerned only with those former colonies or mandated territories which have since 1945 gained, or after a longish period regained, sovereign status internationally, and have become U.N. members.

Of course, newness and age are relative concepts and any attempt to

* See below, pp. 83-112.
† See table below, pp. 202-4.

discuss neutralist policies by reference to the quality of newness[49] is helpful only if its relative arbitrariness is recognized. Yet the very fact that so many of the present day neutralist states are new sovereignties internationally is too important a coincidence to be neglected. New states born into Cold War conditions have many problems similar to those of other neutralist states; but precisely because they are new states, they face all their problems at once and right from the moment of independence. For newly independent countries now have to make, often in a very short time, certain basic decisions which will determine for many years thereafter the patterns of their national life, as well as their relationships with the rest of the world. These decisions—about trade relations, monetary and banking systems, aid agreements, property rights, and a whole range of appropriate international affiliations— often have to be made rapidly and at a time when the country still lacks a clear notion of its assets and liabilities. Many of these decisions are not easily reversible, and whatever their paucity of resources, the leaders of all new states are inevitably involved in the task of making and maintaining the viability and reputation of their state.

Many of the factors already mentioned* which persuade other states to adopt a neutralist policy — most notably, the impracticability of isolation, the quest for material improvement, and the desire to keep free of Cold War ties — all converge to impel new states along a neutralist course. What the leaders of all new neutralist states want, above all, is to show their new states' independence internationally and to convince their nationals that this independence is genuine. Here, forms may be as important as realities.

Four points, all connected, must be mentioned again as they are especially important in understanding new state neutralism. First, is the concern with national unity. Second, is the importance of membership in the United Nations. Third, is the diminishing significance of foreign military bases as a necessary disqualification of neutralist status. And fourth, is the relevance of economic factors in shaping a neutralist course.

National self-determination,[50] with all its ambiguous power, has been the principle for justifying the existence of all the new states, irrespective of whether or not a broadly based national movement preceded the achievement of independent statehood, and regardless of whether or

---

[49] For discussions of the quality of newness, see Akzin, op. cit., and Emerson, From Empire to Nation, chapter 20, 397-419.

[50] It should be remembered that some version of national self-determination has been a battlecry of Liberal, Communist and Fascist movements. See Alfred Cobban, R.I.I.A., National Self-Determination (1945); Elie Kedourie, Nationalism, chapter 5; and Emerson, From Empire to Nation, pp. 295-359.

* See above, chapter iii.

not national unity is at all attainable. National unity is thus the over-riding and unavoidable concern of all nationalist leaders in new states. Yet it is not a measurable commodity, it is more often noticeable for its absence than assessable by its presence. In all the new states an awareness that national unity is either non-existent or precarious has been a powerful influence keeping the state out of Cold War alliances. Two factors seem especially relevant. Firstly, the neutralist state has one important advantage over the aligned state in that its interests and, hence, its efforts can be almost wholly local and limited, it does not have to strive to concert closely and continually with the policies of its alliance partners. The leaders of a new state can thus stress the independence of action enjoyed in virtue of not being a member of an alliance, and can insist that the *national* interest is their dominant concern, whereas membership in an alliance would involve at least some compromise in the interests of coalition diplomacy, and may even involve subordination to the stronger powers. Secondly, any obvious military alignment with a foreign power inevitably becomes a move in domestic politics too, and the government thus runs the risk of losing the leadership of the national movement if its opponents can plausibly represent it as 'selling' the new and cherished independence to a foreign power.

Soon after its inception the first government of independent Burma had to face a succession of rebellions and armed threats — from the Karens, Arakanese, Kuomintang Chinese, White and Red Flag Communists.[51] The survival of U Nu's government and of Burma within its present boundaries in these early post independent years was possible only because its opponents were separate groups of rebels, unwilling or unable to combine with each other, and the government continued to speak in the name of the majority of the nation and of the national independence movement. Alliance with a foreign power would have jeopardized its position by offering a vulnerable target for its opponents to attack. Even small but vital military aid from India in these years had to be given and accepted very discreetly.[52] Indonesia has faced similar difficulties. The fact that this new state is an archipelago of several thousand islands has certainly added to the task of welding an Indonesian national unity.[53] The difficulties of Burma and Indonesia in trying to secure national unity can be roughly paralleled in the experiences of most of the new states.

---

[51] See Hugh Tinker, *The Union of Burma* (2nd ed., London, 1959), chapter 2, "The Background of Civil War 1948-55", and John F. Cady, *A History of Modern Burma* (Cornell U.P., 1958), chapter 17, "Rebellion and Recovery".

[52] See Tinker, p. 355.

[53] See G. M. Kahin, *Nationalism and Revolution in Indonesia* (Cornell U.P.,

The overriding importance of nationalism, and of national leadership in particular, is clearly apparent throughout Africa where new states have arisen, and are still arising, on the basis of administrative units established by the colonial powers. Virtually all these new states are not unified nations but congeries of tribes and parts of tribes. It remains to be seen if these states will eventually create nations, though it seems certain that they need nationalism, in the sense of a community of feeling and will roughly coincidental with the state, if they are to weld together into working units the diverse elements of which they are composed. All these new African states are formally non-aligned in the Cold War, though their neutralism, like their nationalism, is still immature and unsettled. The neutralist policies of these states often closely reflect substantial differences between those 'moderate' nationalist leaders who seem content to work largely within their inherited boundaries, and those 'militants' — President Nkrumah of Ghana is a notable example — who claim to regard their new state as merely a springboard in the creation of larger political units. Although the attractive force of pan-African ideas, at least among some of the African leaders, has been shown in a number of symbolic (so far, none of them could be said to be at all substantive) unions,[54] the vital question remains—who is to head these new and larger unions? Although in Africa there is much talk of the artificiality of state boundaries, this always provides the basis for expansionist claims, never for the view that a state shall voluntarily contract its own territories. In fact, the leaders of new states, however much they may bewail the shape and size of their frontiers, soon come to acquire a vested interest in the territory which they have inherited. Lasting unions between hitherto sovereign states can only be made by conquest or consent—neither way is easily achieved. All the new states are weak, but not meek; they have not shown any greater capability than the older states to refrain from squabbles with their neighbours. And as yet, the 'African nation' seems even less ripe for a take-over than does the 'Arab nation'.

One of the most effective arguments neutralist leaders have been able to use against indigenous Communists is that they give their primary allegiance to a foreign power and are thus subversive of national unity. Irredentism, too, may be one way of trying to solidify the national movement behind the leadership; though in as much as a neutralist state seeks the support of other states in the furtherance of its irreden-

---

1952), and James Mossman, *Rebels in Paradise. Indonesia's Civil War* (London, 1961).

[54] The Union of Ghana and Guinea proclaimed in May 1959 does not seem to have progressed much further than this proclamation; the union of Senegal and Soudan (now known as Mali) lasted only two months—June-July 1960—after independence.

tist claims, most of them have had to rely on fellow neutralists or on Communist powers, as the satisfaction of such claims must nearly always be at the expense of a Western or Western-aligned power. Even so, it is to be remembered that irredentist claims are made in the name of 'the nation' and a distinction between new state neutralists in terms of 'moderate' and 'militant' nationalism is likely to be more profitable than one in terms of whether they are pro-Western or pro-Communist. The 'militants' would want to deny most 'moderates' the right to be considered truly non-aligned, on the ground that they are still too closely connected with their former colonial power.

The initial direction of a new state neutralist's course will be strongly influenced by the way in which the new state breaks with the metropolitan power. Where the parting is amicable, as with Ceylon and all the former French West African territories, except Guinea, the new state's neutralism is likely to show, initially at least, a markedly pro-Western bent. When the severing of colonial ties is less smooth, as in the cases of Indonesia and Guinea,[55] the new state's neutralist course is immediately and almost inevitably anti-Western and militant in support of national claims.

Where leadership is conspicuously strong the absence of national unity or social cohesion appears to be less important. One of the striking differences between Cambodia and Laos since 1954 has been the presence of a single undoubted leader, Norodom Sihanouk, in Cambodia and the lack of any similar dominating personality in Laos. Similarly, Nigeria has no one man who has attained a pre-eminence comparable with that of Dr Nkrumah in Ghana. Strong and undoubted leadership gives a purpose and a direction to a country's foreign policy. Leaders like Nehru, Sihanouk and Sukarno not only seem to personify their nations, but because of their pre-eminence they become the embodiment of their country's neutralism to the outside world.

Membership in the United Nations is valued by all new state neutralists as perhaps the most important symbol of recognition and enfranchizement in international society. Membership enables the neutralist to avoid the discomforts of isolation and encourages the making of a wide range of international contacts, many of which would otherwise be difficult for an uncommitted state. Nevertheless, the obligations of United Nations membership can encourage a confusing mingling of precept and practice, of neutralist doctrine and policy. Many of the ambiguities in neutralist doctrine, discussed in Chapter III above, are reflected in neutralist policies, and much of what was said in that chapter about independence, foreign aid, etc. has a direct relevance here. For confusion and ambiguity are perhaps unavoidable, because as

[55] See Harold Silver, "Guinea Red and Black" in *Listener*, 20 July 1961, pp. 81-3.

a U.N. member a new state has to vote and adopt at least declaratory policies on a wide range of international questions, many of them remote from immediate national concerns, and at a time when its substantive policies are often inchoate and groping.

The pattern of a neutralist state's voting behaviour is one rought indication of its international orientation. By this test one survey,[56] published in 1960, suggested that, at that time, three Afro-Asian neutralists—Laos, Liberia, and Malaya—consistently adopted an anti-Communist line; eleven of them—Afghanistan, Burma, Ceylon, Ghana, Guinea, India, Indonesia, Iraq, Sudan, United Arab Republic, and Yemen—constituted a 'hard-core' neutralist vote; while nine—Ethiopia, Cambodia, Jordan, Lebanon, Libya, Morocco, Nepal, Saudi Arabia, Tunisia—were left as 'floating' votes.[57]

For some new states it has been a virtual condition of achieving independence that they should grant or permit the continuance of military bases or some facilities to the departing metropolitan power and/or its allies. Before 1957 the possession of such bases by an independent state was generally regarded as disqualifying it for neutralist status—no one seemed to regard Morocco, Tunis and Libya as neutralist states then, nor was Ceylon generally regarded as neutralist until the evacuation of the British bases at Trincomalee and Katunayake shortly after Mr Bandaranaike's electoral victory in 1956.[58] Since 1957, with the increasing numbers and growing self-confidence of neutralist states, there seems to be a growing opinion amongst them that the presence of foreign military bases within the boundaries of an otherwise independent state does not necessarily preclude neutralist status. Even so, it seems that a state becomes 'more neutralist', as it were, if it is able to fix a terminal date for the final evacuation of such bases as it has on its soil, or if it imposes more stringent conditions upon the power enjoying such facilities.

After negotiations begun in 1957, Morocco had by September 1960 persuaded France to evacuate her bases from Morocco by the end of 1963. Further negotiations led to a supplementary agreement that all these bases would be evacuated by October 1961, two years ahead of the previously agreed schedule.[59] Intermittent negotiations have also

---

[56] See G. Goodwin, "The Expanding United Nations—1", in *International Affairs* (R.I.I.A., Apr. 1960), pp. 174-87. He warns us that "voting figures merely record arithmetical totals. They cannot indicate the intensity of feeling of the majority—or minority; or the extent to which national interests are directly involved; or the degree of actual power rather than voting power which the majority commands relative to that of the minority" (p. 185). More studies would be useful.

[57] *Ibid.*, p. 181.

[58] See Tunstall, *The Commonwealth and Regional Defence*, pp. 54-5.

[59] See *The Times*, 6 Mar. 1961.

been held for the evacuation of the three main United States bases.[60] Tunisia has been negotiating with France since 1958 to secure the withdrawal of French forces from Bizerta, though, until July 1961, in such a moderate manner than in the eyes of many 'militant' neutralists she is probably regarded as being far too pro-Western* in orientation. Senegal and the Malagasy Republic harbour French military bases and would probably be included in a similar indictment. Malaya's position is rather complicated. She has consistently sought to regulate British military rights on her soil; and both Malayan and Singaporean leaders have said that in the event of a union between Malaya and Singapore, as part of the projected Malaysia scheme, Britain's now largest overseas base of Singapore would not be available for the use of S.E.A.T.O., though it would be available for British, Malayan and Commonwealth purposes. Obviously this is a rather nice distinction, open to different interpretations. Malaya has no military ties with the United States, and had experienced eight years of Communist insurrection from the Malay-Chinese before achieving independence in 1957. She maintains close bilateral links with several of the S.E.A.T.O. powers (and especially Britain) and these were probably sufficient to dissuade or debar her from attendance at the Belgrade Neutralist Summit, despite India's proposal that she should attend. The Malayan government does not describe its policy as neutralist. By adroit, stubborn and prolonged negotiation when the terms of independence for Cyprus were being worked out, Archbishop Makarios whittled down the area for Britain's 'sovereign' bases in independent Cyprus, closely defined the conditions by which they were to be occupied and used, and insisted that the agreements should be subject to review after five years.[61] Even Libya, with the largest of America's overseas bases on her soil, was, by the end of 1962, attempting to increase 'the rental' paid by the Americans and was in other ways identifying herself with the neutralist states of Africa.[62]

All the new neutralist states consider themselves to have underdeveloped economies. The only way they could insulate themselves from outside economic pressures would be to give up cherished industrial aspirations and remain agrarian economies. As they are all unwilling to do this, they have to seek trade with and aid from other states, and

[60] See ibid., also M.S.P. 1961, p. 78.
[61] See Cmnd. 1093 (1960); Economist, 28 Feb. 1959, pp. 753-4 and 767; also Guardian, 16 Jan. 1960.
[62] See Roger Owen, Libya. A Brief Political and Economic Survey (R.I.I.A. Memoranda, May 1961); M.S.P. 1961, pp. 77-8—"The very discouraging long range outlook for Libya's economy changed dramatically in 1959 on the discovery of large oil deposits . . . the government should then (i.e. by 1965 or 1966) become independent of foreign assistance to finance normal governmental operations and its development programme."
* See below, p. 183.

this makes them susceptible to economic pressures. In general, all neutralists regard a wide pattern of economic relations, preferably with both of the Cold War blocs, as being the best way to avoid the snares of economic control, though obviously their opportunities to achieve such aims vary considerably. As the number of potential donors and markets has increased and has come to involve both Cold War camps, the possibilities for neutralist states to gain economic advantages from playing off rival powers have increased considerably,[63] as, in general, neither Cold War camp appears anxious to see a neutralist state become an economic, and then perhaps a political dependency of its rival. An article in *The Economist* on 20th January 1962 forcibly underlined the point that European powers can continue to project economic divisions into an area (in this case, West Africa) after their direct political influence has been removed. The article was appropriately headed "All in new African Countries—excepting Guinea—rely heavily on the West for money, manpower and markets. But none of them like it." The same article also pointed out that "Guinea apart, no West African country conducts less than 80% of its foreign trade with the West and the share of the old metropolitan power is usually above 50%. Indeed, in some of France's ex-colonies it is still 90%."

In fact, some of the new and ostensibly neutralist states are almost wholly dependent on Western aid—Jordan[64] and Israel[65] are notable examples—for their economic viability. As yet, no neutralist state has lost its political independence as a result of Soviet economic pressure. Probably the nearest example was Syria[66] in the two or three years

---

[63] Cambodia has hitherto been a very successful practitioner of this art. See Fifield, *op. cit.*, pp. 366-93. See also *Economist*, 11 May 1957, p. 508; *Observer*, 16 June 1957 and 3 July 1960; *The Times*, 20 June and 31 Dec. 1960.

[64] This dependence on Western aid was certainly true of Jordan from 1948-57, see *The Middle East*, chapter 7, esp. pp. 345-9; see also M.S.P. 1961, p. 84—"Jordan is not a viable economic unit, yet preservation of its stability remains vital to preservation of peace in the area. Therefore the United States, and to a lesser degree the United Kingdom, contribute substantial direct support for Jordan's national budget."

[65] See *The Middle East*, pp. 312-14; see also special *Economist* survey on Israel,, 16 May 1959, pp. 1-24—"Israel gets financial help from the U.S.; credits, jets and sympathy from France; reparations on the generous side from West Germany; warships from Britain. All this is welcome—and necessary—but does not alter the fact of Israel's basic isolation", p. 7. The survey does, however, suggest that Israel is reducing this isolation by developing friendships with such neutralist states as Yugoslavia, Burma and Ghana. Even so, Israel's policy is generally regarded as pro-Western despite the lack of formal ties. Neutralism is thought of as a possible 'new line', not as descriptive of present policies; see W. Z. Laqueur, "Israel's Great Foreign Policy Debate" in *Commentary*, Aug. 1955, p. 110.

[66] See Walter Z. Laqueur, *The Soviet Union and the Middle East* (London, 1959), esp. pp. 247-80; George Kirk, "The Syrian Crisis of 1957; Fact and Fiction" in *International Affairs* (R.I.I.A.), Jan. 1960, pp. 58-61, and M. S. Agwani, "The

H

before it joined with Egypt in the United Arab Republic in early 1958; but even here other factors — especially the pan-Arabism of Syria's Baathist leaders—need to be adduced also in order to explain fully why she joined with Egypt in Fabruary 1958.

We have been concerned with the question why virtually all new states are neutralist, not with the next, and more perplexing, problem of what kinds of neutralism do the new states practise. An easy way out would be to say that each new state is unique, but this pleonasm cannot be the last word on this subject. There are a whole host of currently popular generalizations about new states, most of them worth —and needing—investigation. But they lie to the side of this short study. It is not possible here to try to see to what extent new states are incipient anarchies or embryonic totalitarianisms, whether they are doomed to military rule (as Professor Finer's book *The Man on Horseback* strongly suggests), whether their way is to peace, progress and prosperity or to war, stagnation and poverty. These would be searches for generalizations that must seek to straddle states as small as Rwanda and Burundi and as large as India and Nigeria, as wealthy as Malaya and as poor as Somalia, with local Communist parties as strong and as important as in Indonesia or as insignificant as at present in Sierra Leone; the contrasts are interminable, the uniformities not so obvious. One line of investigation is especially inviting for the student of neutralism, and this is the extent to which public opinion prescribes or encourages a neutralist course. Writing for the American quarterly *Foreign Affairs* in July 1957, President Bourguiba (then an opponent of neutralism and later no more than a sceptical recruit to neutralist ranks) drew attention to the relevance, and in his view the dangers, of popular sentiment in these matters:

"As the people of Tunisia are idealistic and peace-loving they are instinctively attracted to neutralism. They do not wish to be drawn into armed conflict nor to find their country once more a battle-ground over issues that chiefly concern the Great Powers . . . "

Many neutralist leaders might admit to feeling similar pressures, but not many would openly go on, as Bourguiba went on, to say: "Neutralism in the cold war and neutrality in a 'hot' one are equally precarious."

Yet not quite all the new states are neutralist.

Two exceptions

There are two marked exceptions to the general tendency that new states become neutralist. These are the Philippines and Pakistan.

The close alignment of the Philippines with the United States stems

---

Ba'th: A Study in Contemporary Arab Politics" in *International Studies* (New Delhi), July 1961, pp. 6-24.

not only from the agreements made on the eve of independence[67] in 1946, but also from her unique status and experience as America's only Asian 'colony' before 1945. Certainly, Filipino-American relations seem to reflect a mutuality of interests which have continued with surprisingly few strains since 1946.[68] This is not to say that the Philippines could not become a neutralist state, it is to say that neutralism has not, so far, become a dominating force in Filipino politics.

Pakistan[69] is a much less strong exception to the tendency for new states to be neutralist than is the Philippines. She was without formal commitments to either Cold War camp prior to 1954.[70] Then at least five factors helped to bring about an abandonment of non-alignment. These were: the patent failure of attempts to put Pakistan at the head of an association of Islamic states, or even to establish cordial relations with most Arab states; worsening relations both with Afghanistan and with India; a real sense of vulnerability especially strong in a state divided into two parts and separated by more than a thousand miles of territory occupied by an unfriendly neighbour; famine in 1953 in what had hitherto been a country producing a surplus of grain; and American enthusiasm—at that time—for making aid agreements mostly with formal military allies. Together these were powerful enough influences to pull Pakistan into Western alliances. Pakistan has always been a vociferous champion of anti-colonial causes, and since Ayub Khan's accession to power in 1958 Pakistani spokesmen have increasingly questioned the value to their country of membership of S.E.A.T.O. and C.E.N.T.O. In large measure Pakistani complaints have centred on the fact that India is not only getting increasing amounts of aid from the Soviet Union but also from the United States, and several other Western aligned states. Soviet reactions after the American U-2 plane had been shot down over Soviet territory after taking off from Pakistani soil in April 1960, heightened controversy within Pakistan about the advantages and disadvantages of alignment. Some of the most notable side effects of the Sino-Indian clashes in the autumn of 1962 were the steadfast refusal of Pakistan to aid India, the openly voiced suspicion that arms supplied by the Western powers to India were just as likely to be

---

[67] See Fifield, pp. 60-6.

[68] Ibid., pp. 60-107; Hahn, Peters and Rosenthal, "The United States and the Philippines" in *American-Asian Tensions*, ed. Strausz-Hupe, Cottrell and Dougherty (New York, 1956), pp. 123-46; and H. B. Jacobini, "Main Patterns of Philippine Foreign Policy" in *Review of Politics*, Oct. 1961, pp. 507-30.

[69] See Keith Callard, *Pakistan. A Political Study* (London, 1957), esp. chapter 10, "Pakistan and the World".

[70] See *ibid.*; James W. Spain, "Military Assistance for Pakistan" in A.P.S.R., Sept. 1953, pp. 738-51; and B. C. Rastogi, "Alignment and Non-alignment in Pakistan's Foreign Policy, 1947-60" in *International Studies* (New Delhi), Oct. 1961, pp. 159-80.

used against Pakistan as against China, and Pakistan's own efforts to reach a frontier agreement with China concerning Kashmir. Pakistan's policies in the years 1960-2 aptly illustrate the general trend for differences between aligned and non-aligned states to become blurred. For some weeks before the Belgrade Neutralist Summit there were a number of rumours bruited in the Anglo-American press that Pakistan would be attending this gathering. In fact, she did not, though she was represented at the Cairo Economic Conference of "Neutralists", so-called in the British press, in June 1962. Perhaps Pakistan will be the first state to become widely described as neutralist, while still officially a member of Western multilateral military alliances.

Three awkward cases

Finally, there are three awkward cases—Iraq, Cuba, and Albania. None of these is a new state and each was definitely aligned in the Cold War before 1958; but their respective positions have been radically altered subsequently.

Cuba and Iraq are so far the only two states to become neutralist by defecting from multilateral Western alliances—Cuba from the Rio Pact, and Iraq from the former Baghdad Pact. Both of them did so by means of revolutions which overthrew staunchly pro-Western regimes, and installed a dominant revolutionary leader in power—Castro in Cuba, and Kassem in Iraq—in the name of social reform and national independence. Both states became, in a sense, 'pioneers' just by defecting from Western alliances. Both states sent full delegations to the Belgrade Neutralist Summit in September 1961, where they were welcomed as symbols of neutralist desires for the sundering of Cold War alliances. But it is doubtful if their subsequent fortunes have, as yet, provided inspiring examples for other neutralist, or would-be neutralist, states.

Iraq, though avowedly a 'positive neutralist' under Kassem's rule, was notable more for internal convulsions than for anything else. Between 1958 and his death in February 1963 General Kassem merely managed shakily to maintain himself as head of state within the boundaries inherited in 1958, despite attempts to absorb Kuwait and bloody attempts to subdue the Kurds. In March 1959 it was announced that Iraq had withdrawn from the Baghdad Pact, thus formalizing a situation which had existed in effect since the overthrow of the monarchy in July 1958. In June 1959 Iraq renounced American military aid on the ground that it conflicted with the policy of 'positive neutrality', and the American government was informed that the military assistance agreement of 1954, the supplement to a military agreement signed a year later, and a minor economic assistance agreement of 1957, were all terminated. After Kassem had been shot, following a successful *coup d'état* in February 1963, his successors announced that they would practise a policy of 'positive neutrality' and said that Kassem had betrayed the revolutionary ideals of 1958 and had co-operated too closely with Communists. But, as in the immediate aftermath of the Egyptian revolution of 1952, a month after Kassem's overthrow it was, to outsiders, still far from clear who were the real rulers of the country, let alone what the substantive policies of the new government would be. The events of 1958 to February 1963 seemed to underline the present ascendancy of 'positive neutrality' in Iraq, if not its precise content. In Iraq, as in other states, neutralism is now what the leaders of the state can make it be.

Cuba's[71] erratic course since Fidel Castro's accession to power in January 1959 suggests that for Cuba both neutralism and Communism are mostly what Castro says they are, and that the hitherto volatile associations with neutralist and Communist states are overwhelmingly conditioned by the quirks of Castro's circumstances and character. Castro seized power more because of the collapse of Batista's government than through the strength of his following. He was without a party or a programme, though opposition to Batista and all forms of 'Yanqui imperialism' were enough to secure him a popular following, immediately after his accession to power. Relations with the United States soon deteriorated even though President Eisenhower did not break off diplomatic relations with the Castro regime until January 1961. On 5th September 1960 Castro announced to a cheering, shouting throng of more than 300,000 in the civic plaza in Havana that Cuba had recognized Communist China and denounced the bilateral military aid treaty with the United States signed in 1952. Castro also expressed acceptance and appreciation of the Soviet offer of atomic missiles to defend Cuba. Within Cuba Castro soon gave prominence to the hitherto insignificant Cuban Communists, and abroad he turned to the militantly anti-Western neutralist states and to the Communist powers to obtain the support and connections he wanted. In April 1961 there was an abortive attempt by Cuban exiles, with the connivance but without the active support of the American government, to invade Cuba from the United States. From the time of this incident Cuba began to consort closely with neutralist states, especially those of the Casablanca grouping. And it was at the time of this abortive invasion in the Bay of Pigs that Castro first used the word "Socialist" to describe the Cuban revolution. But apparently the idea that neutralist states could be Cuba's closest friends was shortlived: after the Belgrade Conference of September 1961 Cuba seemed to show less interest in the

[71] This paragraph is based on Theodore Draper, *Castro's Revolution, Myths and Realities* (London, 1962) on an article in *Round Table*, no. ccix, Dec. 1962, pp. 7-18, on British press reports, and on *Cuba and the Rule of Law* (Geneva, 1962).

neutralist states and far more in the Communist powers, particularly the Soviet Union. This was perhaps because of disappointment with the generally tepid response Cuba got to her obvious desire for substantive support from the neutralists at Belgrade; but, more likely, it was because only the Soviet Union could, and seemed willing to, provide adequate countervailing force to the United States and provide Castro with some insurance against the possibility of a large-scale American invasion of Cuba. During the last four years Castro's own comments about whether or not he is a Communist have been enigmatic to say the least. In a celebrated speech on 1st December 1961 Castro did not, as many people believe, admit to having always been a Communist, but expressed regret at not having always been a Marxist-Leninist. But this did not mean that Cuba was now ruled wholly by the Cuban Communist Party or by Russians. What it did mean was that Cuba was the declared ally of the Soviet Union and her associates. In the months leading up to October 1962 the Soviets built missile bases on Cuban soil and though these were dismantled following the Soviet-American confrontation on this issue,* Mr Khrushchov did secure from President Kennedy a promise that the United States would not initiate an invasion of Cuba nor permit an invasion by Cuban exiles to be launched from American soil. By December 1962, however disillusioned Castro may have been by the recent coming and going of Russian missiles, and however unwilling he might be to become merely a docile follower of Soviet policies (the distance between Havana and Moscow giving him some useful leverage), his government was still heavily dependent on Russian military and economic aid (and was getting far more ideological than material assistance from China) and therefore he had reason to stay on good terms with the Soviet Union. Cuba had become, for the time being at least, a novel associate member of the Communist camp.

Albania, by December 1962, had become the second European Communist state to sever ties with Moscow. It was ironic that Yugoslavia was the first. For Albania's newly anomalous international position resulted from the interaction of active resurgence of deep-rooted Albanian-Yugoslav rivalry, Soviet-Yugoslav rapprochements, Mr Khrushchov's so-called 'de-Stalinization' programmes, and China's interest in having an ally in Europe. When in December 1961 the Soviet Union broke off diplomatic relations with Albania it was the first time that this had happened in the Communist bloc. Even in 1948 when Stalin's quarrel with Tito was at its height, and Yugoslavia was expelled from the Cominform, the two countries maintained diplomatic relations. Following the rupture of Soviet-Albanian relations, Russian submarines were withdrawn from their Albanian base and Albanian

---

* See above, pp. 57-8.

delegates were no longer invited to attend meetings of the Warsaw Pact countries or of Comecon. Albania seemed threatened with total isolation but for Chinese support. Yet, so far, she has only been suspended and not expelled from the Warsaw Pact so, strictly, she cannot be described as a non-aligned state. Effectively she has merely changed from being a Soviet to a Chinese dependency. By the end of 1962, with no sign that Russia and China would soon resolve their differences, Albania seemed very heavily dependent on Chinese support. In January 1963 it was announced that Cuba and Albania had signed a cultural agreement. Insignificant in itself, such a move was unimaginable five years earlier. The vicissitudes of great power rivalries can have bizarre consequences.

CHAPTER V

NEUTRALISM AS STATE POLICY — SOME CASE STUDIES

"There is room for a more detailed analysis of the logic of situations."   Karl Popper, *The Open Society and its Enemies.*

"It is extremely difficult to put together or unfold historical events before the eyes of a reader in such a way as is necessary, in order to use them as proofs; for the writer very often wants the means, and can neither afford the time nor the requisite space; but we maintain that, when the object is to establish a new or doubtful opinion, one single example, thoroughly analyzed, is far more instructive than ten which are superficially treated."
       Carl von Clausewitz, *On War.*

INDIA, YUGOSLAVIA AND THE UNITED ARAB REPUBLIC — THREE PIONEER NEUTRALISTS

INDIA, Yugoslavia, and the United Arab Republic[1] are the contemporary neutralist states *par excellence.* Each of them has pioneered policies which are now, in some respects at least, generally regarded as being typically neutralist. All three of them provide articulate, even vehement, spokesmen for anti-colonial causes; all three seek foreign aid to forward their ambitious plans for national development; and all three are 'revisionist' rather than *status quo* powers, though the quality of their revisionism differs. Awareness of their affinities, and the currents of contemporary international politics, has encouraged them to develop diplomatic contacts with each other. Together their three leaders, Mr Nehru, President Tito and President Nasser, make up a formidable triumvirate, each coming from a different continent and each aspiring to play an influential part in world affairs. None of these leaders regards a neutralist foreign policy merely as a way of keeping out of Cold War quarrels. On the contrary, they each aspire to a position of importance and of leadership in international affairs. Both the Cold War struggle and the emergence of new states have enabled them to realise these ambitions, though in different ways, to the extent that

[1] The United Arab Republic came into being by the union of Egypt and Syria in Feb. 1958. The Union was dissolved by Syria's secession in Sept. 1961, though the Egyptian half retained the title the United Arab Republic. Here we are concerned almost exclusively with the Egyptian half of the United Arab Republic, with Egypt from 1945 to 1958, and with the United Arab Republic 1958 to 1962. For convenience I have used the term Egypt in the text of this chapter.

by early 1963 India, Yugoslavia, and Egypt were the leading neutralist states in the world. Here the three states will be considered separately before comparing them together.

India

For many people India's foreign policy is the paradigm of a neutralist foreign policy. For not only is India the first, the largest and perhaps the most predictable of the new state neutralists of the Cold War (and occupying a pivotal position in Asia), but in the quality of her leadership and the scrupulousness of her diplomacy she is perhaps the most convincingly independent of the new state neutralists.

Any analysis of India's neutralist policy must begin by acknowledging the paramount rôle and importance of the man who continuously since 1947 has been both Prime Minister and Foreign Minister of independent India. But Mr Nehru's[2] great influence goes back further than 1947, to his work and influence in the Congress Party from the 1920s onwards and to his intimate association with Gandhi. Mr Nehru's habit of public comment on the outstanding international issues of the day also dates from the 1920s, for he has always conceived of India being able to play an important rôle in world politics in harmony with the promotion of India's immediate interests. Though it would be wrong to say that the precise course of India's foreign policy was charted before 1947, it is nevertheless true that many of her post-1947 preoccupations—concern with world peace, sympathy for anti-colonialist and anti-racialist causes, a conception of India's importance in world affairs—were prefigured in Mr Nehru's writings and speeches before she emerged as an independent state.

This preceding period of verbal formulation of India's policy, and Mr Nehru's insistence from the 1920s onwards that the Congress Party must have an international outlook, has a threefold relevance today. Firstly, it helped to create an impression from the earliest days of Indian independence that India's favourite foreign policy methods were generally well thought out and related to a general pattern of policy. These favourite methods have been well summarized by a leading Indian scholar, Professor Appadorai, as: "To keep the peace, by peaceful means—negotiation, inquiry, mediation, conciliation and arbitration; listen to the viewpoint of both parties to a dispute expressed by their duly constituted representatives; hesitate to condemn either party as an aggressor, until facts proved by international enquiry indisputably testify to aggression; believe the *bona fides* of both until proof to the contrary; and explore fully the possibilities of negotiation and at least localize

[2] The three best of the many studies of Nehru are Frank Moraes, *Jawaharlal Nehru* (New York, 1956); Michael Brecher, *Nehru. A Political Biography* (London, 1959); and Vincent Sheean, *Nehru. The Years of Power* (London, 1960).

war—this is India's view."[3] Secondly, it goes a long way towards explaining why Indians themselves seem to place such importance on 'correct thinking' and 'the intrinsic power of ideas'. Thirdly, and most relevant to neutralism generally, it indicates why it was that India, through the person of Mr Nehru, was able to pioneer the notion that neutralism could be a carefully thought out, intelligible and respectable policy. Not only was he the first internationally influential exponent of neutralist doctrine,[4] but he showed that he could translate his ideas into practice with some considerable success, even though Indian policy had to be alert to the vicissitudes of the Cold War. While it is probably true to say that the intentions of India's policy makers have remained broadly the same since 1947, the actual course of India's neutralist policy[5] has gone through three stages.

Between 1947 and 1950 India was preoccupied with immediate tasks flowing from the newly achieved independence following the partition of British India. Domestic and foreign policy tasks were closely linked, for not only was the promotion and consolidation of national unity essential, but Nehru clearly saw that popular support for foreign policy could become an important cement of national unity. Great stress, too, was laid on India's need to industrialize. It was perhaps inevitable that Indo-Pakistan relations should be strained from the start, considering the circumstances of their mutual origin, but the unresolved fate of Kashmir undoubtedly magnified mutual animosities, and has been a major reason for continuous Indo-Pakistan tensions. India's continuing close relationship with Great Britain should be seen, therefore, not only in terms of a large legacy of goodwill, expressed especially in good relations with the Attlee government and in close economic ties, but also as a means of preventing Pakistan developing exclusive relations with Britain to the detriment of India. Apart from the Kashmir issue, India's championship of Indonesian independence was her most active

[3] Quoted in Benjamin Akzin, *New States and International Organizations* (Paris, 1955), p. 174.

[4] See *Independence and After. A collection of the more important speeches of Jawaharlal Nehru from September 1946 to May 1949* (Delhi, 1949), esp. pp. 199-338.

[5] Brecher reports that "the term to describe Indian foreign policy has undergone frequent change. It began with 'neutrality' or 'dynamic neutrality', later became 'neutralism' and then 'non-alignment'. Nehru prefers the phrase 'positive policy for peace', he told the author in New Delhi on 13 June 1956." Michael Brecher, *Nehru. A Political Biography* (London, 1959), p. 563, n. 2. Mr Nehru's testimonies on other occasions have been somewhat different: "I do not like the word neutralism which is commonly used in wartime. In peacetime it indicates a sort of war mentality. India's neutralism meant simply that they had an independent policy and judged questions on their merits." Mr Nehru reported in *The Times*, 7 July 1956. Cf. Mr Nehru's speech in *Lok Sabha Debates*, 29 Mar. 1956, cols. 3729-30. It is important to remember that Mr Nehru is a votary of parliamentary democracy.

international concern in these first three years of independence.[6] At this time Indian neutralism seemed to have a pro-Western orientation. This was partly shown in India's success in being the first Asian state to reconcile independent status with Commonwealth membership (though her relations with the United States were merely correct and tepid, as Mr Nehru's visit to that country in 1949[7] seemed to underline). More significantly, this apparent pro-Western inclination was the unavoidable consequence of Soviet propaganda, and of the Asian Communist parties' persistence in portraying India as not, in fact, independent at all, but as still tied to the 'imperialists'.

From 1951 to 1956 India pursued a fairly active mediatorial rôle and moved from a Western-orientated neutralism towards a more strictly middle-of-the-road position. The strengths and limitations of Indian neutralist diplomacy were shown by her action, or inaction, on such issues as the Korean, Indo-Chinese and Suez wars and the Hungarian Revolution.[8] It was a period during which Indian relations both with Russia and with China generally improved, while those with the United States deteriorated, and those with Britain showed some considerable fluctuations. In 1951 India launched her First Five Year Plan for the national economy and her insistence that aid must be "without strings", just when the Americans were tightening up the conditions under which they would grant aid, was a factor (of course, there were other reasons too) in restricting the amount of help India got from abroad. From June 1952 there was a new note of criticism in the Indian government's reaction to Western alliances. Previously India had been content to say that her membership in the Commonwealth, and belief in "its healing touch" (to use Nehru's words), in no way associated India with N.A.T.O. When, at the N.A.T.O. Council meeting at Lisbon in 1952, Portugal appealed to her N.A.T.O. partners to support Portuguese sovereignty in Goa, and the appeal did not go entirely unheeded, India quickly, and thereafter clearly and consistently, expressed her strong disapproval of all Western alliances and of Western colonial empires. Two working assumptions of Indian diplomacy, always there, but particularly evident throughout 1951-6, are that Asian affairs should be decided by Asians and that all remaining vestiges of "colonialism" must be removed.[9]

In effect, the policies flowing from these assumptions tended to

[6] For details, see K. P. Karunakaran, *India in World Affairs 1947-50* (Bombay, 1952).
[7] See Brecher, pp. 419-20, and Sheean, pp. 137-8.
[8] For details, see K. P. Karunakaran, *India in World Affairs, 1950-3* (Bombay, 1958), and Brecher, chapter 19.
[9] The above paragraph is heavily based on N. Mansergh, R.I.I.A., *Survey of British Commonwealth Affairs, 1939-52*, pp. 357-60, esp. 360.

improve Indian relations with the Communist powers, and in particular with Communist China,[10] and to embarrass or put strain on her relations with the Western powers. During these years Indian leaders tended to stress China's Asian, rather than her Communist, character; and to hint that she was a potential neutralist, perhaps an Asian Titoist. Certainly, both during the Korean and the Indo-China war, India cast herself in the rôle of intermediary between the Communist powers and the West, showed great solicitude for Chinese feelings, great suspicion of American aggressiveness, and worked hard to secure satisfactory compromises and peaceful settlement.

Even so, this period of ostensible friendship with China was not developed without difficulty and some misgivings on India's side. Though at the time of the Korean war India was the only non-Communist country able at that time to have a genuine dialogue with the Peking government, Chinese actions to bring Tibet effectively within Chinese rule provoked some asperities from India in the diplomatic notes exchanged between the two countries from October 1950 onwards. First India asserted her 'protective' interest over Nepal, Sikkim, and Bhutan.* Then it took four years to accomplish the agreement proclaimed in the five principles of peaceful co-existence (the *Panch Sheel*) attached to the preamble of the Sino-Indian treaty of trade and friendship on Tibet, signed in April 1954. In the light of the recent evidence about Sino-Indian border disputes, evidence published by the Indian government between 1959 and 1961,[11] the real charge against Indian policy makers in the years 1954 to 1959 is not that they fully believed in Chinese *bona fides*, but that being uncertain of their reliability they did nothing substantial to prepare for the eventuality that Chinese 'friendship' might prove to be spurious. Two major distractions account for this failing. First, continual obsession with Pakistan meant that whatever military planning and expenditure was undertaken (and it is worth noticing that Indian defence expenditure was only two and a half per cent of national income throughout these years) was done in terms of possible war with Pakistan. Second, India was at this time actively developing a world rôle as was shown in such matters as: advising on settlements for the Austrian and Algerian questions, her initiatives in proposing that a world disarmament agreement should begin with a nuclear test ban, her acceptance of the chairmanship of

[10] See Brecher, pp. 588-92.
[11] See *Ministry of External Affairs, Government of India, White Paper 1 :* Notes, Memoranda and Letters exchanged and agreements signed between the Governments of India and China 1954 - September 1959; *White Paper II :* Notes, etc., Sept. - Nov. 1959; *White Paper III :* Notes, etc., Nov. 1959 - March 1960 (New Delhi, 1959-60) and *Report by the Officials of the Governments of India and the People's Republic of China on the Boundary Question* (New Delhi, 1961).
* See above, pp. 95-7.

the Committee appointed to supervise the implementation of the 1954 Geneva agreements on Laos, and her active rôle in the meetings of "the Colombo powers", and at Bandung in April 1955; and there was the meeting with Tito and Nasser at Brioni in Yugoslavia in July 1956.[12]

An undramatic yet significant aspect of India's diplomacy in the years 1951-6 was her close continuing contacts and, at times, working co-operation with Great Britain. Commonwealth ties here probably aided co-operation where no conflicting interests were involved. By contrast, British and, more importantly, Pakistan adhesion to the Baghdad Pact and to S.E.A.T.O. called forth much criticism of Britain, both from India's official leadership and from Indian opinion at large.[13] Bulganin and Khrushchov, when they paid a state visit to India in 1955, received such an apparently enthusiastic welcome that widespread alarms were expressed in many Western countries. These probably exaggerated the diplomatic implications of India's reception of these two Communist leaders, for it is far more likely that such a reception was compounded of public curiosity, genuine hospitality, and relief on the part of the official leadership now that Soviet policies towards India had changed for the better.[14]

From 1951 onwards India had assiduously striven to build up close relations with a number of fellow neutralist states, and soon came to be widely regarded as the leader of the so-called Arab-Asian bloc[15] in the United Nations. With the rapid expansion of Asian and African membership of the United Nations, this bloc grew correspondingly, became known as the Afro-Asian bloc,[16] became more unwieldy, and India's

[12] Economist, 14 July 1956, p. 111; Scotsman, 19 July 1956; Time and Tide, 21 July 1956. The final communiqué of the Brioni meeting is given in R.I.I.A., Documents for 1956, pp. 70-2. See below, pp. 126, 135, 143-4.

[13] See M. S. Rajan, "Stresses and Strains in Indo-British Relations, 1954-6" in International Studies (Delhi), Oct. 1960, pp. 153-89. In 1954 Nehru had to take action to restrain Indians from trying to occupy the Portuguese enclave in India of Goa.

[14] See Geoffrey Tyson, "India and the Russian Visitors", R.I.I.A., International Affairs, Apr. 1956, pp. 173-80. It was Tyson's view (p. 180) that "Mr Nehru's political neutralism has now been extended to the economic sphere, where its practical application means that India will consider herself free to accept assistance of every kind from the Communist world without prejudice to her relations with the West". An Economist survey of 26 Mar. 1960, pp. 1263-85, showed that 90% of foreign aid to India came from Western sources and only 10% from the Soviet bloc; see esp. p. 1281. Another Economist appraisal of the Indian economy, 28 Jan. 1961, pp. 342-50, concluded that "India will not find economic independence in the next decade". What, precisely, "economic independence" meant was not made clear.

[15] Early Arab-Asian co-operation is discussed in Egypt and the United Nations (New York, 1957), pp. 73-5.

[16] See Triska and Koch, "The Asian-African Nations and International Organisation", in Review of Politics, Apr. 1959, pp. 417-56.

undisputed leadership began to diminish. Even so, between 1954 and the first half of 1956 India seemed to be developing especially close diplomatic ties with Egypt and Yugoslavia—and it was the Brioni meeting of July 1956[17] that seemed to symbolize the undoubted emergence of these three as the world's leading neutralists.

The Brioni meeting was the culmination of several similar meetings[18] held between any two of the three statesmen in the previous two or three years. But in retrospect this meeting in Yugoslavia also seems to mark the point when Nehru had already begun to expect less from, and so to show less enthusiasm for, diplomacy by conference of this kind. The three leaders met to exchange views and, in Nehru's view at least, not to concert together on anything specific. There were earlier reports that Nehru had not been particularly enthusiastic either at the prospect or the outcome of the Colombo or Bandung conferences and it is probable that he felt by 1956 that India had achieved a position of independence and respect sufficient to play a useful rôle in world affairs by herself. In short, Egypt and Yugoslavia needed Indian friendship more than India needed theirs, and from Brioni onwards there were signs that Tito and Nasser were closer together than either of them was with Nehru. This did not mean that there were no more Brioni-like meetings, but it did mean that Nehru was never the instigator of them.

Yet, ironically, the limitations of India's mediatory rôle were soon to be made clear. For with the eruption of the Suez and Hungarian crises in 1956, India's neutralist policies were less effective than during the Korean and Indo-China wars. With Britain a belligerent in the Suez war (and with Hungary part of the Soviet 'empire'), it was not possible to resume Indo-British compromise procedures like those which had worked at the time of the Korean and Indo-China wars. Though in the Suez question India approved of the active mediatorial rôle of her fellow Commonwealth member Canada, after her own initiatives had failed,[19] she herself came to support her neutralist friend Egypt, with whose plight she had a great deal of sympathy. Mr Nehru's initial public reaction to the Hungarian Revolution was vacillating and then rather evasive. This caused great annoyance in the Western world and among a sizeable segment of Indian opinion, and he was accused of applying double standards, either as between the Suez and Hungary questions,

[17] See references in n. 12 above; also L. Radovanovic, *From Bandung to Beograd* (Yugoslav information services, 1961).

[18] See R.I.I.A., *Documents for 1955* for: joint statement by Tito and Nehru, 6 July 1955, pp. 281-3; *communiqué* on talks between Nehru and Nasser, 16 Feb. 1955, p. 331; treaty of friendship between Egypt and India, 6 Apr. 1955, pp. 334-6; joint statement by Nehru and Nasser, 12 July 1955, p. 334.

[19] See Sheean, p. 161: "it was obvious that Nasser counted on India to attain some kind of acceptable settlement". See also Wint and Calvocoressi, *Middle East Crisis* (London, 1957), pp. 70, 74.

or as between Asian and European questions. His own explanation about his early reaction to Hungarian events was that it was difficult to find out exactly what was happening, and this may have been true if, as was likely, he was relying on President Tito as his prime source for information[20]—for Tito's reaction to the Hungarian Revolution was equally equivocal.[21] Another factor which was very probably influencing the course of Indian neutralism was the development of Soviet aid programmes to India, from 1954 onwards. From a neutralist point of view, this had the political advantage of removing a wholesale dependence on the Western powers for vital foreign aid to fulfil the goals of her five-year plans, and also eventually stimulated increased offers of aid from the Western powers. By the end of 1956 India had evolved a neutralist foreign policy recognized by both Cold War camps as independent, and, if only by contrast with the years 1947-51, it seemed slightly inclined in favour of the Soviet bloc.[22]

Since 1957 India has tended to be content with a rather quieter rôle internationally than hitherto; by contrast with either Egypt or Yugoslavia to be more moderate, less stridently radical and revisionist, even on anti-colonial issues. These contrasts were particularly evident throughout 1960-2 in the policies of these three states towards the problems arising from the civil war in the former Belgian Congo. In a manner somewhat reminiscent of the Spanish Civil War of the 1930s the Congolese civil war soon took on an international character and Egypt and Yugoslavia soon came to support Lumumba (the advocate of a unitary Congolese state under his own leadership). In contrast, India approached the whole Congo imbroglio more cautiously at first, shrank from identifying itself with any one of the rival Congolese factions and came to back strongly the U.N. Secretary-General's efforts to tranquillize the situation—even to the extent of sending a large detachment of Indian troops to serve in a U.N. 'police' force.

This generally quieter rôle India has played internationally since 1957 is not only to be explained in terms of the free inclinations of India's leaders—their distaste for belligerent methods and their preference for trying to reconcile "anti-colonial" with "repentant colonial"[23]

[20] I owe this point to Richard Lowenthal, "Tito's Gamble" in *Encounter*, Oct. 1958, p. 61. See also Sheean, p. 161.
[21] See studies cited in n. 44 below, and below p. 135.
[22] See Brecher, pp. 582-8.
[23] The obvious "exception" here seems to be the Indian absorption of Goa in Dec. 1961. The prompting forces behind this act could have been many—the mounting anti-colonial clamour in India, the unrest and frustration of an army anxious to do battle with the Chinese, the desire to restore prestige with Afro-Asian anti-colonials, the feeling that Portugal was in no way a "repentant" colonial power and that the securing of this irredenta could only be achieved by a show of force. And, however much the Indian seizure of Goa may have upset

states—but also because they have felt the need to attend to mounting economic difficulties, to try to reduce and repair the growing rifts in the hitherto broadly based national unity about India's neutralist policy, and generally to devote more energy to pressing foreign policy tasks nearer home. Above all, since October 1962 the dispute with China had made all other issues subordinate.

In India's present predicament problems about economic development, defence, national unity and her overall international posture are all intimately interlinked.

An American study,[24] published in August 1962, showed clearly that India had received more foreign aid, in sheer money terms, from both the Soviet Union and from the United States, than had any other state. But, looked at in *per capita* terms, this large amount of aid is less impressive. India's large and growing population (approximately 450 million in 1962) is one of her biggest handicaps here. For most of the first decade of independence India had at her disposal large sterling reserves mainly accumulated in the Second World War. These had been exhausted by 1957 and ever since she has had a heavy and continuing deficit in her trade balance. Even before the Chinese invasion, in the last quarter of 1962, India's Third Five Year Plan (1961-6) was not being fulfilled. Since the invasion defence costs have mounted steeply, and as it is unlikely that foreign aid will be made available to account for all the extra defence expenditure envisaged, the Indian economy[25] will be subject to unprecedented strains.

Again, even before the large-scale eruption with China the hitherto

or disappointed people in the Western world, however difficult or easy Mr Nehru found it to take the decision, it should be remembered that the act was widely popular in Asia and Africa, vociferously applauded by Communist spokesmen— and was achieved with very little bloodshed.

[24] A volume of testimony about foreign aid, given before the American House of Representatives appropriations sub-committee early in 1962, was published in Aug. 1962. *The Times* of 30 Aug. 1962, in summarizing the report, gave the following table which is a list of the countries which received more than $100 m. from one or the other source (in millions of dollars):

United States		Sino-Soviet block	
India	2,726	India	963
Pakistan	1,329	Indonesia	641
Turkey	980	U.A.R. (Egypt)	615
Brazil	961	Cuba	357
Yugoslavia	794	Iraq	216
Iran	411	Afghanistan	204
U.A.R. (Egypt)	394	Ghana	182
Argentina	360	Syria	178
Indonesia	308	Ethiopia	114
Tunisia	267	Yugoslavia	111
Cambodia	195	Guinea	110
Afghanistan	138	Argentina	104
Ethiopia	115		

[25] See "India, Emergency and Plan" in *Economist*, 23 Feb. 1963, pp. 698-700.

broadly based national unity about India's non-aligned foreign policy had shown some signs of weakening.[26] Chinese behaviour in Tibet and along her borders[27] with India, and the vigorous reaction of Indian opinion to these events gave Indian leaders considerable worries. The growing demands of linguistic-nationalism—or even separatism, as in the case of the Nagas—and the continuation of bad relations with a now militarily stronger Pakistan, gave Indian leaders further reasons for disquiet. Since October 1962 Mr Nehru (though, like the Chinese, forbearing from a formal declaration of war) has said that India is engaged in her "first war of independence" and that even though there would be lulls it would go on for some considerable time to come. Clearly Mr Nehru places considerable reliance on the spirit of national solidarity generated by the fighting with China. It remains to be seen whether this solidarity will be sustained sufficiently to help improve national defences and the national economy.

In New Delhi, on 25th October 1962, Mr Nehru said "that massive invasion of India by China" had made India realize that she had been "out of touch with reality" and that he and his supporters had been shocked out of "the artificial atmosphere of our own creation". Two collateral disillusionments have accompanied India's clash with China. First, Indo-Pakistan tensions have not lessened but heightened as a result of India's military build-up to meet China's challenge, and in fact Pakistan and China have moved closer together against their common enemy. Second, the six non-aligned nations (Burma, Indonesia, Cambodia, the United Arab Republic, Ghana and Ceylon) that met in Colombo in December 1962, after China's unilateral cease-fire, were at pains to make clear that they regarded themselves as mediators not arbitrators; they saw their task to be that of pacification, not adjudication. Only the U.A.R. showed a marked disposition to support the Indian cause, and India thus learned that open support from fellow non-aligned states was not to be counted on. While the United States,

[26] See, e.g., two articles by Cyril Dunn in *Observer*, 10 and 17 Apr. 1960. The most telling arguments have not been directed against the fact of India's neutralism—this is still broadly accepted as right—but whether the methods adopted are best designed to secure India's interests. Less attention to world problems and more attention to Indian problems is what is wanted, say Nehru's critics. One of the ablest of these is Acharya Kripalani (leader of the Praja Socialist Party); see his article, "For a Principled Neutrality" in *Foreign Affairs*, Oct. 1959, pp. 46-60. The Indian interests most referred to by critics are Kashmir and Goa (at least until Dec. 1961), and relations with China, Pakistan, Nepal, and Ceylon.

[27] See "India's Ring of Troubles" in *Economist*, 27 Oct. 1962, pp. 329-30, and two penetrating articles by my colleague, William Kirk, "The Sino-Indian Frontier Dispute" in *Scottish Geographical Magazine*, 1960, pp. 3-13, and "The Inner Asian Frontier of India" in *Transactions and Papers of the Institute of British Geographers*, 1962, no. 31, pp. 131-68.

I

Canada, Australia and Britain proffered material support it seemed as if
at least five of the Colombo powers were inclined to cling to India's old
illusions and not to learn from her present plight. For one report of the
Colombo conference said that "the neutralist nations . . . hold that
non-alignment is still a viable force and that more Asians, Africans and
Latin Americans may see the attractions and add to their collective
strength. India's present entanglement is regarded as an active danger
to these aspirations." [28]

India is undoubtedly undergoing a period of "agonizing reappraisal",
with great stress being laid on the need for adequate defences—a stress
which may, perhaps, lead to the production or at least the acquisition
of nuclear weapons. [29] But it is important not to exaggerate the likely
immediate changes in Indian foreign policy. It is likely that India will
continue to describe her foreign policy as "non-alignment", that she
will not accept foreign bases on her soil, nor enter any formal military
alliance. For some time there is unlikely to be a lasting settlement with
Pakistan, or with China. India will attempt to keep on good terms with
both the United States and the Soviet Union (it is too often forgotten
in the West that in Indian eyes the Soviet Union has on the whole
been a good friend to India ever since 1955), and will try to maintain
(and, if possible, to increase) her flow of aid from abroad.

Yet the paradox of India's position remains. Though territorially
large and with a large population, she is neither militarily nor economically strong. She is neither a small state, nor a world power. Though
the world's leading neutralist power, she is not able in time of adversity
to rely on the undoubted support of other neutralist states. In the years
1954-6 India proclaimed the gospel of "peaceful co-existence" between
Communist and non-aligned states. Increasingly since 1959 it has been
her fate, at the hands of Communist China, to test whether she has the
will and the means to safeguard what she regards as vital national
interests. India, the pioneer of neutralist idealism, may yet become the
pioneer of a new neutralist realism.

Yugoslavia

Yugoslavia's neutralist policy originated with her excommunication
from the Cominform in June 1948. It sprang from Tito's determination
to resist, and Stalin's determination to impose, a strict ideological and
political conformity on Yugoslavia under Soviet leadership. [30] The seeds

[28] Quoted from *Economist*, 22 Dec. 1962, p. 1210; see also *Observer*, 4 Nov. 1962
and 13 Jan. 1963, and *New York Times*, 14 Dec. 1962.

[29] One well-informed study claimed that the Indian government believes that
the acquisition of nuclear weapons from Western powers would be less objection-
able morally than an Indian bomb; see Beaton and Maddox, *The Spread of
Nuclear Weapons* (London, 1962), chapter viii—India.

[30] For an account of the dispute, see H. F. Armstrong, *Tito and Goliath*

of the clash, and the most powerful reasons for Tito's successful resistance, lay in the unique Second World War experiences of Yugoslavia[31] among the eventual east European satellites of the Soviet Union. Altogether three factors were most important: (1) Yugoslavia was the only east European fighting ally of both the Soviet Union and the Allied powers simultaneously: (2) Yugoslavia was not subjected to Soviet occupation and so the Yugoslav Communist leadership was not beholden to the Red Army for its power; (3) geographically, Yugoslavia is the largest Balkan state and is, except for Albania, at the remotest corner of the Soviet's European system. It is probable that Soviet pressures on Yugoslavia, especially between 1947 and 1949, did much to consolidate Tito's regime in power and perhaps to forge a greater sense of Yugoslav national unity than hitherto. This latter point is admittedly conjectural, but Soviet bloc pressure in these years was the first time that a substantial external threat seemed to work against the whole and not a part of the mosaic of nationalities[32] which make up Yugoslavia. Though the Soviet-Yugoslav dispute inevitably took on the appearance of an ideological struggle,[33] its real substance centred upon Yugoslav insistence upon maintaining the independence of their state and Tito's policies concerning Communism in the Balkans.[34] Yugoslavia's success in resisting Soviet pressures was the first dramatic instance of the ability of a non-aligned state to resist considerable great power pressure in Cold War conditions, while remaining formally uncommitted to the other Cold War camp. Since June 1948 Yugoslavia's neutralist policy has varied with the fluctuations in Soviet-Yugoslav relations, and correspondingly these have reflected fairly closely the major vicissitudes of the Cold War.

The years from 1948 to 1953 were marked by the unrelenting hostility of all Communist states towards Yugoslavia, against whom they imposed a complete boycott and blockade. For more than a year after she left the Cominform Yugoslavia was completely isolated. For as

---

(London, 1951), esp. chapters 2-11; and Adam B. Ulam, *Titoism and the Cominform* (Cambridge, Mass., 1952).

[31] See Hugh Seton-Watson, *The East European Revolution* (2nd ed., London, 1952), pp. 118-31, 157-61, 219-25; and Vladimir Dedijer, *Tito Speaks* (London, 1953), part 2, pp. 95-248.

[32] For a fascinating pre-war picture of this diversity, see Rebecca West's *Black Lamb and Grey Falcon* (2 vols., London, 1942). For some more recent discussions of the significance of Yugoslavia's multi-national composition, see J. Frankel, "Federalism in Yugoslavia" in *A.P.S.R. 1955*, pp. 416-30, and Richard Goold-Adams, "Yugoslavia Between Two Worlds" in *Listener*, 12 July 1956, pp. 41-2.

[33] The published correspondence at the time of the Yugoslav break with the Cominform is collected and edited in *Soviet-Jugoslav Dispute* (R.I.I.A., London, 1948).

[34] See Vladimir Dedijer, *Tito Speaks*, pp. 249-384.

a Communist state she was regarded with suspicion by all the Western powers (and, in particular, she was at loggerheads with Italy over Trieste, and with Greece because of Yugoslav aid to Greek Communists), and, having seceded from the Soviet bloc in the name of the sovereign independence of small states, she was under a political necessity not to enter subserviently a rival bloc. Then she began, of necessity, to work for a *détente* with the Western powers.[35] Tito needed economic aid to counteract the Cominform's blockade and to forward his economic plans, and he needed military aid to deter or, if necessary, to repel Soviet attacks. He got both[36] (American economic aid in 1949 and military aid from 1951) and—of great significance in the history of neutralism—he got them on terms he could accept without endangering his standing in his own country. In effect, the unremitting hostility of the Soviet bloc and such acts (in addition to taking Western aid) as the verbal condemnation of North Korean aggression,[37] the conclusion of a treaty of friendship and co-operation with the two newest N.A.T.O. powers—Greece and Turkey—in February 1953,[38] and Tito's state visit to Britain in March 1953, all gave a strong impression of a pro-Western orientation. Yet Tito was constantly at pains to stress Yugoslav independence of either Cold War camp, to insist that Western aid was "without strings", to criticize either camp whenever he saw fit, and to develop an ideological intermediacy[39] distinguishing Yugoslavia from either "capitalism" or "Stalinism" in the name of "true" Marxist-Leninism.

Following the death of Stalin in March 1953, a gradual Soviet-Yugoslav *détente* began to unfold with gestures of conciliation and, at times, even of contrition being made by Soviet leaders, though these were, at first, regarded with some scepticism or, at least, coolness by President Tito.[40] The first half of 1955 saw a definite broadening in

[35] For details, see R.I.I.A., *Survey for 1949-50*, pp. 258-81.

[36] For details, see R.I.I.A., *Survey for 1951*, pp. 240-54.

[37] This was a difficult decision for the Yugoslav leadership. After more than two months' vacillation, she declared in Sept. 1950 that North Korea was the aggressor, though she excused herself even a symbolic part in the military action by maintaining that as she was threatened herself her best service to the cause of peace would be to concentrate her forces in the protection of her own frontiers.

[38] In fact, this Balkan alliance—the Ankara Pact, as it is sometimes called—fell into abeyance soon after its inauguration as the Cyprus dispute divided Greece and Turkey. After the Cyprus settlement Yugoslavia was too far committed to neutralism to wish to be reminded of her links with military blocs. Its demise was officially announced in June 1960. See *The Times*, 25 June 1960.

[39] This did not emerge clearly until the 6th Yugoslav Communist Party Congress in Nov. 1952; see R. Barry Farrell, *Jugoslavia and the Soviet Union, 1948-1956. An Analysis with Documents* (Yale U.P., 1957), esp. pp. 125-41 and 146-60.

[40] See Ernst Halperin, *The Triumphant Heretic. Tito's Struggle Against Stalin* (London, 1958), pp. 260-77.

Yugoslav policy. Though one aspect of this was the growing rapprochement with the Soviet bloc, this renewed amity was restrained, not only by the legacy of past years of enmity, but also because Tito in his journeyings in Asia between 17th December 1954 and 11th February 1955 was developing contacts with Asian neutralist states,[41] and giving his hitherto proclaimed policy of independence of the two World War blocs a more positive content. Hitherto, Yugoslav neutralism had been mainly rather negative, concerned to show that Yugoslavia was not subservient to either Cold War camp, now it was to be shown that she had friends and influence among other uncommitted states. This was a shrewd (or, at least, fortunate) anticipation of developing trends, for not only did it open the way for future Yugoslav identification and co-operation with the Bandung neutralists, but in so doing it gave her a lead over the Soviets when they, too, began to develop friendly relations with Asian and African neutralists.

The reconciliation between the Soviets and Yugoslavia[42] was developed first by improving economic relations, and consummated with Khrushchov's public apology in Belgrade in May 1955, when he admitted that the previous policy of the Soviet Union towards Yugoslavia had been mistaken, and blamed these mistakes on the executed Beria. The official Yugoslav reaction to this visit was to reaffirm her determination to continue to pursue an independent policy internationally, to express satisfaction at improving relations with the Soviet Union, while emphasizing that the rapprochement was between the two states, not between two Communist parties. Though during the next twelve months Tito came to agree to the restoration of amicable party contacts and to endorse Soviet stands on a number of major international issues[43]—especially Germany—he continued to emphasize his determination to belong to neither Cold War camp. His problem was, in fact, to establish and maintain good relations with all three groups in world politics—the Western powers, the Soviet bloc, and the uncommitted countries—while avoiding the danger (always a real one to governments without clearly settled positions) of being thought a nuisance by all three. Improved relations with the Soviet bloc reduced

[41] See R.I.I.A., *Survey for 1955-6*, pp. 54-6. The authors suggest that as a result of this tour Tito's policy "acquired the essential points d'appui which it had hitherto lacked". Though Tito repeatedly opposed the creation of a third bloc, he identified Yugoslavia's policy closely with India's, both of them being "neither 'neutrality' nor 'neutralism' and therefore passivity . . . but . . . a positive, active and constructive policy seeking to lead to collective peace" (*ibid.*, p. 55).

[42] *Ibid.*, pp. 133-8 and 268-72. Yugoslavia became less immediately dependent upon military aid from the United States and was, therefore, able to insist upon more stringent conditions before accepting it.

[43] *Ibid.*, p. 135, n. 3, and p. 270.

his reliance on the Western powers for help and increased his freedom for manoeuvre. Between 1954 and 1957 Tito sought to discover how far Soviet-Yugoslav co-operation could go, short of Yugoslav subservience to the Soviet Union. Good relations with fellow neutralist states here enhanced Tito's bargaining power inasmuch as the Soviets seemed to regard reconciliation with Yugoslavia as an essential part of the Soviet 'new line' of wooing the neutralist states. The Brioni meeting between Nasser, Nehru and Tito, in July 1956, was symbolic of Yugoslavia's place among the neutralist leaders.

May 1955 to June 1956 saw the steady development of this new Soviet-Yugoslav cordiality. Thereafter relations were subject to dramatic fluctuations, probably depending on events inside the Soviet bloc—and particularly on Sino-Soviet relations, as China came to be the most powerfully implacable opponent of 'Titoism'. May 1955 was the time of Khrushchov's journey of reconciliation to Belgrade. In February 1956, at the Soviet 20th Party Congress, Khrushchov spoke of Stalin's "shameful rôle" in the conflict with Yugoslavia. Shortly afterwards Rajk and other victims of various earlier anti-Titoist trials were rehabilitated. Molotov, a symbol of the Stalinist line towards Yugoslavia, was removed from the post of Soviet Foreign Minister; and the Cominform, instrument of Yugoslavia's earlier expulsion from the Soviet camp, was dissolved. In June 1956 Tito was Khrushchov's honoured guest in Moscow.

Thereafter there was a deterioration in Soviet-Yugoslav relations. Riots in Poznan, Poland, soon after Tito's visit to Moscow, led to strong Soviet hints that they were opposed to any spread of 'Titoist' influences inside the Communist camp. Yugoslav policies between June 1956 and November 1957, when she refused to rejoin the Soviet camp, are shrouded in ambiguity and their significance has been a subject of considerable controversy among Western scholars,[44] though at least it seems clear that Tito was endeavouring to encourage 'de-Stalinization' in eastern Europe without dismembering the Communist camp. Yugoslav moves in this period, some idea of their confusing meanderings, can be conveniently portrayed by means of a short chronological table:

June 1956	Tito visits Moscow (deliberately avoiding Hungarian territory en route).
	Riots in Poland. Gomulka — the Polish 'Titoist' — becomes Poland's Prime Minister.

[44] Cf. Fitzroy Maclean, *Disputed Barricade. The Life and Times of Josip Broz-Tito* (London, 1957), pp. 457-60; R. Lowenthal, "Tito's Gamble" in *Encounter*, Oct. 1958, pp. 56-65; Bromke and Drachkovitch, "Poland and Yugoslavia : The Abortive Alliance" in *Problems of Communism*, Mar.-Apr. 1961, pp. 26-33; A. Barcan, "Yugoslavia and the Hungarian Revolution" in *Australian Outlook*, Apr. 1960, pp. 30-9.

July	Brioni talks between Nehru, Nasser, and Tito. U.S. aid to Yugoslavia severely cut.
August	New Soviet-Yugoslavia aid agreement severely cut.
Aug. - Feb. 1957	Tito supports Nasser in Suez crisis.
27 Sept. - 5 Oct.	Tito in Crimea for discussions with Khrushchov, reportedly to reach agreement concerning Hungary.
15-23 Oct.	Delegation from Central Committee of Hungarian Workers' Party visited Yugoslavia (this delegation had been immediately preceded by similar Italian, Polish and Bulgarian delegations, and was followed by a Roumanian one—signs that Belgrade might become a focal point for a new Balkan Communist alliance).
23 Oct.	Fighting broke out in Budapest, capital of Hungary.
24 Oct.	Nagy, a known sympathizer with Tito, took over the Hungarian Premiership. Geroe invited in Soviet troops, though he was himself succeeded as head of Hungarian Communist Party by Kadar the next day.
28 Oct.	The question of holding a debate on Hungarian crisis was discussed in U.N. Security Council. The Yugoslav delegate said that a debate might only aggravate the situation and Yugoslavia would normally have opposed it. As, however, his government was opposed to the use of foreign troops on the territory of other countries, he would abstain from voting.
1 Nov.	Nagy's government renounced the Warsaw Pact, declared Hungary's neutrality and asked for Four Power guarantees and for the question of Hungary to be placed before the United Nations.
1-23 Nov.	Nagy and seventeen others took refuge in Yugoslav embassy in Budapest. When they left, following guarantees of security by Kadar, they were immediately taken into custody by the Soviet authorities.
11 Nov.	Tito, in a speech at Pula, justified the second Soviet intervention as necessary to crush counter-revolution, but blamed the first intervention for having prevented acceptable reforms.
February	Soviets cancel aid agreement with Yugoslavia.
April	Tito, in a speech from Brioni, plays down significance of Soviet-Yugoslav tensions.
August	Khrushchov and Tito meet for talks in Roumania. The cancelled Soviet-Yugoslav economic aid agreements revived. Tito publicly subscribes to Soviet formula of "proletarian internationalism" as a guide to foreign policy.

1957
September   Gomulka visits Yugoslavia. Tito supports Polish claims
              to permanent recognition of Oder-Neisse frontier.
              Tito grants diplomatic recognition to eastern Germany
              —the first neutralist state to do so—thus breaking off
              diplomatic relations with western Germany.
November   Yugoslav delegates refuse to sign the Moscow declara-
              tion of twelve ruling Communist parties, which faced
              them with the implicit choice of unconditionally
              joining the Warsaw Pact, or being attacked as
              'revisionists' and kept outside the Communist family.

Since November 1957 Yugoslavia's foreign policy has reflected what
are perhaps the three most important facts to remember in an appreciation of her international position: that she is a state which is ruled by
a Communist Party, is seeking rapid economic growth, and is neutralist.
All three of these factors are intimately linked.

The influence of Yugoslavia's Communism in shaping her international relations depends primarily on the state of Soviet-Yugoslav
relations at any particular time. During times of great Soviet-Yugoslav
tension (e.g. November 1957 - December 1958) the Yugoslavs are
inclined to stress, as they did in their Draft Programme of April 1958,
three propositions which are likely to be more favourably received by
fellow neutralists than by other Communist states: (1) that it is
possible to have 'peaceful revolution' to advance to 'socialism' (which
in such a context serves as a conveniently interchangeable synonym for
Communism) without war being fatalistically inevitable; (2) that Communist parties do not possess a monopoly of ability to lead a nation
towards socialism; and that (3) the principal cause of danger in the
world is the existence of the two Cold War blocs. At times of considerable Soviet-Yugoslav amity (e.g. July-December 1962) Yugoslav
policies become virtually identical with Soviet versions of 'proletarian
internationalism'. All that remains of Tito's rejection of the Soviet (and,
more particularly since 1956, the Sino-Albanian) doctrine of the two
camps is simply Yugoslav rejection of outright alliance with Moscow,
and there is a marked tendency to assert that the chief danger to peace
springs from Western policies. Tito has always claimed to be a legiti-
mate heir of Marx and Lenin, and has always rebutted accusations that
Yugoslav Communists are guilty of 'revisionism'. He has also always
denied that there is any real meaning to such terms as 'Titoism' or
'national Communism'[45] and claims to be revising bad practice,

[45] See Tito's 'authorized' biography, *Tito Speaks* by Vladimir Dedijer (London,
1953), esp. pp. 446-50. The Yugoslavs dislike the term "neutralism" which they
say implies passivity or indifference. They prefer "peaceful and active co-
existence". Tito spoke on this question of terminology during a speech made to

which he typifies as Stalinist-type practice, and not Communist theory. At the time of Tito's official visit to the Soviet Union in December 1962[46] it seemed as if Tito and Khrushchov were agreed in condemning 'Stalinism'; and that the Soviet Union attached more importance to good relations with Yugoslavia than with either of her now unremitting opponents, China and Albania.

Secondly, although Yugoslavia's economy had achieved a remarkable rate of growth throughout the years 1957-60, declining growth and serious setbacks throughout 1961 and 1962[47] underlined for Yugoslav leaders the point that exclusion from all economic groupings could create difficulties no more welcome than those envisaged if Yugoslavia had to join a Cold War military alliance. And the risks of economic damage were more likely and immediate, if less dire in their consequences than the costs and risks entailed through membership of military alliances. In 1960 Yugoslavia's requests for permanent observer status on the Communist Council for Mutual Economic Aid (Comecon) were turned down, and she then sought to strengthen existing links with the countries of the O.E.E.C. (reconstituted in 1961 as O.E.C.D.), to become a full member of G.A.T.T., and to undertake currency reform in order to improve trading relations with Western powers. Even so Yugoslavia was caught between Comecon and the Common Market, and she took the initiative in persuading Nasser to convene a conference in Cairo in July 1962 in an attempt to forge closer economic links between "the uncommitted nations". Yugoslavia had already developed bilateral trade and aid relations with some Asian and African neutralist

---

the Yugoslav National Assembly in Belgrade on 7 Mar. 1956. See report in *The Times*, 9 Mar. 1956.

[46] See John C. Campbell, "Yugoslavia's Crisis and Choice" in *Foreign Affairs*, Jan. 1963, pp. 384-97. For an official 1960 Yugoslav rebuttal of Chinese charges against Yugoslavia, see Edvard Kardelj, *Socialism and War, a survey of Chinese criticism of the Policy of Coexistence*, translated from the Serbo-Croatian by Alec Brown (London, 1961).

[47] "Industrial production has increased fivefold since 1946 (when admittedly it was very low). The national income, which between 1948 and 1952 was increasing at an annual rate of 1·9%, has for the past four years been rising, they claim, by nearly 13% a year. This year they are embarking upon their fourth five-year plan, at the end of which they confidently predict that Yugoslavia will have become a developed country." Quoted from *Economist*, 7 Jan. 1961, p. 20. Two years later a different picture emerged. "In industry there is uncertainty, disorganization and a sharply falling rate of growth: from an annual rate of 15% in 1960, to 7% in 1961, to less than 5% in the first half of 1962 . . . it was apparent that the Jugoslav economic experiment had produced no magic formula for success; that the country had not reached the point of self-sustaining growth." Quoted from John C. Campbell, "Jugoslavia Crisis and Choice" in *Foreign Affairs*, Jan. 1963, p. 386. See also *Yugoslav Survey. A Record of Facts and Information* (Belgrade), Apr. 1960, *et seq.*, quarterly, *passim*.

countries, but the Cairo conference[48] clearly showed that any substantial multilateral co-operation between neutralist nations was still a long way off.

Finally, as a neutralist state, Yugoslavia has not only avoided diplomatic isolation but has gained considerable prestige and influence by strengthening and increasing friendly relations with a number of fellow neutralist states. This has been done not only by Tito's extensive international tours[49] and by initiating and sponsoring various neutralist meetings—of which the neutralist summit in Belgrade in September 1961 was the most dramatic instance—but also by developing Yugoslav trade and aid with neutralist states in Asia and Africa and possibly by advising on the theory and practice of Marxism. By the end of 1962 Yugoslavia had become one of the leading neutralists of the world, and was acting as a mentor to other neutralist states.

Egypt

Egypt's neutralist policy has no obvious starting point comparable with Yugoslavia's break with the Cominform or India's achievement of independence. For an Egyptian it might be dated from the onset of the Cold War, or from the July Revolution of 1952, or from the conclusion of the Anglo-Egyptian agreement of October 1954 regarding the British evacuation of the Suez base, or from the actual departure of the last of the British troops from Suez in 1956—a few weeks before Nasser announced the nationalization of the Suez Canal Company. Be this as it may, Egyptian neutralism has always reflected the volatility of Egyptian nationalism and the tensions between specifically Egyptian and pan-Arab interests.

Indeed, it may be thought idle to search for the starting point of Egyptian neutralism, and be maintained instead that Egyptians are neutralists by nature. On this view Egyptian policies merely translate into action such widespread and deep-rooted attitudes as: chronic

---

[48] "In 1959 and 1960 Yugoslavia granted credits of more than $125 m. to African and Asian countries so they could buy capital goods and other products from Yugoslavia . . . The biggest credit, $40 m., went to India . . . Other credits have gone to Ghana, Sudan, Pakistan and the United Arab Republic." See C.S.M., 20 July 1961. For the Cairo economic conference see The Times, 13 Feb. 1962, "Egypt backs Yugoslav Plan for economic conference"; Economist, 7 July 1962, "Temperature on the Nile"; Daily Telegraph, 19 July 1962, "Neutralists wrangle at Cairo economic talks. Cubans lead criticism of E.E.C."; and C. K. Kutty, "The Conference of Economists in Cairo" in Review of International Affairs (Yugoslav), 5-20 July 1962, pp. 1-3.

[49] Tito made a ten-week tour of Asian and Middle Eastern neutralist countries between Dec. 1958 and Mar. 1959. Speaking of this tour, before his departure Tito stressed that he wanted to see neutralist nations more engaged in influencing events. See The Times, 24 Nov. and 2 Dec. 1958.

suspicion of great power policies, the desire for an untrammelled national independence and for recognition and respect in the eyes of the outside world, a willingness to play off great powers against each other, and an urge to promote Arab unity.[50] Certainly, these attitudes are as old as Egyptian nationalism and are all part and parcel of radical Arab nationalism (perhaps all contemporary radical nationalisms) today. By 1962 Egypt's leaders were practising a form of neutralism frankly opportunist and eclectic, propagandist and proselytist, friendly to virulent anti-Western and truculent nationalist movements in the Arab lands and in Africa; a policy which had placed Egypt among the leading neutralist states of the world.

Situated at the junction of Africa and Asia, midway between Morocco and Iraq, with her cultural tradition, relatively large population, and historic sense of identity, Egypt seems to be marked out for leadership in the Arab world. Yet before the July Revolution this seems to have been a rôle which Egyptian leaders were unwilling or unable to perform.[51] Indeed, right up to 1954 Egyptian leaders were preoccupied with winnowing down and removing all traces of British power and privilege within Egypt, as speedily as possible. Since 1882 Egypt had been occupied by Great Britain, following the coincidence of an army revolt in Egypt and a revolt in Sudan against Egyptian rule. Formally neutral in both world wars, Egypt had, in fact, served as an important operational base for Britain in both wars. Declared formally independent by the British in 1922, Egypt had to wait until the Anglo-Egyptian treaty of 1936 before achieving any measure of control in her foreign relations, and even this was circumscribed by the requirement that Britain should be able to maintain a permanent military base in the Suez Canal zone—though with provision for negotiation on the terms of Britain's occupancy after twenty years.[52]

Egypt emerged from the Second World War determined to revise the 1936 treaty; in particular, to secure the removal of British troops from her soil, and to end British control over the Sudan in the expectation of joining Egypt and the Sudan in the "Unity of the Nile Valley".[53] Ironically, it was Great Britain who brought Egypt actively into Arab politics and persuaded her leaders to take a leading rôle in the Arab

---

[50] See Jean and Simonne Lacoutre, *Egypt in Transition* (London, 1958), pp. 221-2; and *Economist*, 27 July 1957 (p. 313), 'Neutralism was not invented by President Nasser and the Syrian socialists. It is almost as old as Arab nationalism itself."

[51] See Anwar G. Chejne, "Egyptian Attitudes Toward Pan-Arabism" in *Middle East Affairs*, Summer 1957, pp. 253-68.

[52] For details, see *The Middle East*, pp. 183-90; and Lenczowski, pp. 393-406.

[53] For details, see Lenczowski, pp. 406-14. Eventual Sudanese independence in 1956 was a rebuff to Egyptian hopes of an Egyptian/Sudanese union.

League,[54] founded in 1945. The creation of the state of Israel in 1948 gave the Arab League a common enemy, and added an immediate and lasting sore to Egyptian and, indeed, to Arab hatred and distrust of great power policies. The humiliation suffered by the Arab, and especially the Egyptian, armies in the Palestine war against Israel was a potent factor making for the creation of the Arab Collective Security Pact of 1950,[55] and in paving the way for the eventual overthrow of the Egyptian monarchy in 1952.[56]

While it is true that prior to the overthrow of the monarchy in July 1952 Egyptian leaders failed to secure the eviction of British troops from Suez and a new settlement of Sudan's status,[57] they nevertheless had endeavoured to demonstrate Egypt's neutralism in the Cold War and dissatisfaction with the continuance of formal ties with Britain by such acts as: concluding trade agreements with the Soviet Union in February 1948 and July 1951,[58] by refusing to contribute forces to the United Nations contingent in Korea as a protest against British "occupation";[59] and by unilaterally repudiating both the Anglo-Egyptian treaty of 1936 and the Anglo-Egyptian agreement on the Sudan of 1899, just two days after the receipt of a proposal that Egypt should join with other Middle Eastern states and with Western powers in a Middle East Defence Organization, in October 1951.[60]

In its first two years of power the new military regime, and Nasser in particular, not only consolidated its power, and inaugurated internal reforms,[61] but also secured an agreement with Britain concerning the future of the Sudan and another one laying down conditions for the evacuation of the Suez Canal base.[62] There was hard bargaining,

[54] See J. S. Raleigh, "Ten Years of the Arab League" in *Middle East Affairs*, Mar., 1955, pp. 65-77.

[55] See Keith Wheelock, *Nasser's New Egypt* (London, 1960), p. 207. It is this pact which Nasser later referred to as "the best possible system to defend our part of the world against any possible aggression".

[56] For an account of the background and course of 'the revolution' see Anwar el Sadat, *Revolt on the Nile* (London, 1955). Gamal Nasser's tract, *The Philosophy of the Revolution*, written about 1953 (Economical books, Buffalo, 1959), has only cursory references to the revolution and is, as Neguib suggests (*Egypt's Destiny*, p. 215), better regarded as giving the psychology of the revolutionaries.

[57] Though the Sidki-Bevin agreement of 1946 proposed terms concerning the Suez Canal Zone quite acceptable to the Egyptians, they eventually refused to ratify the agreement on account of the Sudanese question. See Lenczowski, pp. 410-12.

[58] *Ibid.*, p. 416.

[59] *Ibid.*, p. 418. India, Yugoslavia, and Egypt were all sitting as non-permanent members of the Security Council when the Korean War began. See Eric F. Goldman, *The Crucial Decade and After, 1945-1960* (New York, 1961), pp. 150-61.

[60] See Campbell, pp. 39-47.

[61] For details, see Wheelock, pp. 209-218.

[62] See Wheelock, pp. 209-18.

domestic opposition, and some give and take, on both sides. Though at one stage an Egyptian spokesman "hinted strongly . . . that Egypt would align herself with the neutralist bloc of Asian nations[63] in an effort to end Britain's 'imperialist' occupation of the Suez Canal Zone",[64] on the whole, Egypt seemed to be assuming a markedly pro-Western orientation, if only in expectation of substantial economic and military aid from the West,[65] and Egyptian-Israeli relations were probably less tense than at any previous time since 1948.[66] Even so, the Israelis were neither unaware nor were they undisturbed by the removal of what they had hitherto regarded as British restraint on Egypt. Furthermore, in Western eyes the key to the defence of the Middle East now passed from Egypt to Turkey, and for Britain this was a price she paid for continued co-operation with the United States. The British withdrawal from the Suez base marked a second, decisive, end-point in Britain's traditional strategy. The first had come with the withdrawal from India, which had been the largest reservoir of manpower overseas for British military operations. The pivotal importance of India in British strategy had been based on a continuance of maritime strength and of control of the Suez isthmus linking Asia and Africa. In securing British withdrawal from Suez the Egyptians achieved what they regarded as a great nationalist triumph, for it was the first big Western overseas military base to be disbanded. And however much the British government justified the move on strategic grounds there is little doubt that Egyptian agitation against continued British presence played a part in shaping the British decision. Some idea of the importance of the base may be gained from the fact that it covered an area as large as Wales and the installations were valued at between £500 m. and £700 m.[67]

The time between the signature of the Anglo-Egyptian agreements on Suez in October 1954, and the nationalization of the Suez Canal Company in July 1956, was seminal in the shaping of Nasser's neutralist policy, and it was during this period that its general character began to unfold. Until 1954 Nasser had been content to speak for Egypt, henceforward he assumed the rôle of chief spokesman and champion of the

[63] Official representatives of twelve Afro-Asian countries convening in Cairo on 23 Dec. 1952 held the first meeting of its kind outside the U.N.

[64] Quoted in Wheelock, p. 215; see also F. S. Northedge, *British Foreign Policy* (London, 1962), esp. pp. 215-41.

[65] These expectations did not preclude the expression of such sentiments as "The so-called 'free world', particularly the United States, proclaim they are helping to attain self-determination and are helping underdeveloped countries to advance. We consider such talk as opium administered by the 'free world' to enslaved peoples so that they may remain under its domination and not seek liberation." Nasser, 27 Nov. 1953, quoted in Wheelock, p. 215.

[66] See Lacouture, *Egypt in Transition*, pp. 208-9.

[67] See F. S. Northedge, p. 215.

'Arab People'.[68] Nasser's working assumption from 1954 onwards seems to be that all Arabs, all 'true' nationalists in Afro-Asia, are naturally neutralists. If African or Asian states are not neutralist this is due, on this view, to the perversities of governments, not the desires of their subjects. Since 1954 Egypt has become a home in exile for discontented Arab nationalists and for many other dissident nationalists.

The Israeli commando attack on Egyptian territory in Gaza at the end of February 1955 brought about a swift deterioration in Egyptian/ Israeli relations and heightened Egypt's quest for arms and diplomatic support, especially through co-operation with 'friendly' Arab states.[69] In the following September Nasser announced the purchase of a substantial amount of arms from Czechoslovakia, forced on Egypt, he said, because "the West refuses us the means of defending our existence".[70] Simultaneous bargaining with both Cold War camps was becoming one of Nasser's favourite tactics, and perhaps his most novel and influential contribution to neutralist diplomacy. Certainly, Nasser was the first significant neutralist to pursue a policy of active dalliance[71] with both camps, taking the initiative himself, in attempts to elicit aid. "We have invented positive neutralism",[72] claimed Mohammed Husanain Haykal, one of Nasser's chief spokesmen, the day after the Soviets offered to build Egypt an atomic power station and immediately following the West's first offer to finance the Aswan High Dam.[73] Tito may have led the way in showing that aid could be obtained without sacrificing one's independence, but Nasser was the first neutralist to actively exploit the opportunities latent in the situation created by the new Soviet line—of offering aid and diplomatic support to certain neutralist nations—by

[68] "The dependent peoples, in particular, come (to Cairo) to voice their grievances. Cairo is the capital of malcontents and sans-culottes." Quoted from J. and S. Lacouture, p. 412, see also pp. 216-18, 512.

[69] Egyptian reactions to Israeli action and to Western proposals for regional defence are documented in R.I.I.A., *Documents for 1955*, pp. 284-336; see esp. the Egyptian-Syrian Mutual Defence Pact, 20 Oct. 1955 and the Egyptian-Saudi Arabian Mutual Defence Pact, 27 Oct. 1955.

[70] In Oct. 1954 an Egyptian government spokesman had admitted that Nasser had renounced American military aid—because "the conditions imposed" were "incompatible with respect for our national sovereignty". Lacouture, p. 215.

[71] This is the application in Cold War terms of what the Lacoutures describe (p. 224) as Nasser's principal diplomatic tactic — leverage. "Means: a lever. Objective: to smash one by one the shackles on Egyptian independence. He made excellent use of the American lever against the British . . . Against the Americans he used the Soviet lever."

[72] *Ibid.*, p. 244. Nasser's first recorded use of the term "positive neutrality" was in Sept. 1956 after the Brioni conference, but this usage is not invariable and Nasser sometimes speaks as well, or instead, of "positive peaceful coexistence" or simply of "non-alignment".

[73] For the significance of the Aswan Dam in Nasser's schemes, see *ibid.*, pp. 388, *et. seq.*, also Wheelock, *Nasser's New Egypt*, chapter viii.

pitting Soviet and American offers against each other. Whereas Tito had accepted offers of aid, though after close scrutiny, Nasser was soliciting rival tenders.

One other significant aspect of Egypt's neutralist policy took shape during 1955. This was Egypt's undoubted emergence not only among the ranks of the neutralist states, but among the leaders. The year began with Nasser calling on Tito in Yugoslavia and ended with Tito repaying the visit in Cairo. In between times, Nasser attended the Bandung Conference,[74] where he was accorded a leading rôle, secured Chinese support for the Arabs' case against Israel, and had several long consultations with Nehru. Apart from both being Afro-Asian neutralists, Nehru and Nasser were at this time facing a common problem: both were opposed to the newly created Baghdad Pact. Whatever the intensity of their opposition to 'Cold War moves' near to their own frontiers, this was undoubtedly heightened for Nehru by the fact that Pakistan was associated with the scheme, and for Nasser because of Iraq's membership of the Pact. Egyptian opposition was a contributory factor in limiting the membership of the Baghdad Pact[75] just as, similarly, Indian opposition helped to limit the membership and restrict the operations of S.E.A.T.O.; but whereas Nehru attempted no military-diplomatic countermove, Nasser's opposition led to the conclusion of two military agreements, with Syria and with Saudi Arabia, both during October 1955, each of which placed the signatories' armed forces under a joint command headed by Egyptian generals.[76]

As well as these military measures, Nasser continued to try to strengthen his diplomatic friendships with fellow neutralists, especially with India and with Yugoslavia—as the Brioni meeting between Nehru, Tito and Nasser in July 1956 was, no doubt, intended to show. Yet Nasser, accompanied by Nehru, had only just left Yugoslavia, on 20th July, when he learnt of the abrupt withdrawal of the American

[74] On his return from Bandung, Nasser said, during a speech to a Cairo crowd: "I went to Bandung to announce that Egypt has been liberated, and that it speaks for the cause of self-determination and freedom of the nations, the suppression of imperialism, and the independence of all states." Reported in *New York Times*, 3 May 1955. Many commentators date Nasser's popularity in Egypt and throughout the Arab world from the time of his return from Bandung. For the significance of Bandung for Nasser, see Georgina Stevens, "Arab Neutralism and Bandung" in *Middle East Journal*, Spring 1957, pp. 139-52; Keith Wheelock, *op. cit.*, pp. 225; and "Nasser Imports Bandoengism" in *Economist*, 24 Mar. 1956, p. 649. Nasser first began to talk publicly of Arab 'Socialism' after his return from Bandung.
[75] This applies mostly to Jordan, which was linked to Iraq by dynastic ties and was virtually a client state of Britain. See *Economist*, 20 Apr. 1957, pp. 200-2; also Sir John Glubb, *A Soldier with the Arabs* (London, 1957), pp. 378, 422, 425-6; and *The Middle East*, p. 31, for contrasting views.
[76] See Lenczowski, p. 429; *Economist*, 24 Mar. 1956, p. 649.

offer to provide aid in the building of the Aswan High Dam. It was one of the ironies of this withdrawal that Dulles' success in wresting aid for Yugoslavia from an unwilling Congress had reduced the chances of giving financial assistance to Egypt.[77] Already the same week had brought Nasser two diplomatic setbacks: for the Soviet Union had concluded a sizeable oil deal with Israel which dealt a severe blow to the Arab economic boycott, and Tito and Nehru did not subscribe fully to Nasser's views on Algeria, Israel and east Africa.[78] It seemed that Nasser's prestige and projects might be irretrievably deflated.

Nasser's long and impassioned speech at Alexandria on 26th July[79] marked the beginning of his rebound. In its style and themes it was a striking example of Arab neutralist rhetoric. There was a swift and partial *résumé* of modern Arab history, a lauding of the Brioni Conference for marking the confluence of the strongest neutralist and Arab nationalist currents, bitter denunciation of Western imperialism and especially Israel as the creation and lackey of imperialism, some mild compliments for the Soviet Union, a somewhat cryptic claim that Egypt had achieved economic as well as political independence, and an announcement that Egypt had rejected an alliance with Britain in 1953 because such an agreement would not really have been an alliance but an act of submission. But the real sting and substance of the speech came right at the end with the announcement that the Suez Canal Company had, just that day, been nationalized.

The nationalization of the Suez Canal Company, the Suez War,[80] and their aftermath, restored Nasser's prestige and showed the wide sympathy and diplomatic support that a neutralist state could secure in repelling what is widely believed, or said, to be 'imperialist' pressures. The Soviet Union and Communist China[81] quickly showed that any neutralist state at loggerheads with Western powers could count on their support, and there began a period of close Egyptian/Sino-Soviet accord. By contrast, equivocal American attempts, under the shadow of impending Presidential elections, to reconcile the antagonists only estranged the United States from both sides. Subsequently, Egypt

---

[77] See Wheelock, pp. 195-6; J. and S. Lacouture, p. 419.

[78] See Wheelock, pp. 195, 237, 253, and R. St. John, *The Boss* (1961), pp. 209-16.

[79] See R.I.I.A., *Documents for 1956*, pp. 77-113.

[80] For details, see Wheelock, *passim*; Guy Wint and Peter Calvocoressi, *Middle East Crisis* (Penguin Books, 1957); and R.I.I.A., *Survey for 1956-8*, pp. 3-72.

[81] An English Sinophil has clearly pointed to the significance of this: "When the Suez crisis took place China was probably Egypt's staunchest supporter . . . In August, she made most of her sterling assets available to Egypt after the British Government had frozen Cairo's account . . . " This led Egypt not only to increase trade with China, but also enabled her "to continue trading with other sterling area countries (e.g. India and Ceylon)." Victor Purcell, *China* (London, 1962), pp. 260-1.

abstained on all ten U.N. General Assembly resolutions criticizing Soviet aggression on Hungary.[81]

Throughout Asia and Africa widespread, if somewhat variegated, gestures of support and sympathy for the Egyptian cause during the Suez crisis seemed to encourage Egypt to revive and revitalize ideas of Afro-Asian solidarity, which had languished somewhat since the Bandung Conference. By the end of 1957 Cairo had become the head-quarters of the permanent non-governmental Afro-Asian movement,[82] and Egypt and the Sino-Soviet bloc seemed to be working in close harness.[83]

The identification of Egypt and the Communist powers in the so-called 'Afro-Asian People's Movement'—though uneasy and necessarily temporary—was not unnatural. For continental imperialism[84] of the types represented by international Communism and Nasser's brand of pan-Arab nationalism can work together[85] so long as there is rough agreement about a common enemy—in this case 'imperialism'—and before there is any serious argument as to who should be master and arrange the division of spoils. Communists and Nasserite nationalists each believe that 'the people' are on their side, even if governments are not; that political boundaries are inherently temporary and must, in any case, be re-drawn. Both are self-consciously proletarian movements;[86] and Moscow radio is roughly paralleled by Cairo radio, Communist magazines by Arab nationalist magazines; Communist party zealots by Egypt's expatriate teachers.[87] The analogy must not be pushed too far but there are sufficient similarities to explain why a temporary coinci-

[81] Later Nasser explained that these abstentions were "because the Soviet Union was the only country in the Security Council that supported us in our dispute over Suez. We abstained out of gratitude." See interview reported in *Daily Express*, 11 June 1957.

[82] See P. H. Lyon, "The Pan-Continental Movements of Asia and Africa, 1947-58" in *Australian Outlook*, June 1959, pp. 100-11.

[83] See Wheelock, pp. 254-5, 266-70; and W. Z. Laqueur, *The Soviet Union and the Middle East* (London, 1959), pp. 307-11.

[84] See Hannah Arendt, *The Burden of Our Time* (London, 1951), chapter viii, "Continental imperialism: the Pan-Movements".

[85] This is the main theme of the study by W. Z. Laqueur, cited in n. 83 above. See esp. pp. 316-47.

[86] Though Communists by doctrine and pan-Arab nationalists more by feeling. "The national movements in Africa and Asia, and those in the Middle East most of all, remind one more and more of proletarian associations. They have the same harshness and energy caused by long years of waiting and a lasting sense of frustration. The Arabs as a whole are people who all complain in the same language of the same humiliation, and same hunger." Lacouture, p. 513.

[87] See *The Times*, 8 and 9 Oct. 1958—"African War of Words"; and *Economist*, 27 Apr. 1957, pp. 289-90, "Egypt's Empire-Builders", which says that Egypt's prime instruments of propaganda are Cairo radio, illustrated weekly magazines and the export of teachers.

K

dence of Soviet and Egyptian aims need not be seen as wholly fortuitous.

This apparent Egyptian-Soviet accord lasted until the inauguration of the United Arab Republic in February 1958. Indeed, Egypt, as well as Syria, seemed to be becoming increasingly dependent economically on the Soviet bloc during these years, as the Western powers generally boycotted Egypt and Syria. There are indications that Nasser was disturbed by this growing dependence on the Soviets,[88] but such gestures as his October 1957 decree ordering all branches of the government and the press to present Egypt as a strictly neutralist country, and his reported willingness to substitute for the phrase "positive neutrality", with its unfavourable connotations in the West, the more euphemistic term "non-alignment", were not sufficient to bring about an appreciable *détente* with the West.[89] Egyptian tirades against Western interests and pro-Western elements throughout the Middle East and Africa continued unabated throughout 1957, and tensions in Egyptian relations with the Communist powers did not become fully apparent until the following year.

In fact, Nasser restored a great deal of his freedom of manoeuvre between East and West, following the union of Egypt and Syria in February 1958. Though the initiative came from Syria, in a little more than a year the overwhelming dominance of Egyptian leadership in this new United Arab Republic was patent, as was underlined by the eclipse of the Syrian Arab Socialist Baath Party which (with the Army) had led the movement for union.[90] Indeed, for a while 1958 seemed to be a year in which Egyptian ascendancy throughout the Middle East would be assured: with convulsions in Jordan and in Lebanon, which for a time seemed likely to precipitate pro-Nasser *coups*; and with regicide and revolution in Iraq seeming, at first, to mark a *détente* in the traditional rivalry between Cairo and Baghdad. Soon, however, it became clear that Egyptian ascendancy was not going to be achieved so smoothly. The regimes in Jordan and Lebanon remained in power with British and American support respectively, and Kassem's new regime in Iraq showed no strong enthusiasm for close relations with Egypt. Furthermore, relations with the Soviet Union now became considerably cooler, no doubt because the U.A.R's opposition to domestic Communists was intensified, because Soviet influence in Syria had been nullified, and because Nasser was achieving a *détente* with the United

[88] See Laqueur, chapter v. "Soviet Trade and Economic Aid: 1954-1958".
[89] See Wheelock, p. 256; and *Daily Telegraph*, 10 Oct. 1957.
[90] See Wheelock, pp. 271-4; also *Spectator*, 27 Nov. 1959, p. 757. The union of the U.A.R. with the Yemen, proclaimed as the United Arab States in March 1958, remained merely a paper union. Egyptian support for Yemen's irredentist claims on Aden was obtainable without union. But by the last quarter of 1962 Egyptian troops were fighting in the Yemen for the republicans against the supporters of the Yemen's royal dynasty.

States.[91] Certainly, from mid-1958 onwards Nasser made clear his preference for political connections with neutralist[92] rather than Communist states, and he began to pursue an active line in the pan-African movement to the exclusion of the Soviet Union, and of China.

Again, ever since 1958 Nasser has seemed to strive for a foreign policy which, more clearly than before, is complementary to his domestic policy. He has striven for a fusion of social reform and of Egyptian led pan-Arabism; and this has meant abandoning the loose and fundamentally uneasy connections made with the Arab royal dynasties of Jordan, Saudi Arabia and the Yemen in 1954-7, to stress instead republican-socialist causes throughout the Arab lands. The Union with Syria in 1958 seemed a substantial first move towards pan-Arab-socialist goals, because Nasser not only thereby achieved a foothold in the Fertile Crescent but also because he captured and adopted the Syrian Baathist Socialist programme himself. Nasser then pressed forward with a domestic programme of widespread nationalization and state control, as expressed, for example, in the socialist July Laws of 1961. Though the defection of Syria from the U.A.R., by the action of Syrian army officers in September 1961, was a serious setback to his plans and prestige it was significant that the secession was frankly admitted to be a setback, no more and no less. By December 1962, every Arab government, whatever its political colouring, had to take serious stock of what its relations with President Nasser's regime ought to be. For Jordan and Saudi Arabia this was the dominant issue of their politics; while the greater part of Syria's recent history, notorious for its turbulence, has been shaped by various attempts at a solution. It was a major issue in the 1958 civil war in Lebanon, and was still an unresolved issue in the Yemini civil war still being fought at the end of 1962. It was a continuing concern for Iraq, as it was for the Maghreb states too.

By 1962 Nasser had gained some considerable standing on wider fronts too. He enjoyed circumspect, yet correct, relations with the U.S.S.R. and with the United States, though not now with China. He had been instrumental, with Tito, in arranging for the Belgrade

[91] See Wheelock, ibid., pp. 261-2, 275-6; and Observer, 18 May 1958. On 16 May 1958 Nasser said in a speech in Cairo: "I feel that this policy, for the maintenance of which we have struggled, this independent policy of positive neutralism and non-alignment, has finally triumphed, having been recognized by the two strongest powers in the whole world, the Soviet Union and the United States." See Wheelock, p. 262.

[92] In May 1958 Nasser paid a visit to Moscow where he was careful to present himself as a neutralist and to stress his friendship for Tito, despite an intensification of Soviet bloc tirades against Yugoslavia during his stay. It is reported that before leaving for Moscow Nasser called for the complete file of Nehru's speeches during the latter's recent Russian tour. See Observer, 18 May 1958.

Neutralist Summit conference in 1961. Egypt was playing a leading rôle in the Casablanca grouping of revisionist African states. And Cairo was the venue of the July 1962 economic conference of the non-aligned, called to discuss such questions as (1) the impact of the E.E.C. on outsiders, (2) how to work out schemes for controlling commodity prices in world markets, and (3) the sources and conditions of international aid.

'Positive neutrality'[93] as practised by Nasser since 1955 seems to be a policy which, despite its name, has been sustained principally by two powerful negative themes—by opposition to all that is thought to be great power interference or imperialism, and by advocating a radical Arab nationalism. 'Positive neutrality' demands the right to be left alone but does not leave other states alone. It seeks to proselytize, yet it lacks a distinctive creed of its own.[94] It embodies a radical, resentful, linguistic nationalism, operating across state boundaries believed to be artificial and temporary; yet it appears to lack any precise plans for what has to succeed what is to be overthrown—perhaps because 'anti-imperialism' masks a 'neo-imperialism'. By great tactical skill and flexibility Nasser has raised Egypt's diplomatic standing; he has not produced any substantial measure of pan-Arab unity. Though he has initiated a number of long overdue domestic reforms,[95] population pressure and a still substantial dependence on cotton exports have meant that he has not so far brought about any appreciable increase in the standard of living of Egyptians.

*   *   *

Commenting on the July 1956 Brioni talks between Tito, Nehru and Nasser, a journalist wrote: "Their juxtaposition is a product of the Cold War, which all three condemn; an accurate image may be that of

---

[93] "Even those who try, now, to exploit the slogan of non-alignment and positive neutrality in order to conceal from their peoples their alignment to war camps and imperialism give indirect praise to our people. Our people were the pioneers in raising this slogan. Their sincere belief in, and their struggle for it, issues from a real need for it, in order to progress." The *National Charter* (Information Department, Cairo 1962), p. 82.

[94] Nasser: " . . . as far as ideologies go we still have no final position. We are still at the formative stage. We haven't really made our choice between liberalism and controls in matters of economics and politics. Our decisions will be taken according to specific problems and needs."—Quoted in Lacouture, p. 465. For similar statements, see Wheelock, pp. 216, 227, 236, 263. All this was before 1961. Presumably the *National Charter* of 1962 is intended to provide the official ideology hitherto lacking. If this is so, it cannot be claimed that the Charter is a very profound document. For, fascinating as it is, it is merely a strange mixture of verbal violence, crude Marxism, poetic aphorisms, potted history and panegyric for pan-Arabism. I am referring to an English translation obtained by me from the U.A.R. embassy in London.

[95] Consideration of Nasser's domestic policies is outside the scope of this short study but it is probable that in the eyes of the great majority of Egyptians his

the three men on an ice-floe, congratulating each other on the speed with which the warmth of their bodies is thawing it and yet not fully aware that they owe both their eminence and their close association to the ice-floe's continued existence."[96]

This suggestive but rather condescending image has some truth in it. But the rôles of these three men must not be seen only in terms of similar personal inclinations or without an appreciation of which of the currently popular aspects of neutralism they have each pioneered. For their policies stem not only from the contrasting personalities of their formulators, but also from the basic forces which impelled them to be neutralist.

Nehru began to shape India's neutralist policies at a time when the Cold War seemed to be essentially a European affair, though an admitted non-alignment anywhere was soon regarded with suspicion and hostility by the Cold War protagonists. Nehru provided neutralist policies with respectable arguments and, a little later, popularized the idea that neutralist states were eminently suited to act as moderators and conciliators. He invested neutralism with an air of moral grandeur, and of aloofness from Cold War squabbles. Studied moderation in language and action is Nehru's especial contribution to neutralism. India is the first and foremost of the new state neutralists, and Nehru has stood for a peaceful, moderate neutralism. By 1962 he was also trying to lead a national effort to show that a non-aligned state could resist and repel an invasion of national territory.

Tito was forced to adopt a neutralist course for Yugoslavia originally because of Yugoslavia's expulsion from the Soviet bloc. She became a neutralist state because it seemed the only way her leadership could retain their independent sway to shape Yugoslav Communism themselves. Her initial survival as a neutralist state was due to her willingness to shoulder a very heavy defence burden, to strongly resist Soviet bloc pressures, and to the tacit support of the Western powers. Yugoslavia showed that it was possible for a small state to resist great power pressures without becoming a formal member of a Cold War camp. Though something of a pariah in Europe, Yugoslavia, by virtue of skilful identification of her interests with such different states as Egypt, India, Burma, Ghana, and Indonesia, has subsequently become an honorary Afro-Asian state, thus avoiding diplomatic isolation. And as well as her unique position as an early defector from the Soviet camp,

---

regime is preferable to that of his predecessors. Nasser's domestic policies are analyzed in some detail in both Wheelock's and the Lacoutures' studies. See also the talk by the Irish Arabophil, Erskine Childers, "Nasser's Egypt" in *Listener*, 15 Nov. 1962, pp. 795-97.

[96] In *Economist*, 14 July 1956, p. 111, editorial entitled "Three men on the ice-floe".

willing to educate fellow neutralists about Marxism and the Communist world, she is a striking example of a state which has successfully gained considerable aid from both Cold War camps *and* has herself shown remarkable economic development. Her achievements to date thus chime with the aspirations of many newer neutralist states. Tito stands for a progressive, independent, Marxist neutralism.

Nasser pioneered two currently popular aspects of neutralist policies. Firstly, he successfully negotiated the evacuation of the large British military base in Suez, and in thus ridding the 'national soil' of a foreign base achieved what many neutralists have since done or aspire to do. Secondly, he was the first neutralist leader to actively and blatantly exploit Cold War rivalries, taking advantage of the new situation created when the Communist powers began to develop foreign trade and aid programmes to neutralist states. Another facet of Nasser's neutralism is of especial interest. By deliberately casting himself in the rôle of pupil of Nehru and of Tito, he was able to imply that there was no need for him to produce his own distinctive doctrine or justification for his policies, his neutralism was like that of his associates—even if his methods were more 'positive'. Nasser was thus the first of the frankly opportunist, unconcernedly undoctrinaire neutralists—many African neutralist leaders of the post-1957 period are like this now, their strength and weaknesses, like those of Nasser, depending very much on the nationalist movement they lead. Nasser has become a leading champion of radical, resentful, revisionist nationalism—the kind of nationalism distinguished by the over-estimation of one's own nation and the denigration of others, and by the tendency to attribute anything wrong with one's nation to the evil-doing of others. Nasser stands for a belligerently nationalist neutralist.

There are some striking contrasts in the policies which these three men practise. Tito's domestic Communism contrasts with Nehru's and Nasser's proscription of their domestic Communists. Nehru's long tried appeasement—though in the technical, not in the pejorative sense—of China contrasts with Nasser's continual state of war with Israel. To avert war anywhere, and especially with China or Pakistan, has been a constant principle of Nehru's policy; permanent war with Israel has been Nasser's constant theme. Tito and Nasser are fundamentally anti-Western in their sympathies and suspicions, and far, far more so than Nehru. Tito and Nasser are radical revisionists—though Nasser more so, in fact, than Tito—while Nehru is a meliorist. This list of contrasts could be extended, but we must come back to the fact of their association. Whether fortuitous or deliberated in its origins, it has now acquired a certain logic of its own. The kind of co-operation that now exists between these three states has been evident in such acts as: the joint, and unsuccessful, Indo-Soviet move,[97] in August 1962, to exclude Britain from the three-Power nuclear test ban talks and to replace Britain by India and the United Arab Republic; the meeting of Tito, Nehru and Nasser in Cairo[98] in November 1961, to consider common problems in the light of great power policies after the Belgrade Conference; and, Egypt and Yugoslavia's support for India in her border dispute with China.[99] And while there have been several reports, and at different times,[100] of rifts and strains in the relations between these three men, their consultations are likely to continue, if only because each is now widely recognized as a prominent leader in the neutralist world; and because they all feel they are fellow-travelling neutralists, and not fellow-travellers for either Moscow or Washington.

SWEDEN AND SWITZERLAND — THE TRADITIONAL NEUTRALS

Switzerland and Sweden are neutralist states in the sense that they are not members of any Cold War alliance. Only in this limited but important respect can these two countries be described as neutralist, for the vast majority of their citizens undoubtedly consider that they are part of the Western world. Yet, as if in disdain of the convolutions of the Cold War, these two prosperous states cling to their cherished national traditions of non-involvement in military alliances in peacetime and of neutrality in time of war. They can conveniently be considered together because in important respects they resemble each other and no other states.

Both states take pride in a great military past.[1] Both have now avoided active involvement in war for more than one hundred and forty years, while both have restrained, adapted and canalized their traditional skills into national policies of an alert, armed, but purely defensive, strength based on the skills and application of the most modern military techniques. Neither of them have colonial possessions, nor do they lay claim to any irredenta. Spiritual neutrality has never been demanded of their citizens or of their press.

Yet it would be wrong to assume that it is *merely* a long series of

[97] See *Guardian*, 25 Aug. 1962.

[98] See *New York Times*, 17 Nov. 1961; and *Guardian*, 18 Nov. 1961.

[99] See, e.g., *The Times*, 28 Nov. 1962.

[100] See, e.g., Keith Wheelock, pp. 237, 253; *Guardian*, 14 July 1956 and 20 Mar. 1960; and *Observer*, 24 May 1959.

[1] Both states illustrate Toynbee's principle of the transmigration of the martial spirit. See *A Study of History*, vol. ix, pp. 493-4. Switzerland (strictly "the Old Confederation") was at the height of its power between 1315 and 1515. See C. W. C. Oman, *The Art of War in the Middle Ages* (New York, 1953), pp. 93-116 and 160-72. Sweden's great power period was from 1611 to 1709. See Ingvar Andersson, *A History of Sweden* (New York, 1956).

lucky accidents[2] that has brought about their present prosperity and much envied neutrality. For Swedish, but more especially Swiss, national history is not only a quiet record of commercial progress but is full of narrow escapes from invasion, or at least involvement in war, and there is plenty of evidence that their statesmen have invariably appreciated that national survival depends on defensive strength and a constantly varying approximation of the desirable to the practicable. But a policy which survives through the years, which generations of statesmen practise and modify, gradually begins to take on the aspect of a dogma and to become independent of the purposes for which it was first devised. To a great extent this is now true of both Swiss and Swedish neutrality policies. Public explanations and justifications of present policies have to be placed within the cherished tradition; and so a study of Swiss and Swedish neutrality in the Cold War must first try to make clear the reasons for, and remember the continuing and powerful influence of, these distinct traditions.

*   *   *

The notion of Swiss neutrality is older than the notion of a Swiss nation. For a country—one of the smallest in Europe—which contains three official languages and two religions, and whose unity is achieved only by due respect for all these different elements,[3] neutrality was as much a necessary condition of internal stability as of external security. Swiss concepts of nationality are primarily territorial and to maintain unity between Catholic and Protestant, between Germanic, French and Italian speaking citizens, it has been vital to avoid dividing the national territory either by civil strife or by foreign invasion. Swiss history[4] shows that this has been far from easy. Religion in the seventeenth century, when the policy of neutrality was first developed in the Confederation, was as disruptive as political ideology today. The Swiss could

[2] Though this is a common contention, especially among the nationals of these countries; and it is interesting to note that a best-selling Swedish novel of 1952 —*Paradise for Us*—argued that Sweden's successful neutrality in the Second World War was entirely a matter of luck. Later it was discovered that the pseudonymous author was Gunnar Hagglof, one of the most brilliant younger Swedish diplomats.

[3] The total population at the 1960 census was 5,429,061, made up of German-speaking 69·5%; French-speaking 18·9%; Italian-speaking 9·5%. See *Annuaire Statistique de la Suisse 1961* (Bâle, 1962). Racial, religious, linguistic and territorial boundaries do not correspond. This is very important, because where people are disunited by ethnic background they are often brought together by common religion; see C. J. Hughes, *The Federal Constitution of Switzerland* (Oxford, 1954), pp. 88-9 and 128.

[4] William Martin, *Histoire de la Suisse* (Lausanne, 1943); Edgar Bonjour, *Swiss Neutrality*, translated by Mary Hottingen (London, 1946), and W. E. Rappard, *Collective Security in Swiss Experience* (London, 1948).

only retain their identity and their freedom in diversity by a policy which accommodated theological differences within the Confederation[5] but forbade an active bias towards one's co-religionists abroad Externally, much depended on the ability of her larger neighbours to balance, and so nullify, each other's designs on Swiss territory. Further deterrents were the mountainous topography, the absence of natural resources to capture and the military reputation of Swiss soldiers.

The defeat at Marignano in 1515 terminated Swiss pre-eminence in the Italian wars. Thereafter the Confederation sank into the modest rôle of a buffer between France, Austria, and the Spanish power in Italy; and developed a policy of neutrality which was proclaimed as a principle in 1674 at the beginning of the General Wars of 1672-1713, but as a policy developed only slowly and organically from the old Swiss policy of confederacy. The hope of the confederacy to keep its entire territory out of war by following a restrained foreign policy was realizable only if its neutrality was armed. Fearing that the adoption of international guarantees might be detrimental to its future chances of neutrality and lead to foreign entanglements, the confederacy continually refused to adopt such binding obligations. Even so, in these early years the Confederation's success as a neutral buffer probably owed much to the implicit support of France, though this point is not stressed by Swiss historians. From 1713 to 1789 the policy of Swiss neutrality was exposed to the reactions created by changes in the European equilibrium, and in the midst of these changes it required all the experienced diplomatic art of the old sovereigns to preserve the territorial integrity of the confederacy. Eventually, France became the first despoiler, after being the initial protector of Swiss neutrality. For it was during the French Revolutionary-Napoleonic wars that the most substantial violations of Swiss neutrality occurred: first, when, following the collapse of 1798, the whole of the country was for a time engulfed in the Napoleonic Empire; and, second, when her neutrality was disregarded by the Coalition Powers in 1814. At the end of these wars the independence and territorial integrity of Switzerland was guaranteed by the Great Powers in the "declaration of Vienna" in 1815, and for the first time the permanent neutrality of a small state became part of the law of nations.[6] What was implied by this neutralization

[5] The religious settlement of the Old Confederation followed the principle *cujus regio, ejus religio* of the Peace of Augsburg, 1555. The religious boundaries therefore coincided with the political boundaries, and the religious map of the present day is a patchwork which reproduces the sovereignty-structure of the Old Confederation. See Hughes, pp. 61-4.

[6] C. K. Webster, *Congress of Vienna* (London, 1945), p. 134. Technically, this process amounted to neutralization. In Switzerland today neutrality is part of the material, though not part of the formal, constitution and the "Assembly declares neutrality rather as other nations declare war": Hughes, p. 44, see also

was important: for it suggested that Switzerland had ceased to be a keypoint in the European order.

Whether or not the confederacy would possess sufficient strength to transfer into political actuality these proclaimed principles and whether the Great Powers would observe their solemn assurances remained to be seen. In fact, though the confederacy was subjected to certain restrictions by the Holy Alliance and was subsequently endangered on several occasions, Swiss territorial integrity was respected[7] throughout the nineteenth century and the First World War.[8] At the end of the war the Swiss cantons and people, by a narrow majority,[9] voted in favour of Switzerland's entry into the League of Nations; Geneva became the seat of the new international organization,[10] but Switzerland's special status as a permanently neutral state was recognized by a League Council resolution of 13th February 1920[11] which exempted her from the military obligations contained in the League Covenant.

Sweden, the third largest state in Europe territorially,[12] with a nationally homogeneous population, and situated on the fringes of the traditional European battlefields, achieved her position as a 'traditional' non-aligned state without suffering the process of neutralization, and so evolved a tradition of neutrality in war and non-involvement in alliances in time of peace more voluntarily and more gradually than Switzerland. The Swedes have never shown a marked liking for the terms 'neutral' or 'neutrality' to be applied to their own country's policy. Today they prefer the term 'non-alliance', while during the nineteenth century "the word neutrality tended in the popular vocabulary to become synonymous with a peace policy or a peace-loving

---

169-71. (By contrast, in Sweden neutrality is not deeply embedded in constitutional practices.)

[7] Somewhat precariously in 1847, when the seven R.C. cantons unsuccessfully tried to secede from the Confederation, see Jean Halperin, "The Transformation of Switzerland" in *The Opening of an Era: 1848*, ed. by François Fejto (London, 1948), pp. 50-66; and determinedly in the 1830s and 1856, 1859, 1860, 1866 and 1870, when the threat was rather from outside. See W. E. Rappard, p. 143, *et seq.*

[8] Luigi Albertini, *The Origins of the War*, translated by Isabella M. Massey (O.U.P., 3 vols., 1952-7). In vol. iii Albertini discusses: the neutrality of Switzerland, p. 685; Swiss pro-German sentiment, p. 685; the "Two Colonels" espionage scandal, p. 689.

[9] See André Siegfried, *Switzerland* (London, 1950), pp. 181-2; see also Hughes, p. 94, and George Soloveytchik, *Switzerland in Perspective* (London, 1954), pp. 230-6.

[10] Article 7 of the League Covenant.

[11] See A. J. Toynbee, *The World After the Peace Conference* (R.I.I.A., 1925), pp. 37-8; and David Hunter Miller, *The Drafting of the Covenant* (New York, 1928), pp. 437-8. See also Article 21 of the League Covenant and Article 435 of the Treaty of Versailles.

[12] Excluding European Russia. The two largest are France and Spain. The population of Sweden is approximately seven million.

policy. In reality, however, neutrality had never during those hundred years been a consistent password for Swedish foreign policy."[13]

Enjoying its Great Power period nearly a century after the waning of Switzerland's period of eminence, Sweden played a great part in the wars of Europe in the seventeenth and early eighteenth centuries. With the death of Charles XII in 1718, Swedish power was past its zenith, the resources of the nation had been over-taxed, and the last quarter of the eighteenth century was full of domestic unrest.[14] Despite these acute internal troubles, and her membership of the anti-British Armed Neutrality League between 1778 and 1780, Sweden joined Pitt's Third Coalition against France in 1805; and, until 1814, she was an active participant in the struggle against Napoleon. The Congress of Vienna recognized and confirmed the fortunes of war with respect to Scandinavia. Russia received Finland, which for five hundred and fifty years had been united with Sweden. While, by way of compensation, Sweden obtained Norway—though Castlereagh had to put pressure on Norway before she gave way.[15] Non-alignment as a national tradition only evolved after 1815, and then not because of any strong sense of the need for retirement from international politics, but because realistic appraisals of national strength always moderated any initial impulse to adopt an adventurous foreign policy. Between 1815 and 1914 Sweden was not, in fact, involved in war, though on several occasions her participation seemed imminent[16]—attracted each time by Scandinavian interests. Despite intense hostility to Russia and strong tendencies toward alliance with Germany by her governing and military classes, Sweden declared her neutrality on 4th August 1914.[17] Henceforward she consistently espoused a neutral policy and was instrumental in the unsuccessful attempt to secure respect for neutral rights[18] by co-operative neutral endeavour. At the end of the war, Sweden was one of the thirteen neutral states of the First World War which became original members of the League.[19]

[13] Quoted from *Sweden and the United Nations* (Swedish Institute of International Affairs, New York, 1956), p. 20.

[14] Ingvar Andersson, *A History of Sweden* (New York, 1956).

[15] C. K. Webster, *The Foreign Policy of Castlereagh* (London, 1950), vol. i, pp. 306-9.

[16] Herbert Tingsten, "Issues in Swedish Foreign Policy", *Foreign Affairs*, Apr. 1959, refers to Swedish activist movements in 1854-6; 1864; 1905; 1914; 1921; 1939. There was also an activist movement in 1848 in favour of intervention in Denmark. See F. Tegner, "The Events of 1848 in Scandinavia", in Fejto, pp. 167-79.

[17] Albertini, *op. cit.*, vol. iii, pp. 662, 669-72.

[18] Orvik, *The Decline of Neutrality, 1914-41* (Oslo, 1953), pp. 89-108.

[19] Resolutions to join the League passed by 86 votes to 47 in the Upper Chamber and 152 votes to 67 in the Lower. See *Sweden and the United Nations* (New York, 1956), pp. 17-19.

Far from happy with her new commitments, despite her special status as a League member, Switzerland's League policy was highly individual and somewhat temporizing.[20] Obliged to impose economic sanctions if necessary, the Swiss did not insist that this was the traditional policy nor were they preoccupied with the principle of 'neutrality' as a principle. Their predominant and characteristic concern was to ensure that the Swiss version of 'neutrality' was recognized and respected.[21] Nevertheless, so long as the security system of the League of Nations looked like working, the Swiss were prepared to 'differentiate' their 'neutrality'. But when Germany and Italy left the League and soon laid bare the weaknesses of the League collective security system, the Swiss government became convinced that their only hope of escaping involvement in a general war was for Switzerland to revert to her old policy of absolute 'neutrality'. This she did in 1938.[22] League recognition of this avowal of complete impartiality again illustrated Switzerland's remarkable success in securing international recognition for her peculiar status. The attitude of Hitler's Germany towards Switzerland from 1933 onwards was not characterized by a comparable degree of respect.[23]

Sweden's League policy was distinguished not so much by obsessive fears that her security and material well-being might be compromised by the obligations of League membership, but by an adroit and faithful[24] use of the facilities of the new international organization[25] to safeguard traditional interests. A judicious blend of internationalism with the long established policy of friendly relations with Germany was evinced in Swedish policy towards the Ruhr occupation problem in 1923, and over the question of Germany's admission to the League in 1926. By January 1938, in the face of the obvious collapse of the League collective security system, Sweden was first of the European neutrals of the First

[20] See the critical account of F. P. Walters, A History of the League of Nations (London, 1952), pp. 92-3, 123, 136, 184, 198, 765; a Swiss account by Jacqueline Belin, La Suisse et les Nations Unies (New York, 1956), pp. 39-58); G. Soloveytchik, "The League of Nations and Motta's era" in Switzerland in Perspective (London, 1954), pp. 227-50; and Walter R. Zahlen, "Switzerland and the League of Nations", A.P.S.R., Aug. 1936.
[21] See Rappard, p. 149.
[22] Orvik, p. 182; Hans J. Morgenthau, "The End of Switzerland's Differential Neutrality", A.J.I.L., 1938.
[23] Elizabeth Wiskemann, Undeclared War (London, 1939), pp. 280-309; and Edvard Hambro's exposition and rebuttal of National Socialist doctrines concerning neutrality. See "Ideological Neutrality" in Nordisk tidsskrift for international ret : Acta Scandinavica juris gentium, 1939 (vol. x, n. 2-3), pp. 109-17.
[24] See Aaland Islands question in F. P. Walters, pp. 103-5.
[25] H. Tingsten, The Debate on the Foreign Policy of Sweden 1919-1939 (London, 1949); see also chapter 3, "Sweden—the diplomacy of Oslen Unden" in The Diplomats 1919-1939, ed. by Gordon A. Craig and Felix Gilbert (New York, 1953), pp. 87-93.

World War to announce, in effect, its complete lack of confidence in the League system of security and its determination to rely on the *sauve-qui-peut* of rearmament.[26]

Throughout the Second World War both Switzerland and Sweden preserved their neutrality, though precariously, and not without some infringements.[27] From the politico-strategic point of view, the weakest point in both countries' boundaries was where their borders faced Germany. German invasion of Switzerland, which seemed certain on two occasions at least between 1940 and 1945, was thwarted by a mixture of economic appeasement and military threats. The latter included plans for the destruction of all the tunnels through the Alps, a scorched earth policy in the industrial areas of the north, and the military defence of the fortified Redoubt in the central mountains.[28] Sweden's policy,[29] even more than Switzerland's, shifted like a weathervane pointing the fortunes of war. Yet she sought, not always successfully, to reconcile national preservation with the active policy of giving generous help to other Scandinavian countries—her considerable aid to Finland amounting to non-belligerent intervention. During the war both countries provided humanitarian and diplomatic services, as well as valuable war material to both sides.

Since the Second World War both Switzerland and Sweden have been left much worse off strategically than they were after the First World War—this greater vulnerability has been publicly acknowledged by leading spokesmen in each country.[30] In part, of course, given the power and range of modern weapons, this is a predicament common to all states, but for these two states their security now seems more pre-

[26] Orvik, pp. 79-80; Hans J. Morgenthau, "The Resurrection of Neutrality in Europe", A.P.S.R., June 1939, pp. 473-86.

[27] W. N. Medlicott, *The Economic Blockade* (London, 1952 and 1959), vol. i, chapters 4, 5 (3), 17, 19; and vol. ii, chapters 6, 7, 16, 17

[28] See the memoirs of the British Minister in Berne, Sir David Kelly, *The Ruling Few* (London, 1953), chapter 13, esp. pp. 275-80 and 285; Constance Howard, "Switzerland 1939-46" in *The War and the Neutrals*, ed. by A. and V. M. Toynbee, R.I.I.A. (London, 1956); and Jon Kimche, *Spying for Peace. General Guisan and Swiss Neutrality* (London, 1961).

[29] Agnes H. Hicks, "Sweden" in *The War and the Neutrals*, ibid., pp. 171-99; Annette Baker Fox, *The Power of Small States. Diplomacy in World War II*, chapter 5—"Sweden: Armed Neutral" (London, 1959); and Gunnar Hagglof, "A Test of Neutrality: Sweden in the Second World War" in *International Affairs* (R.I.I.A., Apr. 1960), pp. 153-67. For a harsh Soviet criticism of Hagglof, see A. Pogodin, "Gunnar Hagglof's Short Memory" in *International Affairs* (Moscow, Feb. 1960), pp. 94-5.

[30] In Switzerland, for example, by M. Petitpierre, then Head of Swiss Dept. of Political Affairs, see *New York Times* 20 Mar. 1953, *Christian Science Monitor* 18 Apr. 1953, and *Times* 27 Mar. 1958. See also Professor Rappard reported in *Manchester Guardian* 22 Dec. 1952. In Sweden by her Foreign Minister, Osten Unden, see *Documents on Swedish Foreign Policy 1950-51* (Stockholm, 1957), p. 15.

carious than hitherto because of the eclipse of the European power balance which was one of the principal prerequisites of their success as free, independent states. In the dimensions of world politics, Western Europe has become as central, exposed and almost as small as Switzerland compared with the old European powers. And, as the Cold War alignments took shape, Switzerland, instead of being the still centre of a European system of delicately balanced antagonisms, has found herself surrounded (with the sole exception of post-1955 Austria) by states allied with America. For Sweden, too, the situation is radically changed. The pre-1939 Baltic power-balance has been overthrown. Instead of Germany balancing Russia, Germany is divided and the principal military bases in the Baltic are under the control of the Soviet Union. The semi-encirclement of Sweden was completed with Russian bases at Petsamo and Murmansk in the far north;[31] while, since 1949 (when Norway and Denmark joined N.A.T.O.) the chance that she will be able to keep out of a future third world war seems greatly reduced. Since 1953 Soviet leaders have often said that they are in favour of 'neutralizing' the Baltic, but have never said clearly that this would mean giving up Soviet land, sea and air bases in the Baltic region.

*   *   *

The international policies of these two countries in the post-war world show strongly the influence of their distinctive national traditions and experience. They have broadly similar defence and foreign economic policies but when it comes to associating with other states, Sweden's position has been less rigorous and more pragmatic than that of Switzerland—this last point is well illustrated in their different approaches to questions of European integration and to participation in the United Nations.

For both countries national defence means an armed defensive self-reliance with considerable attention to civil defence. But the problems of defence in the atomic age seem almost insuperable; and, as in other Western democracies, the heavy expenditure required for modern systems (quite apart from the vexed question of their dependability) arouses public controversy. Military leaders in both countries have voiced their disquiet about the efficacy of the old methods, while some people, loudly in Sweden and much more quietly in Switzerland, have advocated membership in, or at least association with, the N.A.T.O. powers.[32] Both countries still rely on long established conscript systems

[31] See Walter Kolarz, *Russia and Her Colonies* (London, 1952), pp. 88-95, for a brief discussion of the historical significance of Petsamo and Murmansk in Suedo-Russian relations.

[32] For Sweden see Tingsten, *Foreign Affairs*, Apr. 1959; and for Switzerland see *Sunday Telegraph*, 12 Feb. 1961, and *Daily Telegraph*, 10 Oct. 1961.

and not on standing armies, and pride themselves on the speed with which a large national army can be raised in this way within forty-eight hours,[33] with each man specially trained to fight on his national territory. Both countries have built up their air strength considerably since 1945, particularly since the Korean War and the advent of nuclear weapons.[34] Switzerland, naturally, has no navy, though, curiously, Great Britain keeps a naval attaché at Berne. Sweden has shown that hers is an 'active' form of non-alliance policy by allowing her navy, on occasions, to conduct manoeuvres with units of the fleets of the N.A.T.O. powers.[35]

Basically, both countries follow a strategy of deterrence—aimed at convincing a would-be aggressor that the cost of aggression would be disproportionate to any likely gains. As it is often argued that the only way to deter a nuclear aggressor is to possess nuclear weapons oneself (the directly opposite argument is that the mere possession of such weapons ensures that an aggressor must nullify that nuclear capability at the outbreak of war), there has been some debate in both countries whether they should equip themselves with nuclear weapons. The situation at the end of 1962[36] was that both countries had postponed taking a decision on this matter. Quite apart from the enormous cost of manufacturing these weapons, while the present nuclear powers are reputedly unwilling to sell (and for Switzerland, particularly, there would be difficulties in testing all but the smallest weapons), it may be that both countries have been influenced, while officially repudiating, the Soviet Union's oft repeated contention that possession of nuclear weapons is incompatible with 'neutrality'.[37] In both countries civil

[33] See The Swedish Army (London, 1955) and Economist Supplement on Sweden (29 Oct. 1955). Sweden makes nearly all her purchases of arms in Britain. See E. Wiskemann, "The State of Switzerland in 1956" in International Affairs (R.I.I.A., Oct. 1956), pp. 436-45; The Times Supplement on Switzerland (5 Oct. 1959); Hughes, op. cit., pp. 13-19; and George A. Codding, Jnr., "The New Swiss Capability" in Foreign Affairs (Apr. 1962), pp. 489-94.

[34] The growth can be traced in the annual volumes of Jane's All the World's Aircraft. Both countries have modern jet fighters. In 1955 Sweden had the fourth largest air force in the world with a front line strength of 1,200 planes. The Swiss bought 100 British Hunter jet fighters in 1958.

[35] Documents on Sweden's Foreign Policy 1950-51 (Stockholm, 1957), p. 27. Cf. India whose navy has conducted manoeuvres in Asian waters with the fleets of fellow Commonwealth members.

[36] For a lucid and informed discussion, see Beaton and Maddox, The Spread of Nuclear Weapons (Chatto and Windus for the Institute for Strategic Studies, 1962). See chapter 9—Sweden; and chapter 10—Switzerland.

[37] For illustrations of typical Soviet attitudes, see O. Afanasyera, "Switzerland. Neutrality Armed with the Hydrogen Bomb" in International Affairs (Moscow), Oct. 1958, pp. 92-3; and D. Melnikov, "Scandinavia Today: Sweden", ibid., Dec. 1958, pp. 53-7.

defence is regarded as an integral and important part of their country's defence, and is given far more attention than in most countries within N.A.T.O.[38]

In the age-long argument between the two main schools of Swiss military strategy, Cold War conditions seem to have favoured, for psychological as well as purely military reasons, the advocates of a flexible defence of the frontier. For it is this policy which has gained official approval since 1945, as against the alternative policy of retirement to 'the alpine redoubt'.[39]

For Sweden the American project to create N.A.T.O. compelled her to re-examine her non-alliance policy, to reappraise her relations with her immediate neighbours, and it touched off a domestic debate of great importance and complexity.[40] Swedish army leaders argued, in effect, that the military basis of Sweden's traditional policy was now virtually untenable and were in favour of joining N.A.T.O. But the government leaders replied that their concern was with the political as well as the military aspects of the problem, that Sweden's traditional policy did much to allay Russian suspicions, and Russian hostility would be too high a price for the limited military assistance they were likely to receive on joining N.A.T.O. The position and importance of Finland weighed heavily in the arguments of both sides, and especially in Swedish appraisals of Soviet policy. For in the political and the military sense, Finland is Sweden's 'alarm clock'. There was never any strong probability that Sweden would join N.A.T.O., and the Swedish government's alternative proposal for a Ten Year Neutral Nordic Defence Union was rejected by Denmark and Norway, mainly because their experiences of neutrality had been less happy than Sweden, and the economic sacrifices involved were considered too great. Furthermore, Sweden was economically and militarily the strongest of the three, and it is also noticeable that both Norway and Denmark are North Atlantic powers, whereas Sweden is wholly a Baltic state.[41] Conflicting conceptions of national interest had again shown the flimsiness of pan-Scandinavianism. Sweden has remained attached, however, to most non-military forms of

[38] For Swedish civil defence, see Philip Noel Baker, *The Arms Race* (London, 1958), pp. 168-9; and *Guardian*, 8 Dec. 1961. For Swiss civil defence, see *The Times*, 9 Oct. 1959.

[39] See esp. the speech of the Chief of the Swiss General Staff, Colonel Annasohn, reported in *Guardian*, 3 Dec. 1959; and *Bulletin Sténographique officiel de l'Assemblée fédérale* (Bern, 1960), session d'automne, 4e session de la 36e legislature, esp. pp. 619-28.

[40] See Harald Wigforss, "Sweden and the Atlantic Pact", *International Organization*, Aug. 1949, pp. 434-43; and I. William Zartman, "Neutralism and Neutrality in Scandinavia" in *Western Political Quarterly*, June 1954, pp. 143-60.

[41] For Danish and Norwegian neutralism, see Zartman, *op. cit.*, pp. 125-44.

co-operation with her Scandinavian neighbours.[42] As soon as Norway and Denmark joined N.A.T.O., Sweden immediately devoted attention to the strengthening of her air force and to the provision of defences against submarines and mines in the Baltic.

In both Switzerland and Sweden military leaders have said that in the event of their territory being attacked, their aim would be to hold off the aggressor until they could secure help from the N.A.T.O. powers. The diplomatic implications of this are important and tend to contradict, or at least dilute, their claims of self-reliance and non-committedness. Yet effective military co-operation cannot be built up overnight—as the Belgians found in 1940—though unless actual invasion is thought of as highly likely, it can hardly be maintained that the soldiers' diplomatic indiscretions prove the anachronistic nature of their military policy.

In their foreign economic policies Sweden and Switzerland are directly dependent on foreign trade for the continuance of their present national ways of life, which presuppose the need for both a high defence capability and the preservation of a high standard of living for their nationals. The greatest problem in this connection is a pressing shortage of certain raw materials. Sweden regularly imports coal, iron, oil and petroleum products and textile fibres. Switzerland normally imports nine-tenths of her raw materials, particularly oil, coal and iron. Both countries usually have an adverse trading balance of imports against exports on their current accounts, though Switzerland much more so than Sweden. Receipts from her mercantile shipping enable Sweden to more than offset her trading deficit, while overseas investments, banking, insurance and the tourist industry enable Switzerland to achieve a favourable overall balance of payments position. Since 1945 both countries have increased their trade with each of the superpowers, though trade with the Soviet Union is still relatively small. Both countries feel a greater dependence on the United States than their trading figures indicate, for they fear that their own prosperity is inextricably linked with the continuance of American prosperity, an American recession could mean a Swiss or Swedish depression.[43] Because both countries favour liberalization and multilateralism in trade and avoid associations which they feel might compromise their 'neutrality', they

[42] See Raymond E. Lindgren, "International Co-operation in Scandinavia", Y.B.W.A. 1959, pp. 95-114.

[43] For details on the above points see the annual volumes of the U.N. Yearbook of International Trade Statistics. Specifically, see "Switzerland. Oasis of Free Enterprise" by Blair Bolles in Foreign Policy Reports, New York, 15 Jan. 1950, and G. Soloveytchik, "Switzerland Copes with Prosperity" in Lloyds Bank Review, July 1957; Economist Supplement on Sweden, 29 Oct. 1955. In 1946 Switzerland and U.S.S.R. resumed diplomatic and commercial relations after a break of 22 years. In 1946 Sweden signed a highly controversial Trade and Credit Agreement with the U.S.S.R., and a far less controversial trade pact in Jan. 1959.

L

both have joined the 'Outer Seven' of the European Free Trade Association (E.F.T.A., launched in 1959), rather than the 'Six' of the European
Common Market (E.E.C., launched in 1957). It is typical that Sweden
(with Britain) played a leading part in the formation of the 'Seven' and
—during the first eighteen months of E.F.T.A's life—in the efforts at
'bridge-building' with the 'Six',[44] while Switzerland played a very quiet
rôle.[45]

Since the British government announced its decision in July 1961 to
begin negotiations under Article 237 of the Rome Treaty to see if she
could become a full member of the E.E.C., both countries began to
reappraise their policies towards the Common Market and see if, and
on what terms, they were prepared to see 'association' with the E.E.C.
While both countries were at one in stressing that their policies must
neither involve them in formal political or military commitments, nor
decrease the likelihood that they would be able to be neutral in any
actual war, this need to re-define their respective positions towards the
E.E.C. posed more acute problems for Switzerland than for Sweden.
Swedish spokesmen seemed to prefer a course that would secure their
country associate status under Article 238 of the Rome Treaty, though
this did not seem to be looked on as an unavoidable necessity. By contrast, Switzerland seemed to regard associate status under Article 238
with great misgivings, and yet to be very fearful of the consequences of
not reaching some understanding with the E.E.C. powers. Switzerland
suffers some embarrassments from which Sweden is free. Both geographically and economically Switzerland is in the middle of the E.E.C.
area, whereas Sweden is at the fringes. The Swiss Federal constitution
gives important economic powers to the cantons, which the Federal
Government cannot of its own volition and without complex internal
procedures bargain away. Not only are Switzerland's major trade
channels through two E.E.C. countries, Italy and Western Germany,
but her growing dependence on foreign—mostly Italian[46]—labour could
expose her to future discomforts if the implementation of the labour

[44] See *Observer*, 10 May 1959, and *Economist*, 27 Feb. 1960, pp. 819-22, also
Negotiations for a European Free Trade Area 1956-1958 (The Royal Ministry for
Foreign Affairs, Stockholm, 1959).

[45] See "Sixes and Sevens" in *The Times Supplement*, 5 Oct. 1959, p. vii; and
Henri Stanner, *Neutralité Suisse et Solidarité Européene* (Lausanne, 1959), who
points out that two-thirds of Swiss foreign trade is with Western Europe and
argues for Swiss association with the Common Market. See also the Swiss statement of 24 Sept. 1962 before the Commission of the E.E.C. which gave the official
Swiss viewpoint about neutrality and European integration; and the statement
by Mr Gunnar Lange, Swedish Minister of Trade, on 28 July 1962.

[46] By late 1960 the number of foreigners, mostly Italians, working in Switzerland was, with their families, 550,000, about one-tenth of the population, and
one-fifth of the working population.

clauses of the Rome Treaty were to lead to restrictions on this supply. It is not surprising that the keynote of Switzerland's official attitude is caution, while that of Sweden is of flexible pragmatism.

The failure of Britain's quest to join the E.E.C. in January 1963 relieved the pressure on both states to define and justify their policies in terms simultaneously satisfying both to their own nationals and to their potential E.E.C. associates, and led immediately to attempts to re-invigorate E.F.T.A. But the dilemma of being within a western Europe straining for greater co-operation, while wishing to retain full national identity without isolation, is now the continual preoccupation of both powers.

Their contrasting national positions are again evident if one compares the policies of the two states towards international organization. Sweden became a member of the United Nations in November 1946, though warily and without much enthusiasm, and her policy inside the organization is characterized by a careful, mediatory, form of co-operation which serves as the basis of all Swedish international action beyond the scope of immediate Swedish interests.[47] Switzerland has not joined the United Nations and there has never been a thorough public discussion of this question,[48] though no doubt memories of her difficulties as a member of the League and the intention of giving executive authority to the Security Council were sufficient deterrents in 1945. Nevertheless, the Swiss, just as much as the Swedes, are conscious that their 'neutrality' is more likely to be respected if, as well as benefiting themselves, it can be used to provide international services. And while both powers are at pains to ensure that if war breaks out their neutrality will not be violated, they both realize that prevention of war is the prior concern and endeavour to contribute towards this task. Sweden here makes use of the opportunities afforded by her membership of the United Nations.[49] As well as her membership of the Commission of Neutral Nations in Korea, Sweden contributed military contingents to the U.N. forces in Sinai in 1957 and in the Congo in 1960, and has played an active part in disarmament conferences held under U.N. auspices—where she has been widely regarded as a prime spokesman for 'neutralist' nations. Switzerland shows that hers is not a completely introverted policy by such acts as serving with Sweden on the Neutral

[47] See *Sweden and the United Nations*, report by the Swedish Institute of International Affairs (New York, 1956).

[48] See Jacqueline Belin, *La Suisse et les Nations Unies* (New York, 1956); W. E. Rappard, "Switzerland and the United Nations" (A.A.A.P.S.S., July 1946); and Walther Hofer, *Neutrality as the Principle of Swiss Policy* (Zürich, 1957), esp. p. 28, *et seq*.

[49] Both the Swiss and the Swedes found this is a disagreeable task. See Jacques Freymond, "Supervising Agreements. The Korean Experience" in *Foreign Affairs*, Apr. 1959, pp. 496-503.

Nations Supervisory Commission on Korea;[49] by representing British
and French interests in Egypt after the break of 1956; and, above all,
by encouraging the frequent use of her national territory for important
international conferences, and for the headquarters of international
organizations.[50] The tension between neutrality and international
solidarity is thus eased by the twin conceptions of international services
and humanitarian mission, the most cherished expression of which is
the International Red Cross with its headquarters in Geneva and a
directing personnel recruited only among Swiss citizens.

There is no doubt that the sympathies of the vast majority of Swiss
and Swedish citizens lie with the N.A.T.O. powers in the struggle with
the Soviet Union and its associates. Yet, more emphatically, their traditional foreign policies have a time-tested sacredness, almost a talismanic
quality. Public discussion of foreign policy in Sweden concentrates
almost exclusively on adjusting and justifying Sweden's 'alliance-free'
policy,[51] and the Swiss remain true to their national custom of not
discussing among themselves why they are neutral while assuring other
people that Swiss neutrality is unique, internationally beneficial,
deserves respect, and is not susceptible of being duplicated on the international plane. The Swedish concept of non-alignment is liberal and
pragmatic; the Swiss is conservative and impermeable. It is inconceivable
that either country will easily abandon its traditional policy, though, of
course, in the event of war the choice of neutrality is not confined to
those traditionally given to choosing it, nor does the fact of successful
neutrality in the past guarantee similar success in the future. Yet, whatever dangers belief in a 'magic charm' neutrality may contain, it
remains true that the actual policies of both powers are remarkably free
from illusions.

AUSTRIA — A NEUTRALIZED STATE

Prior to 1955, neutralization[1]—the institution of a status of permanent neutrality—had seemed to be an obsolete nineteenth century

[50] In Geneva alone there were 142 international organizations in 1959. See
The Times Supplement, 5 Oct. 1959, p. xvi.
[51] See I. William Zartman, pp. 143-57; and *Sweden and the United Nations*,
pp. 157-60, for brief discussions of the public debate about the kind of neutrality
Sweden should pursue.
[1] Neutralization requires an international treaty between the great powers and
the state concerned, whereby the former guarantee collectively the independence
and integrity of the latter, which must agree to abstain from any hostile action
or any international agreement likely to involve it in hostilities. In the past
neutralization has been applied only to small, weak states and to situations where
a rough balance of power prevails. See Fred Greene, "Neutralization and the
Balance of Power", A.P.S.R., vol. xlvii, pp. 1041-57; and C. R. M. F. Cruttwell,
A History of Peaceful Change in the Modern World (London, 1937), pp. 183-92.

practice. The neutralization of Austria in that year revived public interest in the device of neutralization and led to much rather loose talk about "the Austrian example". Yet it is doubtful if the success of Austria in achieving some degree of immunization from the struggles of the Cold War can provide a truly heartening example for other states. After all, it took nine years of occupation and the cumbersome method of four-power control to restore the sovereignty of a small country with a population of only seven million people; and, even so, the progress of the negotiations for Austrian independence was extremely hazardous and influenced at all stages by the general climate of East-West relations. Austria's new status, which involved shouldering some onerous burdens, sprang almost entirely from her insignificance as a military factor; and, more specifically, from a coincidence of Russian strategic re-assessments and propaganda aims in the context of 1955.

Indeed, Austria's strategic position, her experiences since 1918, and, more particularly, the power constellations of the Cold War, seem to have confirmed her position as the new cross-roads of Europe, in place of Switzerland. Bounded to the north-west by the Federal Republic of Germany, with its north-eastern frontiers merging into part of the Iron Curtain, with Switzerland and Italy to its west and south-west, and Yugoslavia on its southern frontier, the Austrian Federal Republic has common frontiers with six states. Her newly found unity and prosperity stand in relief with the declining years of Habsburg rule, and even more markedly with the divisions, poverty and ignominy of the inter-war period; and her present independence contrasts sharply with the occupation of 1945 to 1955.

For more than a hundred years political leaders in Austria, whether advocates of Imperial or of Republican rule, have had to face the twin problems of how to find a satisfactory "state idea", and how to come to terms with the impulses of nationalism. While there may be good reason for doubting a popular assertion that the last effective Habsburg ruler, Francis Joseph (1848-1916), played off one nationality against another within his empire, and that "*Divide et Impera*" was his guiding political principle, it is nevertheless doubtful if that monarch's actual maxim of government, "*Viribus Unitis*", was more happily designed for his age.[2] Though it is true that Francis Joseph's personal rule was in defiance of a 'solution' to the nationalities problem of the Habsburg lands, it is also true that the truncated rump of that polyglot empire—constituted the

[2] See A. F. Pribram, *Austria-Hungary and Great Britain 1908-1914*, translated by Ian D. F. Morrow (London, 1951), p. 61. The tensions caused by nationalism within the Habsburg Empire are examined by R. A. Kann, *The Multinational Empire* (London, 1950); and "The Fall of Habsburg Austria" in *The Times Literary Supplement*, 20 July 1951, pp. 445-7, is a penetrating essay on Austrian failures to find a 'state idea' during the same period.

Republic of Austria,[3] by the peacemakers in 1919, as a state comprising mostly of German speaking peoples—lacked either the will or the means to existence, and between the wars it scarcely had an active foreign policy. The original wish of most German speaking Austrians was for an Anschluss with Germany,[4] but this was forbidden by the Allies.[5] The state was only kept in being during its first years by means of substantial League of Nations reconstruction loans; while as early as 1927 the final overthrow of Austrian liberties and the destruction of national independence was prefigured in the bloody 15th July—one of the four fateful days for Austrian liberties.[6] The difficulties of adaptation from being the centre of the vast Danubian Empire of the Habsburgs to playing the part of a small autonomous state (burdened by a now over-large capital city) among the fiercely nationalistic successor states, were magnified by the great depression. The Austrians were easily persuaded by National Socialist propaganda that their state was not economically viable, that a high proportion of unemployed was therefore inevitable, and that the only 'solution' lay in union with Germany. Though Italian and French opposition was sufficient to stifle at birth the Austro-German customs union of March 1931, in March 1938 Hitler's Germany forced through the Anschluss without encountering much opposition from either the League Powers or the Austrian people.[7]

Ironically, it was the German and subsequently the four-power occupations which helped to forge a sense of national unity and to lay some of the economic foundations of Austria's present prosperity. Certainly, the experience of foreign occupation since 1938 seems to have induced a greater national solidarity than previously. For whereas in the inter-war period antagonism between the Austrian Clericals and

[3] The name "German-Austria", used at first by the new Republic, was forbidden by the Allies, and the name Austria accepted. The Austrian Republic comprises nine provinces—Vienna, Lower Austria, Upper Austria, Salzburg, Tyrol, Vorarlberg, Carinthia, Styria and Burgenland.
[4] See S. W. Gould, "Austrian Attitudes towards Anschluss, Oct. 1918 - Sept. 1919", J.M.H., Sept. 1950, pp. 220-31.
[5] In Article 80 of the Treaty of Versailles; but under this clause Austria could be united to Germany "with the consent of the Council of the League of Nations". Cf. also Article 88 of the Treaty of St. Germain.
[6] The other three being the suppression of Parliament by Dollfuss in Mar. 1933 and the two 12ths of Feb.—that of the Counter Revolution of 1934, and that of the Berchtesgaden meeting of 1938, which through the German invasion and Nazi revolution brought the Schuschnigg regime to an end just one month later on 11 Mar. 1938. See G. E. R. Gedye, Fallen Bastions (London, 1939), p. 35.
[7] Frank Borkenau, Austria and After (London, 1938); Kurt von Schuschnigg, Farewell Austria (London, 1938) and Austrian Requiem (London, 1947). Schuschnigg was Chancellor of the Austrian Federal Republic July 1934 to Mar. 1938. See G. E. R. Gedye's assessment of Schuschnigg, chap. 12.

Socialists was so great that civil war broke out between them in 1934, their successors have combined to form a coalition which since 1945 has governed the country without a major split.[8] Furthermore, it was during the occupations that the Germans prospected further oilfields in Lower Austria and the Russians developed and worked them. After 1945, with Russia determined to treat Austria as a defeated nation and to wring as much reparation as possible, Austrian leaders could only turn to the Western Powers for the foreign aid necessary to economic recovery. It was their considerable achievement that Austria became a member of the Marshall Plan organization and of the European Payments Union without driving the Soviet authorities to believe that Austria was bound irretrievably to the Western camp.

Indeed, in many respects the period of four-power occupation now appears as a trying and extremely difficult training for the post-1955 rôle of permanent diplomatic neutrality. From 1945 until 1955[9] Austria, though divided into four occupation zones, had a government whose authority was recognized throughout the country and by all four occupying powers—by the Russians equally, despite the constant electoral resistance of the Austrians to Communism. If the evacuation of all foreign forces was to be achieved — for in the heyday of their co-operation the Allied Powers had stated, in the Moscow Declaration of 1st November 1943, that they wished "to see re-established a free and independent Austria"—Austrian bona fides had to be acceptable to both of the Cold War camps.

This tour de force was achieved, despite the ten years of occupation and the trials of several hundred great power meetings before the conclusion of the Austrian State Treaty. The end to the deadlock sprang entirely from a dramatic reversal of Soviet policy,[10] though patient Austrian diplomacy had prepared the ground. (This included canvassing India's support and good offices to promote Austria's cause with the

[8] Though, inevitably, there have been frictions. See Gordon Shepherd, The Austrian Odyssey (London, 1957); U. W. Kitzinger, "The Electoral System in Austria" in Parliamentary Affairs, Autumn 1959. In Jan. 1963 Austria still had a caretaker government, three months after the election of October 1962 had seen a swing to the Volkspartei, and these results underlined the delicacy of the proportz system which had been operated ever since 1945.

[9] There is no completely satisfactory history in English of these nine years. But see Cary Travers Grayson, Jnr., Austria's International Position 1938-53 (Geneva, 1953); R. Hiscocks, The Rebirth of Austria (London, 1953); Philip Mosely, "The Treaty with Austria", International Organization, vol. iv (1950), pp. 219-35; D. C. Watt, "Some Reflections on Austrian Foreign Policy 1945-1955" in International Relations, vol. i (6), Oct. 1956, pp. 259-69.

[10] See Full Circle. The Memoirs of Sir Anthony Eden (London, 1960), p. 290; and Gerald Stourzh, "Austrian neutrality. Its establishment and its significance" in International Spectator, 8 Mar. 1960, pp. 107-32.

Soviet Union.)[11] There were strategic as well as diplomatic advantages for the Soviets in conceding Austria's neutralization at this time. For as well as conforming with the post-Stalin 'new look'—a diplomacy which was seeking a *détente* with Tito and improved relations with Asian neutralists—there were strategic advantages for the Soviet Union in thus separating two N.A.T.O. powers (Italy and West Germany) and seeing the Swiss-Austrian wedge of neutral territory hindering the logistic consolidation of N.A.T.O. And Austria's neutralization entailed the transfer of 5,000 American troops from Salzburg to south of the Brenner.

The process which swiftly produced Austria's neutralization began with Mr Molotov's speech to the Supreme Soviet at the beginning of March 1955, when he declared that delay in concluding an Austrian State Treaty was unjustified but that guarantees must be found against another Anschluss and against Austria's participation in any alliance before the treaty could be signed. Later he amplified these remarks to Austria's ambassador in Moscow, making it clear that agreement between the powers about Germany was no longer regarded by the Soviet government as an indispensable prerequisite to any settlement of Austria's status. At the end of March the Austrian Federal Chancellor was invited to Moscow and an Austrian delegation duly arrived there on 12th April where, after two days' negotiations, a memorandum[12] was signed on 15th April by which Austria: agreed to make a declaration "in a form imposing upon Austria an international obligation, that Austria will maintain permanent neutrality of the same type as that maintained by Switzerland";[13] agreed to delivery of goods to the U.S.S.R. in payment of the value of the Soviet enterprises in Austria to be transferred in accordance with the Austrian State Treaty;[14] agreed that Austria should pay (one million tons of crude oil annually for ten years) for the transfer of oil properties belonging to the U.S.S.R. in Austria, and in United States dollars for the transfer of the assets of the

[11] See Stourzh, p. 114.

[12] Text, in English translation, printed in *New Times* (Moscow), No. 22, 28 May 1955—Supplement of Documents, pp. 5-7.

[13] Mr Molotov's oft-repeated comparison of Austria's position with Switzerland was inexact. Switzerland suffers no constitutional or international limitation on the kind of armaments it can possess, as Austria does in Article 13 of the State Treaty. But such a limitation has not, traditionally, been regarded as incompatible with neutralization. In 1914 Luxembourg was forbidden to keep a standing army. It is interesting to note that two years later Mr Mikoyan was recommending to Austrian leaders that they should follow the model of Finnish neutrality, stressing that whenever he referred to Austrian neutrality he meant "a neutrality without any reservations whatever". *Daily Telegraph*, 23 Apr. 1957.

[14] See detailed list in Article 22 of State Treaty. The Russians obtained compensation worth $150 m. for these assets (Western estimates placed their value at only $40 m.).

Soviet-held Danube Shipping Company in eastern Austria; and, agreed that the two countries should conclude trade, barter and payments agreements to last, in the first instance, for five years. Exactly one month later the Foreign Ministers of the four occupying powers signed in Vienna the Austrian State Treaty[15] providing for the establishment of a sovereign and democratic Austria within the frontiers of 1938.[16] An Anschluss was forbidden and the rights of non-German minorities were guaranteed.[17] Austria was allowed to keep an army of whatever size it wished, but atomic and other special weapons were forbidden.[18] There were to be no reparations but the onerous terms of the Moscow Memorandum were to be fulfilled by Austria.[19]

These two instruments, together with the Constitutional Law of Neutrality of 26th October 1955[20]—which came into force and was given international publicity on 5th November 1955—regulate Austria's new international status. General international recognition of this new status was soon forthcoming, and in December 1955 Austria was one of sixteen states admitted to the United Nations under the East-West package deal. On a strict reading of the Charter, and one that prevailed at the San Francisco Conference in 1945,[21] neutrality and United Nations membership are incompatible; but a more flexible interpretation allows that the Charter admits neutrality by implication.[22] In line with this latter view a leading Austrian international lawyer[23] has argued,

[15] For text, see *British Treaty Series no. 58*, 1957, Cmd. 214. The treaty bears many marks of hasty drafting and the need to gloss over doctrinal differences. For criticism on this score, see Janko Musulin, "Austria after the Hungarian Rising" in *International Affairs*, Apr. 1957, pp. 133-42.

[16] State Treaty, Articles 1 and 5.

[17] *Ibid.*, Articles 4 and 7.

[18] Article 13.

[19] Articles 21 and 22.

[20] The neutrality declaration which became an integral part of the Constitution on 5 Nov. 1955 contained the following passage: "For the purpose of the lasting maintenance of her independence externally, and for the purpose of the inviolability of her territory, Austria declares of her own free will her perpetual neutrality. Austria will maintain and defend this with all means at her disposal. For the securing of this purpose in all future times Austria will not join any military alliances and will not permit the establishment of any foreign military bases on her territory." See R.I.I.A., *Documents for 1955*, p. 239. See further the argument between a Soviet scholar and an Austrian scholar, Dr. Stourzh, in the March and April numbers of *International Affairs* (Moscow), 1957.

[21] *Documents of the United Nations Conference on International Organisation* (San Francisco, 1945), vol. vi, p. 459; vol. vii, p. 327.

[22] In Articles 43 (3) and 48 (1) where member states *may* be called upon to act for the maintenance of international peace and security as the Security Council *may* determine; it is arguable that in certain circumstances a state may be excluded from these provisions.

[23] Alfred Verdross, "Austria's Permanent Neutrality and the U.N.", A.J.I.L., Jan. 1956, pp. 61-8. See also Stourzh's discussion, esp. pp. 123-31.

plausibly, that by the time Austria was admitted to the United Nations her neutrality had already received almost universal recognition and that in consequence members are obliged to respect this status if sanctions are invoked. The then Austrian State Secretary for Foreign Affairs, Dr Bruno Kreisky,[24] defined the official Austrian conception of neutrality in an article he wrote for a leading American journal:

"Actually it is not accurate to speak of neutrality in peacetime, because what the term means is non-participation in war. An attitude of indifference toward the ideological struggle has more properly been called neutralism (as opposed to neutrality). But this should not be taken to mean that neutrality does not impose any obligations whatever upon a country in peacetime. Such obligations can be summarized as follows:

(1) A neutral country cannot join a military alliance in time of peace because in so doing it would destroy its ability to remain neutral in time of war.

(2) Similarly, a neutral country must bar foreign military bases from its territory, since they would diminish its former freedom of action —or rather non-action—in time of war.

(3) A neutral country must not accept any obligations—political, economic or other—which would tend to impair its neutrality in wartime."[25]

Dr Kreisky maintained that Austria's permanent neutrality was a question of Hobson's choice if Austria was to become independent: "To venture out into the open without having sought shelter with one of the blocs seemed fraught with grave consequences. Whatever the merit of this argument, it had the flaw of pre-supposing a choice between neutrality and the *status quo*. At no time could we choose between neutrality and alignment with a bloc. And in fact what did the *status quo* amount to? Was it not itself a form of passive neutralization— neutralization by occupation? Under the circumstances, what alternative was open to a nation which longed to be master once again of its own destiny?"[26]

Nevertheless, the Austrians have shown great skill in making a

[24] Dr Kreisky, at one time a career diplomat (before his rapid rise in the Austrian Socialist party), succeeded Dr Leopold Figl as Austrian Foreign Minister in July 1959, and for the first time the Foreign Minister was permitted to be independent head of his Ministry, now freed from the Federal Chancellor's office. It is interesting to note that Dr Kreisky spent the entire war years in Sweden and that he has a Swedish wife.

[25] Bruno Kreisky, "Austria Draws the Balance" in *Foreign Affairs*, Jan. 1959, pp. 269-81. This is in part a paraphrase of the Austrian Constitutional Federal Statute of 26 Oct. 1955, which expressly mentions these three duties. See further Josef L. Kunz, "Austria's Permanent Neutrality", A.J.I.L., Apr. 1956, p. 413.

[26] Kreisky, *ibid.*, p. 273.

friend of necessity and in evolving a form of diplomacy which is, perhaps surprisingly,[27] more like that of Sweden than of their Western neighbour, Switzerland. By joining the Council of Europe,[28] like Sweden and unlike Switzerland,[29] Austria openly demonstrated its affinities with the West. However, as a vital condition of her continued independence, she has been scrupulous in the maintenance of her military and diplomatic neutrality between both blocs; providing a neutral stage for international conferences of all political complexions; performing neutral good offices during and after the Hungarian Revolution, despite strained relations with neighbouring Communist states; and protesting strongly at the violation of Austrian air space by American military transport planes *en route* southwards during the crisis in Jordan and Lebanon in the summer of 1958.

In dealing with these difficulties, Austrian leaders have shown considerable diplomatic skill, a skill which is equally evident in the way Austria manages to keep on generally favourable terms with both superpowers. Since 1945 relations with the United States have been consistently amicable. In addition to vital American economic aid, given during the nine years of occupation, subsequently the United States Export-Import Bank has advanced substantial loans for developing Austria's iron industry. Only two relatively minor, and related, issues have threatened to impair relations. These were the question of the settlement of the claims of American oil companies whose properties were confiscated by Hitler's Germany in 1938, and the question of the release of 2,000 million schillings in counterpart funds held in a blocked account to the credit of the United States. Both of these issues were settled, virtually, by the end of 1959.[30] Equally, and in sharp contrast to the pre-1955 period, there has been marked evidence since 1955 of official Austro-Russian cordiality. The visit of Mr Mikoyan in April 1957 was an undoubted success and produced a Soviet promise that

[27] See Stourzh, *op. cit.*, pp. 112-13. Writing before the State Treaty, both Elizabeth Wiskemann, *Undeclared War* (London, 1939), p. 5, and Oscar Halecki, *The Limits and Divisions of European History* (London, 1950), pp. 134-5, mention the relevance of the Swiss example for Austria. But by 1957 Elizabeth Wiskemann, "Resurgent Austria" in *Contemporary Review*, No. 1099, July 1957, p. 8, was writing "Austria has developed a new kind of neutralism. Something less negative and more actively European in spirit than the neutrality of Switzerland."

[28] When Austria joined the Council of Europe—a purely advisory, non-military organization—the Austrian Foreign Minister was reported as saying "We are a militarily neutral state, but there is no neutralism": *New York Times*, 22 Feb. 1956. Cf. Professor Wiskemann's opinion, in the preceding note.

[29] Though in Nov. 1961 the Swiss government, having previously kept aloof from the Council of Europe, accepted an invitation to send observers to the Council in future on the ground—surely, not new—that it was the only organization embracing all the Western European countries.

[30] *New York Times*, 17 Nov. 1959; and C.S.M., 14 June 1961.

Austrian deliveries of oil to Russia would be reduced, provided trade in general between the two countries continued to rise. In the following year the Russians agreed to reduce by one half Austrian oil delivery obligations under the State Treaty.[31] The Russians, who had never had vital need of Austrian crude oil, now seemed more interested in stimulating Danubian trade and in underlining the power of 'the Austrian example'.[32] Mr Khrushchov's eight-day official visit to Austria in July 1960 produced some further, though small, economic concessions by the Soviets. But the Austrians had to suffer Mr Khrushchov's frequent sallies into the delicate field of defining Austria's international status. Their distinguished visitor insisted, *inter alia*, that if Austria were to join the Common Market, or to suffer the passage over her territory of American rockets from Italy, her neutrality would be violated. These embarrassing remarks elicited from the host government a reply to the effect that it was Austria's sovereign right to decide for itself whether or not its neutrality was threatened or violated, and what countermeasures to take if this occurred. While it would welcome a joint guarantee of its territorial integrity by all four powers, it could not agree to such a guarantee by one power only.[33] Even so, the Austrians wisely realize that it is in their every interest to do all they can to agree with Soviet claims that peaceful and profitable relations can be maintained between a 'bourgeois' and a 'socialist' state.

Most states, and especially small states, have some difficulties with their neighbours. Austria is no exception. Only relations with Switzerland seem entirely trouble-free. Her relations with neighbouring Communist states are invariably uneasy, not least because of the refugees who seek refuge in Austria—strained relations with Hungary during and after the Hungarian Revolution were thus, in a sense, an unusually

[31] The desire to stimulate Danubian trade is the probable explanation of the curiously roundabout method chosen by the Soviet leaders to effect this reduction (Austria to continue to deliver one million tons of crude oil to Russia for the next seven years as stipulated by the treaty, but from 1959 Russia to compensate her by delivering half that amount of her own oil from Baku to Austria via the Danube—see *The Times*, 27 Aug. 1958). The tacit *quid pro quo* seems to have been that Austria would join—as she did in Apr. 1959—with the Communist powers who were parties to the 1947 Belgrade Convention on the navigation of the Danube. The Russians said frankly that they hoped the Federal Republic of Germany would also adhere to the Convention. No doubt, the revival of the old tradition of expanding trade down the Danube is seen by some Austrians as a pull away from the strong economic ties with Western Germany.

[32] See, for example, S. Okhantsev, "An Example of Peaceful Coexistence" in *International Affairs* (Moscow), Sept. 1958, pp. 85-6. For an earlier example, see A. Markov, "Austrian Neutrality—the First Year" in *New Times* (Moscow), Oct. 1956, pp. 9-11.

[33] See *Economist*, 16 July 1960; *Daily Telegraph*, 30 June 1960; and 7 and 9 July 1960.

severe eruption of a general problem. With Italy, the only continual source of tension is the question of the treatment of the German speaking population in the Italian province of Alto Adige.[34] This issue has a long history but to date there is no sign of it becoming a dominating factor in Austrian domestic politics. Another constant, though minor, source of irritation is Yugoslavia's active interest in Austria's Slovene and Croatian minorities in the south-eastern provinces of Carinthia and Styria. In general, though, Austro-Yugoslav relations seem to have improved steadily since early 1958.[35]

Undoubtedly, however, economic ties and sentiment, as well as long intertwined histories, make Western Germany the most important of Austria's neighbours. The Austrian State Treaty, the chief 'charter' of neutralized Austria, expressly forbids "all agreements having the effect, either directly or indirectly, of promoting political or economic union with Germany".[36] As the majority of Austrian industrialists are *grossdeutsch* by tradition and interest,[37] and as Germany is the most important customer and supplier in Austria's close overall links with the six European Common Market countries,[38] it seems that the government's reason for joining the 'Outer Seven' of the European Free Trade Association was based not on economic considerations, but rather because of a strict regard for Austria's neutral status.[39]

If non-Communist Europe is really to congeal into two separate economic blocs, then Austria, like Switzerland, will find herself separated from her main markets. And in terms of the Cold War as well as of Western European rivalries, the political and economic factors

[34] Known to the Austrians as South Tyrol. For a brief account of the history of this dispute, see "Tensions in South Tyrol" in *World Today*, Jan. 1958; and *The Times*, 16 Sept. 1961.

[35] Hugh Seton-Watson, *The East European Revolution* (London, 1950), pp. 369-71; and cf. *The Times*, 1 Mar. 1962.

[36] In Article 4, para. 2.

[37] See E. Wiskemann, *op. cit.*; and Gordon Shepherd's argument that Austria will be forced into the German orbit by sheer economic pressure—*The Austrian Odyssey* (London, 1957).

[38] In 1959 50% of Austria's exports went to Common Market countries; and between 50 and 60% of her imports came from these countries. 26% of her exports went to Western Germany.

[39] The government's view of neutrality was expressed by Professor Alfred Verdross (a legal adviser to the Austrian Foreign Office) in these terms: "A permanently neutral state cannot join a multinational economic group such as the Common Market because (such an organization) aims at fusion of the national economies concerned, and to this end it deputes authority to a central organ to follow a united economic policy which is binding on the member states." Verdross further argues that in case of war Austria must be able to free itself from restrictions on the course of its trade which might hamper it in the protection of its physical independence. Quoted in "Austria's European Choice" in *Economist*, 30 Jan. 1960, pp. 437-8.

converge to emphasize that Austria, more than Switzerland, is at the blocked crossroads of Europe: "The eastern frontier of the Common Market, just like the western frontier of the Soviet bloc, cuts across the natural trade routes of central Europe. Since these are political as well as economic frontiers, they leave no room for a stable position for a country placed as Austria is. Austria's problem of association probably cannot be really settled until the relationships between western and eastern Europe changes, and what used to be central Europe can, in some form, come into existence again. Until then, the Austrians can only improvise."[40] The task of working out an association with the Common Market without seriously impairing her permanently neutral status, especially in Soviet eyes, is a task to tax all the Austrian powers of improvisation.[41]

Though analogies between Austria and Germany are often made, there are many reasons why 'the Austrian example' of neutralization is far from suggesting a clear precedent for Germany, despite the attractions of this idea for some Germans.[42] The most compelling differences are that Austria has a population of seven million while there would be over seventy million in a neutral Germany, made up of the two Germanies of today; Austria's is an armed neutrality with no limit on the size of her army—a freedom hardly likely to be granted to a "neutralized" Germany. Moreover, Germany cannot be compared to a small, unambitious state with no revisionist demands or ability to impose its will on others. Even if Germany stayed aloof from Cold War entanglements, its neighbours would be concerned over its foreign policy to an extent which would make neutralization an essentially unreal status. As long as Germany is divided, the fact of division is likely to deter increases in the strength of the old *Alldeutsch* impulses within Austria towards a new *Anschluss*—though Professor Wiskemann maintains that there are signs that such sentiments are still present in the Tyrol, Salzburg and in Styria.[43] Their influence in Austria's political life so far seems small. For most Austrians actual experience of the consequences of union with Germany may now have made independence seem more attractive than it did between 1918 and 1938. The *Handbook of the Austrian National and Federal Assemblies* for 1959 showed that 92 of the National Assembly's 165 members were

[40] *Economist*, 13 Feb. 1960, p. 598. Such dilemmas are far from being merely contemporary. For similar problems of orientation are as old as the idea of Austria. See J. M. Thompson, *An Historical Geography of Europe, 800-1789* (Oxford, 1929), pp. 21 and 139.

[41] See *Guardian*, 22 Mar. 1961; *The Times*, 21 July 1961; and C.S.M., 16 Dec. 1961.

[42] See Terence Prittie, "The Impact of the Austrian Treaty on Germany" in *Listener*, 16 June 1955, pp. 1057-8.

[43] E. Wiskemann, "Resurgent Austria", p. 10.

in prisons or concentration camps of Hitler's Germany or in prisons of pre-Nazi authoritarian regimes in Austria. Prison camp friendships are probably an underestimated source of post-war Austria's greater political stability than hitherto. For the non-German minorities[44] of the 'new' Austria, separatism seems to be a negligible force, though in order to fortify "the Austrian idea"[45] new and inexpensive books on Austrian history are being published and generously circulated under government sponsorship.

Few would now dispute the contention of Herr Raab, the Austrian Chancellor, who during his visit to Moscow in July 1958 said that "the overwhelming majority of Austrians today favour this neutrality, and it is increasingly realized that we took the right decision for our future."[46] It may be that the old tag of Imperial days—"Felix Austria"[47] —has again become appropriate. Less than eight years after the Austrian State Treaty the internal aspect seems as propitious as her external relations. But both are delicately poised. The example of Switzerland and Sweden suggests that a successful neutral needs, as well as restraint and care in her external relations, national unity and stability in internal politics, undoubted viability in economic life and military strength sufficient to deter a would-be aggressor from achieving easy conquest. To date, Austrian leaders have amply shown their diplomatic skills, but it is too early to be confident of the country's national unity or its economic strength, and its puny defences have already caused its military leaders much disquiet.[48]

[44] At the 1951 census these were only 2% of the total population, and were mostly Slovene in Carinthia.

[45] A. J. P. Taylor—who is rather sceptical about a "distinctively" Austrian idea, insisting, with some reason, that so much depends on the larger neighbour, Germany—has traced some of the past vicissitudes and ambiguities of "the Austrian idea" in his book *The Habsburg Monarchy 1809-1918* (2nd ed., 1948), see esp. the epilogue, pp. 252-61. The political significance of national history has been clearly appreciated, and so rewritten, by each twentieth-century Austrian regime in turn. See R. John Rath, "History of Citizenship Training—An Austrian Example", *J.M.H.*, Sept. 1949, pp. 227-38.

[46] Quoted in *The Times*, 27 Aug. 1958.

[47] This was a recognition of diplomatic finesse, as opposed to armed might. For Austria was once known as Felix Austria because the Habsburg Monarchy acquired an empire by marriage compacts rather than by conquest, "*Bella gerant alii, tu felix Austria, nube*".

[48] The strength of the Austrian army varies between 35,000 and 55,000 men, owing to the nine-month conscription period. By April 1961 some 110,000 trained reservists were available. It was reported in 1958 (though by September 1961 neither aim had been achieved) that in order to provide some effective protction of neutrality the Austrian government proposed "to build up a strong protective fighter unit and also to obtain the revision of clause 13 of the Austrian Treaty, which prohibits the possession of anti-aircraft missiles". Quoted from Lajos Lederer, "Austria's Arms Talks with Russia" in *Observer*, 12 Oct. 1958. See also *The Times*, 23 Apr. 1959; and *Daily Telegraph*, 25 Apr. 1961.

The "failure and downfall" of the Austrian Empire was due to its "efforts to span two worlds",[49] and one remembers the misfortunes of Luxembourg and Belgium in 1914 following the collapse of the balance of power which had initially enabled their neutralization. It would be rash to assert that the post-1955 neutralism of the Austrian Federal Republic is deeply entrenched. So far, it has not been severely tested.

[49] Geoffrey Barraclough, *History in a Changing World* (Oxford, 1957), p. 134.

CHAPTER VI

THE BELGRADE NEUTRALIST SUMMIT,
SEPTEMBER 1961

"It is the ideology of neutralism which is now emerging as a significant feature on the international scene."
Daily Telegraph, leader, 31 Aug. 1961.

"The communiqué issued by the non-aligned nations who have just
finished their meeting at Belgrade . . . is a lazy document, pompous
and pretentious, professing much admirable principle without giving
the slightest indication how it is to be applied."
Daily Telegraph, leader, 7 Sept. 1961.

"These people are not exclusivist, anti-European chauvinistic . . .
they are the makers of a new synthesis which may contain the
germs of a shared and enriched world culture."
Peter Worsley, writing on the Belgrade Conference
in *New Left Review*, Nov. - Dec. 1961.

As the first large meeting of the world's leading neutralists, called
together to discuss common problems and interests, the Belgrade
Conference of Non-aligned Countries is an important landmark
in the history of neutralism. As a microcosm of neutralist diplomacy, at
a time when pressures were growing for an increase in neutralist initiatives and impact in world politics, the Conference was not without its
own intrinsic interest and importance. The meeting was important, or
at least revealing, for the way the decision to hold the Conference was
taken; for the way in which attendance at the Conference was arranged;
for the way in which different neutralist currents clashed and/or combined during the course of the Conference; and, important, above all,
for its ambiguous results.

THE BACKGROUND

Though Tito was the host, the originator and the chief engineer of
the neutralist summit, the preparations for the Belgrade meeting were
neither straightforward nor swiftly agreed, and the actual occasioning
of the Conference owed as much to the pressure of events as to personalities. At least since 1958 Tito, impressed no doubt both by the benefits
of his Brioni meetings with Nasser and Nehru and by repeated evidence
of his definite exclusion from Communist bloc conclaves, was openly

advocating[1] greater co-operation and co-ordination of the uncommitted countries. By his own extensive tours in Asia and Africa and by assiduous efforts in the United Nations he sought to promote this idea. And, working closely with President Nasser, it seemed that Tito regarded the United Nations as the most appropriate agency to use in the forging of greater neutralist solidarity.

By September 1960 Tito's plans seemed to be bearing fruit. While an unprecedented number of the world's political leaders converged on U.N. headquarters at Turtle Bay, enthusiasm for neutralist initiatives ran high among certain neutralist leaders. There were reports[2] of Nehru arriving to find the ground already prepared for him to lead a bloc of neutralists. The preparations had been made by Nasser and Tito, both of them apparently ready to accept Nehru as the leader of an emerging neutralist camp. In the event no wide ranging coherent and cohesive neutralist camp emerged. Perhaps this was because of Nehru's known reluctance to assume the leadership of an organized disciplined bloc, but more likely it was because the emotional and political strength of all the participant's neutralism was within the main stream of Afro-Asian nationalism and anti-colonialism and not as a cold war neutralizing current running alone. The difference can be illustrated by pointing to the different fortunes of two resolutions before the fifteenth General Assembly.[3]

The first resolution,[4] jointly sponsored by Ghana, India, Indonesia, the United Arab Republic and Yugoslavia, called for a meeting à deux between President Kennedy and Chairman Khrushchov as an urgent step in the amelioration of international relations. Eventually the motion was withdrawn because, as Nehru explained, amendments had robbed it of its force. The second resolution,[5] presented by Ceylon on behalf of twenty-six African and Asian countries (including the five mentioned above) stated, inter alia, that: (i) all forms of colonialism were contrary to the U.N. Charter and impediments to world peace; (ii) inadequacy of political, economic, social or educational preparedness should never serve as a pretext for delaying independence; and (iii) immediate steps should be taken in trust and non-self-governing territories to transfer all powers to the people in accordance with their freely expressed will. The motion was adopted by eighty-nine votes to none, with nine abstentions (Portugal, Spain, South Africa, the U.K., the U.S., Australia, Belgium, Dominica, France). Western colonialism was clearly on the defensive, it was less clear that the great powers accepted

---

[1] See The Times, 10 July 1958 and 4 Aug. 1958; and Observer, 6 July 1958.
[2] E.g. Daily Telegraph, 26 Sept. 1960; and Hindu, 25 Sept. 1960.
[3] Y.B.U.N. 1960.
[4] U.N. Docs. A/L 317.
[5] U.N. Docs. A/L 323.

the indispensibility of neutralists as mediators or adjudicators of their quarrels. It was the Bandung rather than the Brioni spirit which had triumphed.

President Sukarno seemed to sense the significance of this, for in March 1961[6] he again publicized one of his favourite pleas—for a second Bandung Conference. But the fact that Communist China was one of his strongest supporters in this move certainly weakened Sukarno's chances of success. Remote were the days of the mid-1950s when China was welcomed as a novitiate in Afro-Asia counsels. China was now unpopular with each of the three leading neutralists. Tito, as well as strongly resenting her support for Albania, also found China's opposition a major obstacle in the way of Yugoslavia achieving a *détente* with the Communist camp; Nasser resented Chinese activity and rivalry in the Afro-Asian Peoples' Movement now centred on Cairo; while Nehru, harbouring a Tibetan government in exile and with the growing strains of frontier clashes with China, now, as on several occasions before, discounted the need for another Bandung-like meeting.

Though Sukarno's plan for a second Bandung had clearly failed by early April, later in the same month Nasser and Tito met in Cairo and successfully launched their project for what eventually became the Belgrade Neutralist Summit. At the time both leaders were being subjected to venomous attacks from Soviet publicity organs while both enjoyed tepidly correct relations with the United States. As they conferred the American-encouraged invasion of Cuba was tried and failed in the Bay of Pigs, and apparently the two Presidents' immediate reaction was that this event, in conjunction with the continuing civil war in Laos, was a part of what they regarded as a steadily worsening international situation, and thus made the need for a general neutralist conference urgent.

The two co-sponsors now moved swiftly and decisively. On 26th April 1961, Nasser and Tito sent a joint letter[7] to the leaders of twenty-

---

[6] *Guardian*, 10 May 1961, reported that in March Sukarno had sent letters to Heads of other Governments suggesting another Bandung to "support the liquidation of colonialism and imperialism in the shortest possible time". Marshall Chen Yi, China's Foreign Minister, welcomed the idea during his visit to Indonesia in April 1961. *The Times*, 11 Apr. 1961, reported the opening of a 53-nation Afro-Asian Solidarity Council Conference at Bandung. Sukarno addressed the 150 delegates at the opening session. He proposed that a second Afro-Asian conference (i.e. at the inter-governmental level) should be held in order to face the new colonialism. It was reported that China and the Soviet Union had sent strong delegations and that a statue of Mr Lumumba was erected in the conference hall. He was described as a martyr of the fight for independence and a victim of assassination by "colonialist stooges".

[7] See Ibrahim Shukrallah, *Non-Alignment: Hope and Fulfilment* (The National Publications House Press, Cairo; n.d. but 1961 or 1962), pp. 39-40.

one non-aligned countries suggesting that in view of recent world developments and the dangerous increase in international tensions a conference of non-aligned states should be held to try to promote improvements in international relations, the relinquishment of policies of force and the constructive settlement of international conflicts. They proposed that such a meeting should be held soon and at any rate before the sixteenth session of the U.N. General Assembly opened, so that the non-aligned countries might participate in the Assembly as effectively as possible in joint endeavours. Tito was later to attribute the actual differences in policy between India and the United Arab Republic and Yugoslavia on Congo issues to the lack of "a more systematic co-ordination".[8]

Tito and Nasser further suggested that a preparatory meeting should be held in Cairo as early as possible to discuss such questions as the agenda, the place and date of the meeting and other relevant matters. The weeks between the Tito-Nasser initiative and the actual opening of the Belgrade Conference on 1st September were rife with speculation in the world's press about the character and likely consequences of this novel meeting—issues fully befogged by prophecy and partisanship. But it is important to remember that Tito and Nasser had already strongly influenced the issue by sending preliminary invitations to twenty-one countries of *their* choice, and that they had already drawn up what was in broad measure a prototype for the Belgrade agenda. And although the sponsors had kept their original list of invitations secret,[9] there seems little doubt that it corresponded closely with those states that actually assembled for the preparatory conference in Cairo and that the ground had been well prepared during Tito's recent journeys in Asia and Africa, and by Nasser with the help of his fellow Casablanca powers. (A Casablanca Charter was signed by Morocco, Ghana, Guinea, Mali, the U.A.R. and the Algerian Provisional Government in Cairo in May 1961, prohibiting accession to foreign military pacts, providing for a joint African High Command, and requiring all signatories strictly to practise policies of non-alignment.)[10] Only Nehru's apparent lack of enthusiasm for their scheme seemed to worry Tito and Nasser. But although until almost the very eve of the Belgrade Conference Nehru seemed reluctant fully to endorse[11] Nasser's and Tito's

[8] See *The Times*, 30 Aug. 1961.
[9] In the *New York Times* of 7 June 1961 it was reported that 23 countries were invited to Cairo, but that Venezuela declined, and Mexico, after first accepting, did not send a delegate.
[10] See Colin Legum, *Pan-Africanism* (London, 1962), pp. 50-2 and 187-8.
[11] Rawle Knox reported from New Delhi on 2 June that "Nasser and Tito had been pressing Mr Nehru for two years to join in a meeting of the 'uncommitted triumvirate' but Mr Nehru had laid low and said nothing"; see *Overseas Foreign News Service*, No. 17011.

plans or to admit publicly that he would attend in person, equally he was unwilling to oppose in the open. So, when formal invitations were sent out on 6th May, fixing the date of the preparatory Cairo meeting for 5th June, the letter signed by Tito, Nasser, and now by Sukarno too, also stated that the Prime Minister of India was happy to join in the invitation to the various governments concerned.

The preparatory meeting, mostly of Foreign Ministers, was held in Cairo as scheduled from 5th - 12th June. It was attended by delegations from Afghanistan, Burma, Cambodia, Ceylon, Cuba, Ethiopia, Ghana, Guinea, India, Indonesia, Iraq, Mali, Morocco, Nepal, Saudi-Arabia, Somalia, Sudan, the United Arab Republic, Yemen, Yugoslavia, and the provisional government of Algeria. Brazil was represented by an observer.

As well as agreeing that the full Summit Conference would convene in Belgrade on 1st September, it was also agreed that the agenda should provide for (i) an exchange of views on the international situation; (ii) a full consideration of all relevant matters concerning the establishment and strengthening of international peace and security; (iii); discussion of problems of unequal economic development; (iv) any other matters. The responsibility for administrative and other preparations were left to the host country, Yugoslavia, to arrange. Only one major item—the question which other states should be invited to Belgrade— was left for an ambassadorial committee of the twenty-one Cairo conferees to decide. But to help them in their deliberations the Foreign Ministers presented a five-point definition of non-alignment.

This definition[12] laid down that no country should be admitted to the Summit meeting unless it complied with the following conditions:
  (1) to follow an independent policy based on peaceful co-existence with other countries of different political and social ideologies, or to show trends towards such a policy;
  (2) always to support popular liberation movements;
  (3) not to become a party to any collective military pact that would involve implication in current East-West wrangles;
  (4) not to become a party to any bilateral treaty with any regional defence bloc, if that would mean involvement in East-West disputes;
  (5) not to have on its territory any foreign military bases set up with their own consent.

Each of these criteria left room for flexibility in interpretation, and while they gave a broad indication of what the Foreign Ministers meant by non-alignment the whole definition was not free from ambiguity. To

---

[12] See *Dawn*, 13 June 1961; *Observer*, 18 June 1961; and Ljubomir Radovanovic, *From Bandung to Beograd* (Yugoslavia Information Service No. 1050, Aug. 1961), p. 23.

an outsider it was not immediately obvious whether these criteria were to refer to past performances or to promises about behaviour in the future. In the event it seems that the former was more important than the latter.

Eleven of the twenty-one states called to Cairo by Tito and Nasser were new states, independent since 1945. Indeed, only five of them (Burma, Cambodia, Ceylon, India, and Indonesia) were independent in 1955, and so represented at the Bandung Conference; the other six (Ghana, Guinea, Mali, Morocco, Somalia, and Sudan) had all secured their independence since 1955, and only Sudan and Somalia were not Casablanca powers. This eleven became twelve on 8th June with the addition of the not yet independent republic of Algeria. And Algeria remained on the list despite the expressed misgivings of some 'moderate' neutralists—most notably, India, Burma, Ethiopia, and Sudan. (After all, could it not be argued that Archbishop Makarios had been an honoured guest at Bandung at a time when his claims to the allegiance of his entire people were more doubtful than those of the Arab leaders of the provisional Algerian government? At Cairo Ghana and Indonesia, as well as the Arabs, strongly urged the admission of Algeria to their talks.) Then there were five older states (Afghanistan, Ethiopia, Nepal, Saudi Arabia, Yemen), each without an active foreign policy before the 1950s; but all five had been represented at Bandung, and all but Ethiopia were to prove themselves at Belgrade as vehemently opposed to "Western colonialism". In joining this company Iraq had the distinction of being the sole defector from a Western "cold war" alliance, just as Yugoslavia had the distinction of being the sole defector from the Communist camp. Saudi Arabia and Morocco were not disqualified by the fact of having American air bases on their soil, presumably because they had already announced that they were making arrangements to secure their removal. The presence of the great American base at Guantanamo in Cuba was not regarded as being there with the "consent" of the Cuban people, and on 6th June the Cuban Foreign Minister urged that the Neutralist Summit Conference should be held in Havana, "the centre of resistance to American imperialism".

So, in fact, much greater emphasis was placed on the requirement "always to support popular liberation movements" than on the invitation to "show trends" towards an "independent policy based on peaceful co-existence". This was underlined by the treatment of Indian proposals. For although it was reported[13] that Indian spokesmen urged that a further nineteen states (Sweden, Ireland, Finland, Paraguay, Argentine, Chile, Costa Rica, Ecuador, Bolivia, Mexico, Brazil, Lebanon, Jordan, Malaya, Tunisia, Nigeria, Sierra Leone, Upper Volta, and Togo)

[13] *Hindu*, 8 July and 1 Aug. 1961; *Observer*, 11 June 1961.

should be invited, this more comprehensive vision of the non-aligned countries was not to be realized. In fact, at the Cairo Foreign Ministers' conference the twenty-one nations agreed that they were themselves non-aligned states, but only four more states (the former Belgian Congo, Cyprus, Lebanon, and Tunisia) were added to the list of states to be represented at the Belgrade Conference, which also now included Bolivia and Ecuador, as well as Brazil, as official observers. Though India was no doubt glad to see Lebanon and Tunisia, and probably glad to see a fellow Commonwealth country, Cyprus, added to the list of acceptable neutralists, it was known that she disliked the idea of inviting representatives from one or more of the warring factions in the Congo.[14] Furthermore, it is doubtful if the invitations were sent to Lebanon, Cyprus or Tunisia because of Indian urging, Lebanon was another anti-Israeli voice to add to the Arab opposition to Israel. President Makarios managed to be on a week's official visit to Cairo when the ambassadorial committee was scrutinizing the final invitation list to Belgrade, and it was while assuring Nasser that Cypriots would never allow British bases to be used for an attack on any Arab countries[15] that Makarios probably gained his neutralist spurs. Tunisia, besides being another Arab League state, was, after the July battle[16] with the French garrison around the French base of Bizerta, widely regarded as a victim of "imperialist" attack. Though, hitherto, Tunisia had been estranged from the Casablanca powers (mainly because of its support for an independent Mauritania in the face of Morocco's claim that Mauritania was Moroccan territory), the Bizerta incident brought about a temporary abatement of 'fraternal' squabbles in the interests of a common Arab and African front against French 'aggression'. France refused to attend the special session of the U.N. General Assembly called solely to discuss the Bizerta situation. Tunisia was very strongly supported by African and Asian states at this special session— and was invited to Belgrade. None of the Brazzaville group[17] of newly independent African states were invited to Belgrade; all of them were former French colonies, and in the view of the Casablanca powers all of them were still far too closely tied to France.

Right up to the very opening of the Conference the world's press kept alive a sense of uncertainty about the composition and probable

[14] See Robert C. Good, "Congo Crisis: the rôle of the New States" in *Neutralism* (The Washington Center of Foreign Policy Research, 1961, mimeograph), pp. 1-46; and *Daily Telegraph*, 1 Sept. 1961.
[15] See *Observer*, 11 June 1961.
[16] See *Economist*, 29 July 1961, pp. 433-4 and 448; also *ibid.*, 7 Oct. 1961, p. 20, and Y.B.U.N., 1961. In August 1961 Tunisia had signed its first aid agreement with the Soviet Union, a loan of £10 m. for technical and scientific assistance, valid until 1964.
[17] See Colin Legum, *Pan-Africanism*, pp. 50 and 176-82.

character of the neutralist summit. The Indian paper *Hindu* on 17th August, having earlier reported that the Casablanca powers had overcome the opposition of India, Ethiopia, Burma and Sudan to the presence of Congo and Algeria at Belgrade, now reported that the Casablanca caucus was to meet in Cairo before the Belgrade talks and drew the inference that this made "it pretty clear where the initiative will be". The same paper also announced that Mr Nehru would be accompanied to Belgrade by Mrs Bandaranaike, that he was to have talks with King Mahendra and U Nu in New Delhi before departing, and that Sukarno had already refused an invitation to stop off at Delhi en route to Belgrade. Clearly the Indian-led Colombo powers' caucus of 1954 was no more. The Pakistani paper *Dawn* reported on 31st August that Yugoslavia had invited Chile on Monday to send an observer to the Conference which was to open on Friday. It was not revealed whether this was with the approval or disapproval of Cuba—which had hitherto truculently assumed major rights for itself as the judge of Latin American neutralist inclinations. Anyway, the Chilean Foreign Minister announced, with regret, that there was no time to appoint a delegate. This was but a calmer rejoinder to a similarly late invitation Nigeria had received, and refused—mostly because of its humiliating lateness and because of resentment against recent Ghanaian policies. Also on 31st August the *Daily Telegraph* reported that the Conference organizers had again rejected an East German request to send official observers with the comment that "only those who are invited to send observers may do so". It was also pointed out that as a member of the Warsaw Pact Eastern Germany could hardly claim to be non-aligned. The Bonn government sent a diplomatic note to each of the Conference delegations (save the host country with which Bonn had no diplomatic relations) gravely informing them of Western rights in Berlin and of the Bonn viewpoint on the situation of the two Germanies.

It was Berlin and the tense German situation which made the diplomatic skirmishing which took place before the Belgrade Conference trivial when compared with the apparently looming threat of a Soviet-American clash of arms. After much cautious preparation President Kennedy and Chairman Khrushchov had met for two days of private conversation in Vienna on 3rd and 4th June. Common ground was only established regarding Laos, where both leaders were agreed on the need for, though not the means to achieve, a cease-fire and 'neutral' status. Khrushchov's determination to try to press ahead with the application of his *troika* proposals to the U.N. Secretariat and to nuclear test control and disarmament agencies, and his avowed determination to "settle" the Berlin and German questions in 1961 caused Kennedy to admit their deep disagreement in a television report to the American nation on his return to Washington. On 13th August the East Berliners began building their government's high wall to seal off the eastern from the western sectors of the city. Soon the sense of being under siege was very strong in West Berlin. In the Indian parliament Mr Nehru said that "the drums of war are already beating in Berlin". As the Berlin wall daily grew higher and thicker the two rival superpowers announced partial mobilization and impending increases in their armed strength. On 1st September the Soviet government chose to end its two-year moratorium with the United States on nuclear testing. The Belgrade Neutralist Conference opened to the announcement of a new nuclear dust storm over Siberia.

THE CONFERENCE

It was uncertain at the start whether the Conference would develop along strict "anti-colonialist" lines which when applied to such currently topical places as Angola, Kuwait, Mauritania, West Irian, Aden, Kenya, and Algeria, would have certainly indicated a strong anti-Western bias, or whether it would seek a more studiously peace-making rôle. Prior to announcing its decision to resume nuclear tests and to conduct a first test explosion on the eve of the Belgrade meeting, the Soviet Union had appeared reserved and aloof towards the Conference, and news of its impending opening had not exactly been blazoned forth in the Soviet press. Tito, in his opening speech[18] as host did not refer to the Soviet resumption of nuclear tests, but later expressed "understanding"[19] for its motives. Nasser, Nehru, Nkrumah and some other speakers openly deplored it.

The public part of the Conference was taken up almost entirely with statements by each head of delegation, during what was misleadingly termed the general "debate". Speeches were roughly related to an agenda which included such topics as the causes of international tension, colonialism, and neo-colonialism, military bases and disarmament; peaceful co-existence; the structure and reorganization of the United Nations, and economic development and financial assistance to under-developed countries. But from the start almost[20] every speech fell into two parts;

[18] See the official report of The Conference of Heads of State or Government of Non-Aligned Countries (published by Publicisticko-Izdavacki Zavod, Yugoslavia, 1961), pp. 17-22. (The report is hereafter cited as B.C.R.)

[19] B.C.R., p. 156. Curiously, when this documentary record was published in Dec. 1961 the following sentences were missing from the actual text of Tito's speech, but were on a separate sheet of corrigenda: "We are not surprised so much by the communiqué on the resumption of atomic and hydrogen weapons tests, because we could understand the reasons adduced by the Government of the U.S.S.R. We are surprised more by the fact that this was done on the day of the opening of this conference of peace."

[20] Notable exceptions were Cuba, whose delegate preferred to concentrate on attacking the U.S.A. (see B.C.R., pp. 118-28); the Yemen, whose delegate concen-

first, some attempt to define, or at least describe, the speaker's sense of what were the general principles and preoccupations of non-alignment; and, second, a discussion of world tension.

All were agreed that proponents of non-alignment were now more numerous and more confident. Many were also aware that non-alignment was protean and that they were still groping for definitions and identity, even while they recognized the forces that buoyed them up.

Thus Haile Selassie[21] stated in a powerful, frank and incisive passage:

"We may say that no nation here feels itself so wholly within the sphere of influence of these two great groups that it cannot act independently . . .

"By the word 'neutral', we do not, of course, mean that abstention from political activity which has been for so long the hallmark of a Switzerland. We can no more refrain from political activity in the year 1961 than man today can voluntarily refrain from partaking of the radioactive fall-out which will be bestowed upon him should a nuclear holocaust erupt on this globe. Nor does neutrality mean that without taking sides, we content ourselves with urging that the powers most intimately concerned negotiate in good faith to the solution of the issues in dispute between them; we have passed the point where prayerful pleading serves any purpose other than to debase those who thereby abdicate any responsibility or power to influence events.

"To be neutral is to be impartial, impartial to judge actions and policies objectively, as we see them either contributing to or detracting from the resolution of the world's problems, the preservation of peace and the improvement of the general level of man's living conditions. Thus, we may find ourselves now opposing, now supporting, now voting with, now voting against, first the East, next the West. It is the worth of the policies themselves, and not their source or sponsor, which determines the position of one who is truly neutral. This, we maintain, is the essence of non-alignment."

In general terms what Haile Selassie said was acceptable to all, and his claims that non-alignment could not be isolationism but that it could mean 'objective' judgment were widely echoed in other speeches. But when it came to giving more precise content to these claims, widespread agreement was less obvious. For Haile Selassie clearly identified himself with those who were urging that the conferees concentrate their efforts on endeavouring to mediate between the Cold War camps. He was thus lining up with such 'moderates' as Nehru, Mrs Bandaranaike

---

trated on attacking imperialism, especially "British imperialism, with its notorious deceit" (see B.C.R., pp. 238-42); and Somalia, whose delegate devoted a lengthy passage of thinly veiled references to territorial claims on Ethiopia (while the Emperor listened impassively). See B.C.R., pp. 226-33, esp. pp. 230-1.

[21] B.C.R., p. 86.

and, perhaps, Tito, and not with the 'militants' like Sukarno, or the spokesmen for Cuba, Guinea, Somalia, Mali and the Yemen, who were more concerned with anti-colonial causes. Nasser's position was ambivalent; he appeared to sympathize strongly with the 'militants' while wishing to concert closely with the 'moderates'.

The speech of Prince Sihanouk of Cambodia[22] was very largely a characteristically forthright analysis of his own country's predicament and of the plight of Cambodia's northern neighbour, Laos. With what was in this company rare approval of 'buffer' status, he proposed that a "neutralized zone" embracing Cambodia and Laos would help to solve the problem of Laos and would serve as a valuable buffer between Cold War opponents. But the principal claim Sihanouk made was that the very effort and achievement of national individuality involved in staying outside the Cold War camps was internationally as well as nationally beneficial. This was so, Sihanouk claimed, because an independent stand outside Cold War alliances impeded the dangerous drift towards a total identification of all states with one or other of "the two nuclear blocs" at present deadlocked in global struggle:

"We have often heard neutrality described as the inability to choose between two ideologies; for, as far as each of the two great powers . . . is concerned, there can only be two conflicting tendencies—the good which is its own, and the bad, which is its opponent's . . . to our way of thinking, this simplification is absurd. For its part, Cambodia has espoused its own ideology: a form of Socialism suited to our special economic and social conditions, and having its roots in our past and our religion, Buddhism. Would the blind adoption of Marxist socialism or American-style democracy have been a wise course? We think not."

And Beuvogui Lansana,[23] emphasizing Guinea's "ideology of anti-ideology" said: "for the disinherited peoples, unequal levels of economic development . . . are more important than ideological considerations."

Yet it was the Sudanese soldier and Head of State, General Abboud,[24] who poured most content into the fashionable theme of the needs of underdeveloped economies when he spoke of the growing psychological and material gap between "the northern and southern parts of the globe", alleging that "the developed countries" have in fact "widened the gap by effecting the drop in the prices of the primary products". Abboud further said that assistance should aim "at giving impetus to

[22] B.C.R., pp. 182-196. An example of Sihanouk's frankness was this passage: " . . . during the Angkor period we ourselves were imperialists occupying the whole (sic) of South East Asia, we ourselves were colonialists oppressing the neighbouring peoples. But the wheel of history has turned and from oppressors we have become oppressed." B.C.R., p. 184.

[23] B.C.R., p. 222.

[24] B.C.R., pp. 52-66, and esp. pp. 63-5.

our economy to reach the take-off stage" and that "we expect assistance to help us to come to rely eventually on ourselves, and not to awaken in us the instinct to fill in a temporary gap in our economy. We do not want it to become a permanent element, or take the place of our own initiative and efforts."

Sukarno,[25] too, in himself a personal embodiment and example of the eclectic suppleness of much neutralism, spoke of Indonesian searches for a distinctive national personality:

"Yes, we in Indonesia have already passed through the gruelling process of forming our national ideology and we have now reached our synthesis, i.e. Indonesian socialism . . . Yes, our Indonesian socialism developed through turmoil. In the course of that turmoil we have learnt many things, and we believe that the lessons we have learnt will be of interest to other nations. We have learnt that the basic ingredient of any national ideology must be the national inheritance of that nation itself, its heritage from the past, the traditions which bind its people together and set the pattern of their life. In Indonesia, this is kerakjatan, gotong royong, musjawarah and mufakat—the people as the source, collective effort for a common goal, discussion and deliberation, consensus of opinion. To this basic ingredient add all useful ideas from other countries. In Indonesia, for example, we drew the equality of men from the Jefferson declaration . . . we drew scientific socialism from Marxism. Put this mixture into the mould of the national identity and the result is a national identity which binds the people together and frees all energies for the tremendous tasks of construction."

Nehru's speech[26] with its single-mindedness on the question of how to avoid world war gave a welcome sense of purpose to a very disparate gathering. His main contention was that fear and suspicion between both Cold War camps were the prime and immediate threats to world peace and that "the era of classic colonialism is gone and is dead"— though, characteristically, he added the qualification "though, of course, it survives and gives a lot of trouble". It was not that Nehru was the first to say this; Haile Selassie had said much the same earlier. But Nehru, the only leader to speak extempore, put it at the centre of his short speech and subordinated everything else to it. By "classic colonialism" Nehru obviously meant the occupation of overseas territories by European powers, and the claim that this era essentially "was over" was, *at that time*, far more true of Asia than of Africa. In Asia European government lingered only in a few places (and, for these conferees, most notably in Goa, West Irian, and Aden); whereas in Africa there was palpable European, or white, presence in Algeria, Kenya,

[25] B.C.R., pp. 28-9.
[26] B.C.R., pp. 107-17.

Katanga, the Rhodesias, Angola, Mozambique and the Union of South Africa. Even so, Nehru's claim that the need to try to avoid world war was more urgent and so more worthy of the attention of the delegates than were anti-colonial issues was acceptable to all but the most dedicated and introverted anti-colonialists among them. But these latter few, representatives of the radical African countries, even condemned Nehru as *"vieux jeu"*—though not in their public speeches. It was far more important, they implied, to concentrate on fighting colonialism and on stopping the loss of lives in Algeria and Angola than on trying to prevent a world war. And if they were stressing what was more practicable for a gathering of this kind, rather than what was preferable, perhaps their emphasis was right. However, they were in the minority in urging this. For it was Nehru, the lodestar of neutralism since the earliest days of the Cold War, this fastidious Kashmiri Brahmin who had so often confessed that he was not versed in the ways of the market place, who was to assume decisive leadership in shaping the eventual outcome of the Conference. Most important of all his contributions was his insistence that the Conference should know its own strength and weakness, and address the two greatest world powers in a language relevant to the world as it was and might become and not as some militants thought it ought to be. It was Nehru who devised and drafted the 400-word "peace appeal"[27] to Khrushchov and Kennedy, which was adopted unanimously by the conferees in their closing session.

Nearly every speaker made some reference to the German problem. The existence of two Germanies it was generally felt was a fact which had to be recognized, although not many followed either President Sukarno in demanding the diplomatic recognition of Eastern Germany, or yet President Makarios[28] who opposed the continuance of the barrier preventing freedom of movement between West and East Berlin, and suggested the need for a free plebiscite on German reunification under the United Nations. Though there was much insistence on the need for German self-determination, on the whole the analysis of the German problem was rather facile.

Insistence on the need for general and complete disarmament was well nigh general and complete, even though there seemed to be general unawareness or at least impatience with the complexities of the subject, and condemnation of all nuclear testing was also almost universal. Virtually every speaker wanted Communist China admitted as a full member of the United Nations. Tito and other speakers opposed

[27] B.C.R., pp. 264-5.
[28] B.C.R., pp. 170-3, esp. 173. This speech was remembered with pleasure by West German spokesmen when President Makarios paid a state visit to Bonn the following May; the German Federal Government then gave grants and loans to Cyprus—see *The Times*, 21 and 25 May 1962.

any idea of forming a third bloc between East and West but urged that the uncommitted countries should have more influence in world affairs.

Yet, particularly among some of the Casablanca powers, there was a strong inclination to impose on the meeting a certain discipline and unity, with President Nkrumah[29] appearing as the principal, even peremptory, protagonist of this view. Nkrumah wanted the Conference to make specific demands. These included the demand for complete liquidation of colonialism by the end of 1962, for a declaration of Africa as a nuclear-free zone, and for the appointment of three deputies to the U.N. Secretary-General to represent the East, the West and the uncommitted countries respectively. But specificity was not to be the hallmark of the final Conference declarations, and none of Nkrumah's specific demands appeared there.

As well as the public speeches, the Conference afforded opportunities for private business to be transacted. Presidents Bourgiba and Nasser met twice to resolve their previous differences—successfully, it was reported.[30] Five countries (Yugoslavia, Afghanistan, Cambodia, Ghana and the Congo) granted full *de jure* recognition to the Algerian provisional government, with India thus left out on a limb for granting only *de facto* recognition.[31] A curious document purporting to be a photographic copy of a letter written by a British Conservative M.P. and claiming to disclose secret British plans for keeping control in newly independent African states was put into general circulation, and apparently[32] accepted by some African nationalists as genuine. Reading matter was not in short supply. For during the Conference there arrived twelve messages from Heads of State or Government, ten memorandums, one hundred and eleven letters, messages and telegrams; with fourteen more messages and telegrams arriving after the Conference had broken up.[33] And one evening the heads of delegations were invited to scale the gastronomic heights of Tito's challenging sixteen-course dinner, while other guests jostled for their buffet meal nearby.[34]

But despite all these junketings the conferees had, in the last resort, met to agree. And agree they did on 6th September after prolonging

[29] B.C.R., pp. 98-106.
[30] *Guardian*, 5 Sept. 1961; and "Bourguibism: A Separate Road", chapter ix, pp. 118-28 in *The Arab Rôle in Africa* by Jacques Baulin (Penguin Books, Harmondsworth, 1962).
[31] See K. P. Misra, "Recognition of the Provisional Government of the Algerian Republic: A Study of the Policy of the Government of India" in *Political Studies*, vol. x (2), June 1962, pp. 130-45.
[32] See *Observer*, 10 Sept. 1961; and Andrew Boyd, "Belgrade Notebook" in *Encounter*, Nov. 1961, p. 59. Boyd's whole article, pp. 56-61, well conveys the atmosphere of the conference.
[33] For full list see B.C.R., pp. 266-70.
[34] See report in *Guardian*, 5 Sept. 1961.

their talks an extra day, and by producing their final declarations at 2 a.m. after nearly twelve hours of continuous drafting. Mr Nehru got what he wanted from the Conference—acceptance for his own brief peace appeal to Kennedy and Khrushchov to make, *inter alia*, "the most immediate and direct approach to each other in order to avert imminent conflict and establish peace".[35] The second document, a 4,000-word, twenty-seven-point declaration, on the whole avoided concrete topics, putting them forward briefly and only when particular interests were strongly pressed. There was a paragraph each on Algeria, Angola, Tunisia, and the Congo, a passing mention of "the Arab people of Palestine", two brief references to Cuba and support for the admission of Communist China to the United Nations. Otherwise, the declaration was full of wholly predictable pieties. There was insistence on the need: to end colonialism swiftly; to promote peaceful co-existence; to achieve general, complete and internationally controlled disarmament; to eliminate foreign military bases; to reduce the great and increasing economic inequalities between nations; and to increase neutralist representation in all important international agencies; and, in what was perhaps the most distinctively neutralist item, there was one piece of mildly phrased proselytism:

"The participants in the Conference . . . consider that the further extensions of the non-committed area of the world constitutes the only possible and indispensable alternative to the policy of total division of the world into blocs, and intensification of Cold War policies. The non-aligned countries provide encouragement and support to all peoples fighting for their independence and equality.

The participants in the Conference are convinced that the emergence of newly-liberated countries will further assist in narrowing of the area of bloc antagonisms and thus encourage all tendencies aimed at strengthening peace and promoting peaceful co-operation among independent and equal nations."[36]

THE IMMEDIATE AFTERMATH

What were the lessons of the Belgrade meeting? These were far from clear. We must avoid the temptation to take the agreed proclamations too seriously or the emotions of the conferees too lightly. And just as many incongruities and ambiguities were revealed during the Conference, so there were plenty of parallels for these in the three months following.

All the conferees had professed opposition to the macro-imperialism of big powers; though some had micro-imperialist ambitions of their

[35] B.C.R., p. 252.
[36] B.C.R., p. 256. The whole declaration takes up just over eight pages of the official report, i.e. pp. 253-61.

own. Most claimed that they spoke for "world opinion", though some were personally uncertain of much support from their own "national opinion". Many spoke of the signal importance of the Belgrade meeting, though three Heads of State—Fidel Castro, Karim Kassim, and Sékou Touré—had stayed away because of more pressing business at home. The conferees had ended by calling for more neutralists to join them, yet they had begun by restricting the size of their gathering. But if these contrasts were obscured by the final declaration this was not surprising. For such is the task for final Conference declarations to perform.

Even so, it was ironic that a Conference which had opened just as the prior Kennedy-Khrushchov meeting had been followed not by a *détente* but by an intensification of friction, should itself end by sending emissaries to request another superpower meeting. It was also ironic that a Conference which had in its final declaration given much space to Nehru's moderate ambiguities and very little to the militant powers' minatory pronouncements should send two militants, Sukarno and Keita, as emissaries to Washington bearing Nehru's peace appeal. As it was, both in Washington and in Moscow (whence Nehru and Nkrumah travelled separately, though they were charged jointly to present the peace missive to Khrushchov) the letters were received with formal politeness, were quickly filed, and were heard of no more. All the indications were that each of the superpowers was displeased with the failure of the neutralists openly to have declared themselves neutralist on their side. Yet it was patent that the neutralists were not a bloc and that no single generalized policy designed to embrace all of them would be adequate. It soon appeared that both superpowers were re-appraising their relations with neutralist states. Official American reactions to the Belgrade Conference were studiously non-committal, unlike the American press; but it was clear that there was some disillusionment, especially with Yugoslavia. It was reported[37] that President Kennedy had created a special Cabinet-level group to see how the non-aligned countries could be "educated" into realizing what were their "true" interests. American aid to Yugoslavia was suspended. At the 22nd Soviet Party Congress in October the unprecedented presence of delegations from non-Communist ruling parties—from Ghana, Mali, and Guinea—was proclaimed as a sign of the growing attraction of Communism for all ex-colonial peoples. Cuba was fêted at the Congress as the prime symbol of Latin American liberation from the imperial oppression of the United States, and as the harbinger of similar revolts throughout the Western hemisphere. There were indications that future Soviet aid

[37] See *Daily Telegraph*, 3 Oct. 1961. It was also widely reported that Mr George Kennan, the American ambassador in Belgrade during 1961, was deeply disappointed by Tito's concern not to annoy the Soviet Union during the Belgrade Conference.

would be primarily for those "friendly" neutralists that followed the Soviet foreign policy line, severed their economic ties with the West, organized their economies on a "socialist" basis, and admitted indigenous Communists to their governments. Clearly, Cuba was moving towards such "friendly" neutralism, but, by contrast, Guinea rebelled against Soviet guidance and expelled the Soviet embassador from Conakry in December.

The Anglo-American press was full of righteous indignation because more spokesmen had not openly attacked Soviet misdeeds but had continued to repeat the tediously familiar anti-Western themes. The more disillusioned of these oracles tended to imply that many neutralists were crypto-Communists, stalking horses for Moscow. Such charges did in many ways point to the truth of Abboud's earlier plaint about the psychological gulf between "the north and the south". For, while even the most cursory reading of the speeches delivered at the Belgrade Conference revealed the depth and intensity of anti-Western sentiment, it was remarkable that this still occasioned so much apparently genuine surprise in the West. All the participants regarded themselves as revolutionaries. Their "revolution of rising expectations", as Mrs Bandaranaike described it, significantly borrowing Adlai Stevenson's phrase[38] (or more pointedly, in Sukarno's version— "the revolution of rising demands"), represented demands of a West which was taken to include Soviet Europe. They were, and are, demands voiced in language first spoken in the West. The final declaration of the Conference called for "the transition from an old order based on domination to a new order based on co-operation". But it was the Iraqi Foreign Minister (one of Harold Laski's former pupils) who gave the clearest point to these claims when he spoke of the neutralists' need to embrace "three revolutions"—nationalist, socialist and the scientific-technological.[39] Yet all these 'revolutions' have their roots in the Western world, and these neutralist needs boiled down to the demand to 'Westernize' themselves largely by their own hands and on their own terms, in their own interests as they see them.

It would be quite wrong to assume that some stable form of neutralist doctrine or practice crystallized during or as a result of the Belgrade Conference. We saw that the actual process by which states were designated as neutralists for Belgrade Conference purposes owed much more to the prior arrangements of Tito and Nasser and to the pressure of events than to the formal definition concocted earlier in Cairo. But the fatalistic belief[40] that there is little point in trying to propitiate

[38] See Adlai E. Stevenson, *Call to Greatness* (London, 1955), p. 43.
[39] B.C.R., pp. 144-5.
[40] See, e.g., Peregrine Worsthorne, "The Belgrade Illusion" in *Daily Telegraph*, 5 Sept. 1961.

N

any of the non-aligned states because they will always show a bias against the West and take the Soviet line is not supported by the facts.

For instance, in the opening stages of the 16th General Assembly the Soviet delegation suffered defeats both on nuclear tests and on its proposal to replace the late Secretary-General, Mr Hammarskjold, by a triumvirate, each member of which would hold the power of veto. These Soviet moves were defeated mostly by neutralist votes and the Soviets eventually decided not to oppose the installation of U Thant (one of the Burmese delegation at the Belgrade meeting) as Hammarskjold's successor.

While it was true that the resumption of nuclear testing by the Soviets was not unanimously condemned, the fact that some states chose not to do so cannot necessarily be taken as evidence either of their crypto-Communism or even of their unremitting anti-Westernism.[41] Tito's unwillingness to denounce the resumption of Soviet testing may be understood in terms of his ambivalent yearnings to be with but not in the Communist camp; but the greater number of African participants were probably quite genuinely more concerned about French atom tests in the Sahara than by much larger Soviet ones in Siberia. A small fire in his own backyard will tend to worry a householder more than a bigger fire in the next street.

Of course, most of the governments represented in Belgrade were in fact heavily committed and aligned on one issue or another. Some were obviously inclined to favour the Soviet bloc—Cuba was the most obvious example here—a few (one thinks here especially of Tunisia) were inclined towards the North Atlantic powers. Most of them were involved in cold wars[42] of their own. And while the distinction between 'moderates' and militants at Belgrade had some foundation in fact, it would be wrong to assume that this therefore described permanent postures. After all, India chose to absorb Goa in December, and Nasser suffered the defection of Syria from the United Arab Republic—just three weeks after the Belgrade meeting—with remarkable composure.

The hitherto brief histories of the Brazzaville, Casablanca and Monrovia groupings clearly reveal that there is a fission-fusion process at work in the diplomatic groupings of the non-aligned, just as there is now in international society at large. All the Belgrade neutralist states are transitional, experimental societies internationally as well as domestically. They want to get all the external help they can to enable

[41] See, e.g., David Rees's review of the Official Conference Report, "Castrumbu Follies '61" in *Spectator*, 18 Jan. 1963. And note the contrasting tones of the two excerpts from *Daily Telegraph* used as epigraphs at the start of this chapter.

[42] E.g. the Arab states against Israel; India and Afghanistan against Pakistan; Ghana against Togoland and Ivory Coast; Iraq against Kuwait; the Yemen and Saudi Arabia against British protectorates; Cambodia against Thailand.

them to advance economically; they want to help to create an international order in which non-aligned states can expect to survive and prosper alongside, or instead of, their aligned neighbours. Regardless of tactical and often temporary alignments of their own, they do want to be able to draw upon the more advanced countries for whatever seems relevant to their needs, without necessarily accepting either Western or Communist ways as a complete model. For some time to come it would be unwise to expect to see more than occasionally clear landmarks in the shifting sands of neutralist activity and endeavour.

CHAPTER VII

SI DEFINITIONEM REQUIRIS . . .

"Words borrow their weight from experiences, which can be very
different." Bertrand de Jouvenel.

'NEUTRALISM' and 'neutralist' are popular and mostly pejorative terms nowadays and their use is often convenient. But
they are not terms of art, and this study has made no attempt
to make them so. For it has not been a central aim to make an anthology
of verbal definitions and equivalents of the term 'neutralism', still less
to end up with a single terse definition. What has here been regarded
as neutralism is often described elsewhere as 'non-alignment', as
'positive neutrality', as 'uncommitted', as 'active and peaceful co-
existence', and in many other ways too. Each of these designations has
something to commend it, but more important than the choice of any
one such label is the appreciation of the relevance of them all, in their
several ways and different contexts, for the student of international
politics. Furthermore, I believe it is a mistake and a distraction of
political enquiry from its proper concerns to seek for a quintessential
neutralism. The term at least connotes certain definite states and statesmen, with their similarities and differences, influenced by and
influencing the character of the Cold War. The first reaction to the use
of the term should be: whose neutralism is referred to and what forms
does it take, how general or particular are these forms? For fruitful
generalizations about the significance of neutralism in international
politics should be generalizations about the actual policies of states and
the attitudes and opinions of statesmen, and are to be justified by
reference to and debate about particular instances and examples. The
conclusions that now follow are deliberately terse and depend for their
validity wholly upon the validity of the analysis from which they are
drawn.

*   *   *

All the new states of the post-war world have become neutralist save
two, the Philippines and Pakistan. All these new states are neutralist
at least in the sense that none of them are members of the multilateral
military alliances of either the Soviet Union or the United States, and
all of them have achieved their sovereign independence internationally
since 1945. These new state neutralists were forty-three out of the fifty-

six neutralist states in a total United Nations membership on 1st January 1963 of one hundred and ten; and an overwhelming majority of these new states were from Asia and Africa. In the conjunction of new statehood and non-alignment lies the main key to an understanding of the nature and significance of neutralism in contemporary international politics. Being neutralist has become a well-nigh inevitable consequence of new statehood in the post-war world. New states do not just happen to be neutralist, they are neutralist because they are new. There are at least five other avenues by which a state has become neutralist, and these have sometimes intersected, but, so far, the transition from dependency to new statehood has been the main highway.

Of the other five avenues to neutralism as a state policy, that of three pioneer neutralists—India, Yugoslavia and Egypt—is the most important, as these three states have initiated certain policies which are now widely recognized as being neutralist, and which new states have copied, or at least come to practise themselves. These three states have shown ways for translating certain widespread urges—especially about military pacts, bases, foreign aid, 'imperialism' and national independence—into policy forms, and in so doing they have attained positions of leadership in the neutralist world.

Of the four remaining categories of neutralist policy, three— neutralization, buffer status, traditional neutrality—are survivals, or revivals, of nineteenth-century practices, while the fourth category— the erstwhile isolationists—illustrates the growing impracticability of isolationist policies today. There are only two currently neutralized states—Austria and Laos (the latter a new state too)—and it is unlikely that there will be many more. Buffer status is now generally unpopular, and the conditions which created buffer states in the nineteenth century do not obtain today. The traditional neutrals—Sweden and Switzerland —are together a class apart, because of their prosperity and the fact that they are the only states to have successfully practised policies of non-alignment in peace and neutrality in war from the nineteenth century right up to the present day. These traditions do not guarantee a successful neutrality in any future hot war in Europe.

The Chinese invasion of India in October 1962 has re-emphasized what has always been true but what has so often been neglected; that a policy of non-alignment, such as India pioneered, cannot with any plausibility be regarded as a method of security that certainly confers upon a state immunities from attack not possessed by those that enter alliances. On the other hand, it is also important to note the limits within which this conclusion is valid. It is not true, at any rate not yet true, that either war or cold war is indivisible throughout the world as a whole. There are still circumstances in which it is possible for states to stand aside from some conflicts without serious danger to themselves. Certainly, recent developments have reduced the significance of geographical distance, whether as barriers to intercourse or as safeguards of independence, but they have not yet entirely eliminated them in either capacity, and so long as this remains true, it will follow that states will find their interests unequally engaged in the struggles of other states.

The Cuban crisis in the last quarter of 1962 showed that though the superpowers were not necessarily impervious to neutralist remonstrances, in such a great-power crisis situation the significance of the non-aligned states is at most marginal. The permanent installation of Soviet missiles in Cuba would not necessarily have revolutionized the global balance-of-power in favour of the Soviet Union; but it would have been a massive affront to America's prestige and would have added to her, still sensitively new, national sense of vulnerability. Though Peking radio castigated the Russian "retreat from Havana" in October 1962 as "a second Munich", it was possible that as Mr Khrushchov compiled his private balance sheet of the crisis he was satisfied with the result. What would be interesting to know is whether the crisis retarded or speeded the spread of neutralism in Latin America. Cuba has now become the unicorn in both the communist and neutralist zoos. Cuba is now avowedly opposed to "capitalism" and more dependent on external Communist support than any other neutralist. Yet if to be a Communist state still requires that the country be ruled unmistakably by the indigenous Communist party then can Cuba now rightly be called Communist? Neutralism, Communism and Capitalism, nowadays, jostle each other frequently, making an uncomfortable troika of equivocation.

The dismantling of the overseas empires of the West European powers has proceeded so rapidly in recent years that the creation of new states by this means is often thought of as soon due to come to a halt. But there are signs that for some leaders in Asia and Africa a swift end to the so-called "anti-colonial" struggle is not immediately envisaged. For at an Afro-Asian Peoples' Solidarity Conference at Moshi in Tanganyika in February 1963 delegates spoke of the need to help a further twenty-seven dependencies still "struggling to be free". Such claims, once made public, are not readily retracted. Clearly, not all the tides of nationalism, racialism and irredentism are everywhere ebbing. Though in North America and Western Europe it might well be expected that anti-Western anti-imperialism will soon become a fading force, there is no strong evidence as yet that this is happening. That this is so probably pleases the Communist powers; and it is not without its ironies that it is the fact of Communist expansion since 1945 which shows most clearly that the age of empires is not yet over. Even so, allegations about neutralist gullibility to Soviet claims are often exaggerated and it is more likely that neutralist suspicion of Soviet and Chinese intentions and deeds will grow rather than diminish. But it is also true that understanding that a threat to one's security exists is not of itself a sufficient safeguard. A prudent reluctance to condemn Communist policies openly is not necessarily evidence of naïvety, though it might be taken as a tacit recognition of the limitations of one's own power to resist severe pressures.

Hitherto, the steady growth in the number of neutralist states has given an impression of growing momentum and has caused the superpowers to take increasing account of factors outside their opposed alliance systems. The difficulties of trying simultaneously to forge friendly relations with neutralist nations while preserving material strength and morale within their own alliance systems are now problems common to both superpowers, and seem likely to increase rather than diminish.

The most dramatic example of the growing impact of neutralist states has been shown in the increasing neutralist membership of the United Nations, especially since December 1955, and the greater attention paid in that organization to neutralist themes and interests as a consequence of the changing pattern of membership.

Even so, it would be wrong to lay great stress on the solidarity or agreement of neutralist states among themselves, for they represent a wide range of different and sometimes conflicting interests. Although there has been much talk about the notion of an association bringing together all neutralist states in a neutralist bloc, this has not materialized so far, nor does this seem likely. Indeed, some neutralists regard a bloc of the non-aligned as a contradiction in terms. However, there have been and will, no doubt, continue to be *ad hoc* groupings of some neutralist states bent on pursuing certain specific ends in common. It is not the case that an uncommitted state is in all respects freer than a member of an alliance; one can only say with surety that its commitments are different.

It is probably in the expression of neutralist doctrine, rather than the practices of neutralist states, that neutralist leaders seem to be most in accord. For words can unite where actions may divide. All neutralists are agreed on the truth of their central propositions—the need to abate the Cold War rivalries, the iniquities of colonialism, the need of poor countries for economic aid, the horrors of nuclear weapons. Indeed, such propositions now meet with such general verbal assent that, in this loose sense, it is possible to say that "we are all neutralists now". But the significant fact is that neutralist doctrine in its broader forms seems most convincingly a philosophy of state practice in Africa and Asia, where it is often nourished by new nationalisms, and where it always

serves to explain or excuse measures proposed or performed in the name
of the neutralist state.

Afro-Asian neutralist doctrine, rather paradoxically, expresses both
highly sensitive suspicion of all foreign influences and more or less
tolerance for all modern political doctrines regarded as useful to
neutralists. It is a highly eclectic and pragmatic doctrine, not least
because its most influential proponents are leaders of neutralist states.
Its arguments are not novel but this does not mean that they lack
appeal, rather the reverse. For neutralist doctrine can provide a rationale
and sense of direction for new nationalisms seeking expression in a
world where increasingly there are pressures forcing each state to adopt
at least declaratory policies on a whole host of international problems,
and where national isolation is a virtual impossibility. At the root of
most Afro-Asian neutralist attitudes to the Cold War lie widely popular
demands for national independence, national equality, and for augmenting national power and welfare. Throughout the greater part of Asia
and Africa the effective choice of political attitudes is not a choice
between the Russian brand of Communism or the American brand of
anti-Communism, but between various shades of anti-Western
neutralist-nationalism and various degrees of concern about local and
regional problems.

In retrospect, three popular beliefs about neutralism as a state policy
seem to have been mistaken.

Firstly, there has been a prevalent assumption that if neutralist states
oppose the Soviet bloc on certain issues, they must therefore support
Western policies instead, or *vice versa*. Yet opposition to a particular
policy of one of the Cold War camps does not necessarily mean approval
of the other. In fact, neither Cold War camp can rely on the majority
of neutralists to consistently take their side in Cold War disputes.
Although Cold War protagonists will persist in trying to see to which
of the camps particular neutralists are inclined, it is important to
remember that neutralist leaders are virtually all genuinely concerned
to stay non-aligned, for it is their fundamental conviction that the
benefits of non-alignment outweigh any advantages that commitment
could bring.

Secondly, American fears of "creeping neutralism", the growth of
neutralist feeling and sentiment within her alliances, resulting in the
defection of some of the members, seem, so far, to have been exaggerated.
Of course, it is arguable that the actual voicing of these fears and
warnings helped to prevent their realization, though this is a dubious
contention. Japanese, French, and British neutralist movements, however vocal, have so far been without international significance as they
have not engendered sufficient strength to take command of the state.
Effective neutralism must be an attribute of statehood, the state being

its measure and mould. The only states which have so far become neutralist as a result of defecting from a Western alliance are Iraq and Cuba (with the latter now consorting closely with the Communist powers). It should be borne in mind, however, that these defections have both occurred since 1958. Certainly there is nothing permanent and unalterable about the present states-system, still less in the alliance systems the older states have developed in the past fifteen years. But while it is now fashionable to decry the advantages of both alliances and of statehood it is important to remember that any attempt to supersede them must start from the fact of their existence, and, preferably, with some clear notion of why their supersession is necessary and how this is to be done.

Thirdly, there seems to be little justification so far for the view that neutralism is a first step to Communism. Americans have feared this and Communists may have believed it, but so far no neutralist state has become Communist (the only really doubtful case here is Cuba)—and only one Communist state, Yugoslavia, has become neutralist. The exact international orientation of Albania is still obscure, but she is undoubtedly still ruled by her indigenous Communist party, and is dependent on support from Communist China. The view that neutralism was a step towards Communism has been widely held in both parts of the committed world because of the strongly anti-Western character of nationalism throughout Asia and Africa. Yet, in fact, Afro-Asian national leaders see their neutralism as a natural expression of their state's sovereign independence in international politics. Ironically, although it is the Communist and not the Western powers who look and work for a world where eventually there can be no non-aligned states, neutralist barbs are directed mostly against the Western powers.

To say that a state or person is "neutralist" is now to use an increasingly indefinite label. This is because the label is now used to connote a wide and increasingly complicated pattern of professions and practices, and because the word is now often used to convey imprecise imputations. There is need for much more study and understanding of particular neutralisms. But at least we can advise that in general neutralism should be seen not as a degeneration or departure from some cherished principles of nineteenth-century neutrality, but primarily as the expression of new sovereignties and new nationalisms in prevailing and ever-changing Cold War conditions.

Neutralism has undoubtedly emerged but, like Proteus, can assume many changing forms. *Si definitionem requiris, circumspice.*

TABLE

Showing Cold War affiliation or type of neutralism practised by the
members of the United Nations on 1st January 1963

	Date of Joining the United Nations	Date of Independence if since 1945	Cold War Affiliation	Category of Neutralism
	1	2	3	4
AFGHANISTAN	Nov. 1946			ex-buffer
ALBANIA	Dec. 1955		ex-Warsaw pact	?
ALGERIA	Oct. 1962	1962		new state
ARGENTINA	Oct. 1945		Rio pact	
AUSTRALIA	Nov. 1945		SEATO-ANZUS	
AUSTRIA	Dec. 1955			neutralized
BELGIUM	Dec. 1945		NATO	
BOLIVIA	Nov. 1945		Rio pact	
BRAZIL	Oct. 1945		Rio pact	
BULGARIA	Dec. 1955		Warsaw pact	
BURMA	Apr. 1948	1948		new state
BURUNDI	Sept. 1962	1962		new state
BYELORUSSIAN S.S.R.	Oct. 1945		Soviet satellite	
CAMBODIA	Dec. 1955	1953/4		new state
CAMEROUN	Sept. 1960	1960		new state
CANADA	Nov. 1945		NATO	
CENTRAL AFRICAN REPUBLIC	Sept. 1960	1960		new state
CEYLON	Dec. 1955	1948		new state
CHAD	Sept. 1960	1960		new state
CHILE	Oct. 1945		Rio pact	
CHINA (Formosa)	Oct. 1945		bilateral pact with U.S.	
COLOMBIA	Nov. 1945		Rio pact	
CONGO (Brazzaville)	Sept. 1960	1960		new state
CONGO (Leopoldville)	Sept. 1960	1960		new state
COSTA RICA	Nov. 1945		Rio pact	
CUBA	Oct. 1945		ex-Rio pact	?
CYPRUS	Sept. 1960	1960	British bases	new state
CZECHOSLOVAKIA	Oct. 1945		Warsaw pact	
DAHOMEY	Sept. 1960	1960		new state
DENMARK	Oct. 1945		NATO	
DOMINICAN REPUBLIC	Oct. 1945		Rio pact	
ECUADOR	Dec. 1945		Rio pact	
EL SALVADOR	Oct. 1945		Rio pact	
ETHIOPIA	Nov. 1945			ex-isolationist
Fed. of MALAYA	Sept. 1957	1957	bilateral pact with U.K.	new state
FINLAND	Dec. 1955		bilateral pact with U.S.S.R.	ex-buffer
FRANCE	Oct. 1945		NATO and SEATO	
GABON	Sept. 1960	1960		new state
GHANA	Mar. 1957	1957		new state
GREECE	Oct. 1945		NATO	
GUATEMALA	Nov. 1945		Rio pact	
GUINEA	Dec. 1958	1958		new state
HAITI	Oct. 1945		Rio pact	
HONDURAS	Dec. 1945		Rio pact	
HUNGARY	Dec. 1955		Warsaw pact	

TABLE 203

	Date of Joining the United Nations 1	Date of Independence if since 1945 2	Cold War Affiliation 3	Category of Neutralism 4
ICELAND	Nov. 1946		NATO	
INDIA	Oct. 1945	1947		pioneer (and new)
INDONESIA	Sept. 1950	1947/9		new state
IRAN	Oct. 1945		CENTO	
IRAQ	Dec. 1945		ex-Baghdad pact	?
IRELAND	Dec. 1955			ex-isolationist
ISRAEL	May 1949	1948		new state
ITALY	Dec. 1955		NATO	
IVORY COAST	Sept. 1960	1960		new state
JAMAICA	Sept. 1962	1962		new state
JAPAN	Dec. 1956		bilateral pact with U.S.	
JORDAN	Dec. 1955	1946		new state
LAOS	Dec. 1955	1953/4		new (and neutralized) state
LEBANON	Oct. 1945	1941/6		new state
LIBERIA	Nov. 1945			ex-isolationist
LIBYA	Dec. 1955	1951	U.S. bases	new state
LUXEMBOURG	Oct. 1945		NATO	
MADAGASCAR (Malagasy)	Sept. 1960	1960	French base	new state
MALI	Sept. 1960	1960		new state
MAURITANIA	Oct. 1961	1960		new state
MEXICO	Nov. 1945		Rio pact	
MONGOLIA	Oct. 1961		Soviet satellite	
MOROCCO	Nov. 1956	1956	U.S. and French bases	new state
NEPAL	Dec. 1955			ex-buffer
NETHERLANDS	Dec. 1945		NATO	
NEW ZEALAND	Oct. 1945		SEATO and ANZUS	
NICARAGUA	Oct. 1945		Rio pact	
NIGER	Sept. 1960	1960		new state
NIGERIA	Oct. 1960	1960		new state
NORWAY	Nov. 1945		NATO	
PAKISTAN	Sept. 1947	1947	SEATO and CENTO though new	
PANAMA	Nov. 1945		Rio pact	
PARAGUAY	Oct. 1945		Rio pact	
PERU	Oct. 1945		Rio pact	
PHILIPPINES	Oct. 1945	1946	SEATO/though new	
POLAND	Oct. 1945		Warsaw pact	
PORTUGAL	Dec. 1955		NATO	
ROUMANIA	Dec. 1955		Warsaw pact	
RWANDA	Sept. 1962	1962		new state
SAUDI ARABIA	Oct. 1945		U.S. bases	ex-isolationist
SENEGAL	Sept. 1960	1960	French base	new state
SIERRA LEONE	Sept. 1961	1961		new state
SOMALIA	Sept. 1960	1960		new state
SOUTH AFRICA	Nov. 1945		bilateral pact with U.K.	
SPAIN	Dec. 1955		bilateral pact with U.S.	
SUDAN	Nov. 1956	1956		new state

	Date of Joining the United Nations 1	Date of Independence if since 1945 2	Cold War Affiliation 3	Category of Neutralism 4
SWEDEN	Nov. 1946			traditional neutral
SYRIA	Oct. 1945			new state
TANGANYIKA	Dec. 1961	1961		new state
THAILAND (Siam)	Dec. 1946		SEATO	
TOGO	Sept. 1960	1960		new state
TRINIDAD and TOBAGO	Sept. 1962	1962		new state
TUNISIA	Nov. 1956	1956	French base	new state
TURKEY	Oct. 1945		NATO and CENTO	
UGANDA	Oct. 1962	1962		new state
UKRAINIAN S.S.R.	Oct. 1945		Soviet satellite	
U.S.S.R.	Oct. 1945		Warsaw pact etc.	
UNITED ARAB REPUBLIC	Oct. 1945			pioneer
UNITED KINGDOM	Oct. 1945		NATO, SEATO and CENTO	
UNITED STATES	Oct. 1945		NATO, SEATO and CENTO etc.	
UPPER VOLTA	Sept. 1960	1960		new state
URUGUAY	Dec. 1945		Rio pact	
VENEZUELA	Nov. 1945		Rio pact	
YEMEN	Sept. 1947			ex-isolationist
YUGOSLAVIA	Oct. 1945			pioneer

Notes:
1. In 1958 Egypt and Syria, original members of the U.N., were united in a single state, the United Arab Republic—shortly afterwards Syria ceased to maintain separate representation at the U.N. Syria seceded from the U.A.R. in September 1961, and re-secured separate U.N. representation. The Egyptian half of the former union of the two countries retained the title of the United Arab Republic.
2. Of states dealt with in any detail above only Switzerland (traditional neutral), Bhutan and Sikkim (buffer states) are neutralist states and yet not members of the U.N.
3. India is here counted as a pioneer neutralist and hence not as a new state. Although she was an original member of the U.N. (just as she had been a former member of the League of Nations) she did not become independent until 1947.
4. Neither half of any of the three partitioned states of Germany, Vietnam and Korea is a member of the U.N.

SELECT BIBLIOGRAPHY

As those who have read my notes will already have found there are, to my knowledge, relatively few valuable studies of individual neutralist movements or even studies that centre attention on neutralism at all. But there are many studies of domestic or international politics, law, economics and strategy which contain material useful and relevant in the study of neutralism. There seems to be no point in simply listing all the references already cited in the table of abbreviations and in the notes. My debts to them are extensive and, I hope, patent. But this is best seen in the context in which they are used. This short bibliography contains the titles only of books and articles that I have found generally useful or can recommend to readers who themselves wish to study neutralism on a general basis. Though I was not myself able to make use of any study appearing after December 1962 my list takes account of material I have read up to the end of March 1963. I have put an asterisk against the material that appeared after I had written my study.

Some general surveys of neutralism are:

H. F. Armstrong, "Neutrality: Varying Tunes" in *Foreign Affairs*, October 1956, pp. 57-83.
>A critical view of American and of neutralist profession, especially in the context of 1956, by an American scholar.

The Economist, "Neutralism" in *The Economist* (London), 10 February 1951, pp. 300-1.
>An analysis of public opinion on neutralism in Europe at that time.

Aldo Garosci, "Neutralism" in *European Integration*, edited by C. Grove Haines (John Hopkins Press, Baltimore, 1957), pp. 196-214.
>An Italian view, which draws attention to the nihilist streak in some European neutralism.

Denis Healey, *Neutralism* (Bellman Books, No. 4, Ampersand, London, 1955), 64 pp.
>A clear and forthright attack on neutralism by a leading spokesman on foreign affairs for the British Labour Party.

William Henderson, "The Roots of Neutralism in Southern Asia" in *International Journal*, Toronto, vol. xiii (1), Winter 1957-8, pp. 30-40.
>Stresses the complexity of neutralism and outlines eight main motives for being neutralist: (i) pervasive anti-Westernism; (ii) preoccupation with newly won freedom; (iii) physical weakness and emotional exhaustion; (iv) indifference to and ignorance of foreign affairs; (v) influence of Marxism; (vi) felt need to seek accommodation with Communist China; (vii) conviction that Cold War neutralism can make a positive contribution to peace; and (viii) notion that neutralism can contain Communist expansion.

K. P. Karunakaran, *Alignment and Non-Alignment in Asia*, India and the World 1 (People's Publishing House, New Delhi, August 1961), 24 pp.

An Indian scholar argues that there is an intimate inter-relation between the domestic politics and foreign policies of all Asian countries.

*Peter Lyon, A *Primer of Neutralism* (to be published towards the end of 1963 by Frank Cass, London), circa 150 pp.

A collection of representative writings and speeches of leading neutralists, with an introductory essay and extensive biographical and bibliographical notes.

*Laurence W. Martin (ed.), *Neutralism and Nonalignment*. The New States in World Affairs (Frederick Praeger, New York, 1962; issued by the Pall Mall Press, London, March 1963), 244 pp.

Twelve essays by American scholars on various aspects of neutralism. The early essays focus principally on the nature and policies of the new states, whereas the late essays deal more directly with the significance of neutralism for American foreign policy. This is the most comprehensive study to be published so far. Though it appeared in print too late to be used in this study I did see an earlier and shorter mimeographed version which was kindly sent to me by the Washington Center of Foreign Policy Research. The table of contents is as follows:— Introduction: The Emergence of New States by Laurence W. Martin; I. State-Building as a Determinant of Foreign Policy in the New States by Robert C. Good; II. On Understanding the Unaligned by Charles Burton Marshall; III. The Congo Crisis: A Study of Post-colonial Politics by Robert C. Good; IV. A Conservative View of the New States by Laurence W. Martin; V. The "Third Party": The Rationale of Non-alignment by George Liska; VI. Nehru, Nasser, and Nkrumah on Neutralism by Ernest W. Lefever; VII. The Non-aligned States and the United Nations by Francis O. Willcox; VIII. Allies, Neutrals and Neutralists in the Context of U.S. Defense Policy by Arnold Wolfers; IX. Revolutionary Change and the Strategy of the Status Quo by Vernon V. Aspaturian; X. The Relation of Strength to Weakness in the World Community by Reinhold Niebuhr; and XI. Tripartism: Dilemmas and Strategies.

Hans J. Morgenthau, "Neutrality and Neutralism" in *Dilemmas of Politics* (University of Chicago Press, 1958), pp. 185-209.

A leading American scholar here uses the terms 'neutrality' and 'neutralism' interchangeably rather than distinctively. He argues that neutrality, being a function of the balance of power, partakes of the latter's precarious and unstable nature. He also argues that a nation best serves the purpose of neutrality, which is to stay out of war, by giving up neutrality in order to prevent war from breaking out.

N. Parameswaren Nayar, "Non-alignment in World Affairs" in *India Quarterly*, January-March 1962, pp. 28-57.

A lecturer in Politics at the University of Kerala examines and appraises the origins, evolution, conceptual development and prospects of non-alignment in the light of changing attitudes of the Cold War blocs.

Norman D. Palmer, "Changing Balance of Power: The 'Neutral' Nations in the United Nations" in *Studies in Political Science*, edited by J. S. Bains (Asia Publishing House, London, 1961), pp. 38-76.

A 'national interest' approach which stresses the varieties and many shades of neutralism, the connection with nationalism and the implications for American policy.

Robert A. Scalapino, "Neutralism in Asia" in *The American Political Science Review*, March 1954, pp. 49-62.
An incisive analysis of the ideological aspects of neutralism by an American scholar who is a specialist in Japanese studies.

Some more specialized analyses of neutralism are:
John T. Marcus, "Neutralism in France" in *The Review of Politics*, July 1955, pp. 295-328.
John T. Marcus, *Neutralism and Nationalism in France* (Bookman Associates, New York, 1958), 207 pp.
I. I. Morris, "Japanese Foreign Policy and Neutralism" in *International Affairs*, R.I.I.A., London, January 1960, pp. 7-20.
Marina Salvin, *Neutralism in France and Germany* (New York, Carnegie Endowment for International Peace, 1951).
John H. Wuorinen, "Neutralism in Scandinavia" in *Current History*, 1956, pp. 276-80.
I. William Zartman, "Neutralism and Neutrality in Scandinavia" in *The Western Political Quarterly*, June 1954, pp. 125-60.

Some aspects of Communism and neutralism are dealt with in:
George Ginsburgs, "The Soviet Union, Neutrality and Collective Security, 1945-1959" in *Osteuropa Recht*, October 1959, pp. 77-98.
George Ginsburgs, "Neutrality and Neutralism and the Tactics of Soviet Diplomacy" in *American Slavic and East European Review*, vol. xix, December 1960, pp. 531-60.
These two articles are careful studies by an American scholar, carefully based on Soviet publications.
A. M. Halpern, "The Chinese Communist Line on Neutralism" in *The China Quarterly*, January-March, 1961, pp. 90-115.
E. Korovin, "The Problem of Neutrality Today" in *International Affairs* (Moscow), March 1958, pp. 36-40.
D. Melnikov, "Neutrality and the Current Situation" in *International Affairs* (Moscow), February 1956, pp. 74-81.
L. Modjoryan, "Neutrality" in *New Times* (Moscow), February 1956, pp. 15-18.
*L. Stepanov, "Neutralism—Attack Repelled" in *New Times* (Moscow), March 1963, pp. 3-5.
The above four articles are by leading Soviet publicists.

On 'classical' neutrality, see:
Philip S. Jessup (ed.), *Neutrality: its History, Economics and Law*, 4 vols. (New York, 1935-6).
Still the most comprehensive study.

Nils Orvik, *The Decline of Neutrality, 1914-41* (Tanum, Oslo, 1953), 294 pp.

A Norwegian scholar argues that there has been a radical decline in the chances of maintaining neutrality as defined in the Hague Conventions of 1907.

Nicolas Politis, *Neutrality and Peace* (Washington, Carnegie Endowment for International Peace, 1935), 99 pp.

A distinguished Greek statesman, diplomat, jurist and publicist argues that neutrality appears to have become a true anachronism.

On the Belgrade Neutralist Conference of September 1961 see:

Andrew Boyd, "Belgrade Notebook" in *Encounter*, November 1961, pp. 56-61.

The impressions of the assistant editor of the *Economist* who reported the conference for his journal.

Official Report. *The Conference of the Heads of State or Government of Non-aligned Countries* (Publicisticko-izdavacki zavod, Beograd, Jugoslavija, 1961), 344 pp.

A record of all the public speeches of the conference together with the final resolutions, and with brief biographical notes on the heads of each of the delegations and brief descriptions of the chief characteristics of each of the participating countries.

Ljubomir Radovanovic, *From Bandung to Beograd* (Yugoslavian information service, August 1961), 26 pp.

A brochure prepared before the Belgrade conference designed to show that Belgrade would mark the culmination and confluence of several significant trends.

On nationalism, see especially:

D. W. Brogan, *The Price of Revolution* (Hamish Hamilton, London, 1951), especially pp. 103-7.

Rupert Emerson, *From Empire to Nation. The Rise to Self-Assertion of Asian and African Peoples* (Harvard University Press, 1960), 466 pp.

Thomas Hodgkin, *Nationalism in Colonial Africa* (Muller, London, 1956), 216 pp.

Elie Kedourie, *Nationalism* (Hutchinsons, London, 1960), 151 pp.

Primarily an essay on the intellectual pedigree and pretensions of nationalist doctrine.

On the Cold War and contemporary politics generally, see especially:

Raymond Aron, *The Century of Total War*, translated from the French by E. W. Dickes and O. S. Griffiths (Derek Verschoyle, London, 1954), 379 pp.

Raymond Aron, *On War, Atomic Weapons and Global Diplomacy*, translated by Terence Kilmartin (Secker & Warburg, 1958), pp. 126.

Raymond Aron, *Paix et Guerre Entre Les Nations* (Paris, Calmann-Lévy, 1962), 794 pp.

Hedley Bull, *The Control of the Arms Race*. Disarmament and Arms Control in the Missile Age. Studies in International Security: 2 (Weidenfeld & Nicolson, for the Institute for Strategic Studies, 1961), 215 pp.

Peter Calvocoressi, *World Order and New States*. Studies in International Security: 4 (Chatto & Windus for the Institute for Strategic Studies, London 1962), 113 pp.
Discusses three main themes: the place of the great powers as guardians of peace; the internal problems of new states, and especially their difficulties in trying to ensure law and order within their own boundaries; and the past, present, and potential rôle of the United Nations as an instrument in the fashioning of world order.

Richard Harris, *Independence and After*. Revolution in Under-developed Countries (O.U.P. for the Institute of Race Relations, London, 1962), 69 pp.
An incisive essay warning against the imposition of Cold War analyses on the complexities of local situations, and a plea for an understanding of the nature and necessity of revolution in the new countries.

John H. Kautsky, *Political Change in Underdeveloped Countries: Nationalism and Communism* (John Wiley and Sons, London, 1962), 347 pp.
A collection of twelve essays previously published in various scholarly journals, together with an original essay by the editor who explains the reasons for his selections and discusses the themes of: industrialization for agrarian societies, nationalism, Communism, totalitarianism and the future of politics in the developing countries.

Richard Lowenthal, "Communism and Nationalism" in *Problems of Communism*, vol. xi No. 6, November-December 1962, pp. 37-46.
A rejoinder to Kautsky's views as given in the Introduction, cited above, by the author of one of the papers Kautsky reprints. Lowenthal argues that what Kautsky says about totalitarianism is too wide and too loose, and that his identification of nationalism and totalitarianism is dubious.

C. A. W. Manning, *The Nature of International Society* (G. Bell and Sons, for the London School of Economics and Political Science, 1962), 220 pp.
A unique and subtle essay in metadiplomatics.

Hugh Seton-Watson, *Neither War Nor Peace. The Struggle for Power in the Post-war World* (Methuen, London, 1960), 504 pp.
Two books in one. An account of the main vicissitudes of the Cold War 1945-59 with more about Soviet than American policy; and a series of analytical essays on the forces of revolution, totalitarianism and imperialism.

Arnold Wolfers (ed.), *Alliance Policy in the Cold War* (O.U.P. for John Hopkins Press, Baltimore, 1959), 314 pp.
Ten essays by leading American academics and officials.

INDEX

210